Qatar

Qatar

Politics and the Challenges of Development

Matthew Gray

LYNNE RIENNER PUBLISHERS

BOULDER
LONDON

Published in the United States of America in 2013 by
Lynne Rienner Publishers, Inc.
1800 30th Street, Boulder, Colorado 80301
www.rienner.com

and in the United Kingdom by
Lynne Rienner Publishers, Inc.
3 Henrietta Street, Covent Garden, London WC2E 8LU

Library of Congress Cataloging-in-Publication Data
Gray, Matthew, 1970–
Qatar : politics and the challenges of development / Matthew Gray.
pages cm
Includes bibliographical references and index.
ISBN 978-1-58826-928-7 (alk. paper)
1. Qatar—Politics and government. 2. Qatar—Economic conditions.
3. Qatar—Strategic aspects. 4. Qatar—Foreign relations. I. Title.
DS247.Q35G73 2012
953.63—dc23

2013001380

British Cataloguing in Publication Data
A Cataloguing in Publication record for this book
is available from the British Library.

Printed and bound in the United States of America

∞ The paper used in this publication meets the requirements
of the American National Standard for Permanence of
Paper for Printed Library Materials Z39.48-1992.

5 4 3 2 1

For my parents,
Beth and Barry Gray,
with long-overdue thanks, for everything

Contents

Tables and Figures

Tables

Figure

A Note on Transliteration and Terminology

There is no simple and universally accepted means of transliterating Arabic, and in keeping with this wholly unsatisfactory and confusing state of affairs, I have adopted a hybrid approach here. For words that commonly appear in English, I have used their common English format (e.g., emir, not 'amīr; Doha, not al-Dūha, etc.). At other times, especially with personal names, I have been more precise, but have not opted for an academic style of transliteration with macrons, underdots, and the like. While this is not ideal, I hope that I have been able to clearly distinguish the names and lineages of individual people while avoiding an overly complicated system that would be of little use to most readers and could come at the expense of readability. Where there is a risk of confusion because of the transliteration style, I have clarified this in the text or notes. The only place where an academic transliteration remains is in Figure 2.1, for clarity and precision.

At times I also present personal names in full or with the branches of the family evident, which can include four, five, or more names. For example, the full name of the current emir of Qatar is Hamad bin Khalifa bin Hamad bin Abdallah Al Thani, indicating that he is Hamad, son of Khalifa (the most recent former emir), son of Hamad, son of Abdallah, and from the Al Thani dynasty. Traditionally, as in Hamad's case, this is done to show the lineage of the person. While this may result in some long names in the text that follows, it is often important in identifying the house and branch of a family through whom someone traces their lineage—not least of all in very large families with multiple houses and branches.

Furthermore, many names are similar in Qatar, as in the Arab Gulf more widely, and common names appear a lot: for this reason, while it may seem a small nuisance to general readers, sometimes additional names are used. As an example, given that the emir and the prime minister both have the first name Hamad and are both from the Al Thani dynasty, I have referred to them respectively as Emir Hamad and Hamad bin Jassim, or Prime Minister Hamad, to avoid (or at least minimize) confusion. The names Qasim (or Qasem) and Jassim can also be confusing, especially as some sources use them interchangeably: I have tried to be true to the Arabic in my transliteration of them, except where an individual translates his name a particular way and clearly has a preference for how it is given in English.

Dynastic references are also distinguished from simple cases where the definite article "al-" is used in a name. It is common, for example, to see the name of the ruling family in Qatar referred to as "al-Thani," but in fact "Al Thani" is more accurate, to distinguish "Al" as a dynastic title (meaning something like "of the line of") from "al-" as a definite article, which sometimes appears in Arabic names.

Finally, a note on terminology. Technically, Qatar is ruled by an emir (literally a "prince"), not a king, but I have referred to the Al Thani family as a "royal family" throughout the text because Qatar is a hereditary monarchy and is indistinguishable, in political and protocol senses, from monarchies that have a king at their helm.

Acknowledgments

This book, like most, could not have been written without the help of a great many people: too many to give proper credit to them all here. I apologize in advance for anyone I have omitted, and to the many whom I have not thanked enough.

I received considerable institutional support that allowed me to research and write this book. I would first like to thank the Australian National University, especially the College of Arts and Social Sciences and, within that, the Centre for Arab and Islamic Studies, where I am based, for supporting study leave in the second half of 2011. This gave me the chance to travel to Britain, Jordan, and Qatar and to focus on further research and the drafting of the book. Particular thanks are due to Toni Makkai, Adam Graycar, and Amin Saikal for supporting this study leave and to others at the Centre for Arab and Islamic Studies for taking over my duties during my absence.

I would also like to thank the people at Durham University for hosting me for part of this study leave: they not only gave me the space and facilities to write, but also were gracious hosts. I thank in particular Jim Piscatori, Anoush Ehteshami, Emma Murphy, Jeroen Gunning, Chris Davidson, and Lorraine Holmes, among others, for their friendship, support, and ideas during that wonderful summer.

At a more personal level, I would like to thank my colleagues Kirill Nourzhanov and Bob Bowker at the Centre for Arab and Islamic Studies. The genesis of the idea of late-stage rentierism came about during a vigorous debate with Bob about the weaknesses of earlier rentier theory, which in turn led me to start exploring some of the wealthier Arab Gulf states in more detail. Kirill has been one of my closest friends since the mid-1990s, when we were both graduate students, and continues to be a source of camaraderie, insight, and humor. I would also like to thank Jonathan Cheng and Jessie Moritz for their comments on earlier drafts of the book, which were extremely helpful.

A large number of people gave me their time and insights during three visits to Qatar in 2011 and 2012. Befitting a cosmopolitan society like Qatar's, they came from all over the world, although one surprise was how readily young Qataris opened up to me. They demonstrated to me how much the country is changing and how much potential rests with young Qataris. Nearly all of the people I interviewed asked not to be cited by name or affiliation (and regardless, anonymity was a condition I included in my ethics clearance from Australian National University for the research), but they know who they are, and I would like to thank them here. Several of them met with me more than once, and all were helpful in one way or another. Several of the staff at the Georgetown University campus in Doha offered helpful advice and support during my visits; and the university had also published my paper on late rentierism, from which this book draws for some of its theoretical ideas. Back in Australia, I would like to thank Daryush Baudo for his advice and assistance when I was planning my first visit to Qatar.

At the publishing stage, I thank the book's anonymous reviewer, who provided some great comments and suggestions (and did so with humor and élan). At Lynne Rienner Publishers, I would especially like to thank Lynne herself. Her personal interest in Middle Eastern studies and Arab Gulf studies was obvious from the care and attention she paid to this project, and beyond the reviewer's comments Lynne gave me a number of other great ideas. Thanks are also due to all the others at Lynne Rienner Publishers who helped get the book into print. I would also like to thank the Council on Foreign Relations and the International Monetary Fund for permission to reprint some material, as noted in the text.

Finally, a thank you to my family: to my parents, to whom I dedicate this book, for everything they have done for me; to my wife, Yasmine, for all her support; and to my son, Henry, for the happiness he brings me.

—Matthew Gray

1

The Transformation of Qatar

A visitor in 2010 returning to Qatar's capital, Doha, for the first time since 1990 would have struggled to recognize the city, so dramatically had it changed in those two decades. Back in 1990 Doha was a sleepy city, not poor by any measure but centered around the oil sector with few other industries of note. Its skyline then was a spread of small commercial buildings, apartment blocks, and houses, including some traditional white- and dun-colored Gulf houses now since demolished. The tallest buildings in Doha were the ten-story Sofitel hotel, now the Grand Mercure; the Qatari Central Bank, slightly taller; the Sheraton hotel farther to the north (still a Doha landmark); and a handful of other buildings and office blocks. There were other impressive buildings as well, including the ministries of finance and foreign affairs and the emir's palace—a grand white estate surrounded by manicured lawns and one of the landmarks along the 7-kilometer Corniche, which wraps around the edge of Doha Bay.

What a difference two decades have made. In stark contrast with 1990, by 2010 the city skyline was clustered with skyscrapers, seemingly with almost as many of them under construction as actually completed. In the same twenty years, the population of the city had expanded immensely, from 371,000 in 1990—with only about a quarter of them Qatari citizens and the remainder nearly all foreign workers and their families—to around 1.7 million in 2010, with all but at most 300,000 of them foreign nationals. Doha by then was, moreover, a global city and one increasingly recognized around the world: it had hosted the 2006 Asian Games, had bid for the 2016 and 2020 Summer Olympic Games, and was about to win—with some controversy, in due course—the 2022 FIFA World Cup, soccer's most prestigious international competition. Qatar's satellite news broadcaster, Al-Jazeera, had made the small emirate just as famous—some would say infamous—as a critical and entertaining source of news and current affairs: from a modest start in 1996, initiated with a decree by Qatar's new emir at the time, Hamad bin Khalifa Al Thani, it has since expanded into a global news source in multiple languages. Qatar and its capital, if still not quite household names, were becoming well known in international circles in 2010, and for a small state with a population comparable to that of cities such as San Jose, California, or Birmingham in Britain, it had risen dramatically to become a key actor in the world economy and the global security cnvironment.

What is just as dramatic and interesting is how Qatar's political economy also changed in this period. When Hamad seized power from his father in 1995, he commenced a series of dramatic changes and reforms: the formation of Al-Jazeera, as well as an expansion, diversification, and globalization of the economy, which, while more selective and cautious than many observers typically assume, has been broad and intense nonetheless. Qatar, moreover, is different from its neighbors in the region: it is not Dubai, even though sloppy attempts at a comparison with that emirate are sometimes made; nor is it Saudi Arabia or Kuwait—its economic profile but especially its social dynamics are very different from those of its neighbors, even if some broad characteristics are shared. The changes introduced by Hamad account in large part for the remarkable changes in Qatar since the mid-1990s; however, there is more—much more—to Qatar than its emir, and while simplistic panegyrics to him are to be found, they offer little depth or detail in explaining how and why Qatar is the way it is. Hamad is not a naive leader overeagerly seeking to reconstruct Qatari politics through blind globalization and democratization. There has been little real democratization thus far in the emirate, and the evidence is scant that much will come soon. Even though some liberalization has occurred and been nurtured by the emir, and Qatar is certainly more liberal toward its domestic critics than are the other Arab Gulf states, Hamad and the Qatari regime have not been charting a path toward real political liberalization. Nor is Hamad just an oiled Gulf autocrat who does as he pleases with the emirate, even if there are some autocratic characteristics to his rule. The economy has changed under Hamad, and this has brought some social and cultural change, but the political structure remains largely unaffected, especially the political centrality of the emir and the core elements of the royal family, and the overarching allocative role of the state with all the political implications of such a rentier state-society arrangement.

All the same, the Qatar of the early twenty-first century is more complex than a rudimentary rentier-state simplification would allow, even if a rentier dynamic underlies and informs its politics. When the Arab world erupted into protests in 2011, with leaders in Tunisia and Egypt overthrown and others pushed out of power or their rule threatened, Qatar was one of the few states in the region that was almost completely untouched by the turmoil. However, this was not just a feature of the Qatari regime's co-optive power—oil but especially gas had, by 2011, made Qatar the wealthiest state in the Middle East measured per capita—nor was it the result of the regime having some magical coercive power. The protests were, after all, still famously vigorous and aggressive in Bahrain, where they nearly removed the Al Khalifa dynasty, who had ruled there for over two centuries, and there were smaller protests in Oman as well, while other Gulf leaderships such as the Saudi Arabian royal family were nervous indeed that similar uprisings would visit them. Qatar was a unique case, even within the Gulf Cooperation Council (GCC).[1] Despite the seeming stability enjoyed by the Qatari regime, it still saw fit to raise public sector salaries by some 60 percent in September 2011, something that most observers viewed as a rentier response motivated by the threat of social dissatisfaction and unrest.

All of these dynamics feed into the fundamental questions raised in this book. Those questions revolve, as its title suggests, around Qatar's new political order and its political economy: that is, around who holds power and what they do with it; the ways in which politics and economics intersect and influence each other; and in how actors and forces such as the state, society, civil society, and international figures and institutions appear in both political and economic roles or across the two. Ultimately the book therefore attends to several wide issues. It is a book about where Qatar came from and what has changed or not, and why; the centrality of oil and gas to the political economy; Qatar's diversification of its economy and branding of itself as a distinctive nation-state product; Qatar's active diplomatic role since the late-1990s and why this has economic and not just political goals behind it; and why world-class firms and initiatives such as Al-Jazeera, Qatar Airways, Education City, and Aspire Academy (a sports academy) exist and how they serve economic, social, and indeed political ends concurrently. It is about the transformation of a society and a political economy, and the various political dynamics that have prompted and impacted it and that buttress and elucidate it.

Why a Book on Contemporary Qatar?

The changes in Qatar and its political economy since 1995 have occurred within the same framework that has seen spectacular developments elsewhere in the Gulf. Because the changes in Dubai since the late 1980s have been the most dramatic in the Gulf subregion, several works on its political economy have been published,[2] as well as an increasing number of books on Abu Dhabi, another city in the United Arab Emirates (UAE) that since the turn of the twenty-first century has undergone a striking transformation.[3] Saudi Arabia also has seen published several books on its political economy, perhaps befitting its size and importance to the global energy sector.[4] An increasing number of books on the changes in the Gulf are also being published, covering the region in general—often the GCC states and sometimes Iran and even Iraq as well—but typically focusing on Saudi Arabia and the UAE, and to a lesser extent Kuwait, as the largest or most prominent states and economies in the Gulf.[5]

But little literature has been published on Qatar. Given its small physical size and population, this may not seem strange. Yet in light of its characteristics and the role that it plays in diplomacy and the regional and global economy, this is in fact quite unexpected. Qatar is, after all, one of the wealthiest societies in the world in terms of gross domestic product per capita, and not only produces over 1.7 million barrels of oil per day,[6] but also is emerging as a natural gas superpower as it increasingly exploits the North Dome field, which it shares with Iran and which has total natural gas reserves of 894 trillion cubic feet, or 13.5 percent of the world's proven conventional reserves.[7] Also important are Qatar's diplomatic role, its foreign policy dynamics, and of course, as mentioned, its position in the global media as a result of Al-Jazeera's role and the controversies it has stirred—although there are quite a few works on Al-Jazeera specifically, which unavoidably include some discussion of Qatari politics and international relations.[8] The only recent book-length piece specifically on Qatar is a modern history by Allen Fromherz.[9]

This absence of literature alone justifies a work such as this book, which focuses on the contemporary politics and political economy of Qatar but weaves into that approach pertinent diplomatic and social dynamics. Given the transformation of Qatar in such a short space of time, a work investigating its economic policymaking and approaches, its development strategy, and the political motivations attached to its various economic dimensions is overdue. The few works that do exist specifically on Qatar's economy and economic policy were undertaken in what is now becoming the quite-distant political past; the key works by Ragaei el-Mallakh[10] and Zuhair Nafi[11] were published in the late 1970s and 1980s during the reign of Emir Khalifa bin Hamad Al Thani (r. 1972–1995) and before his son Hamad's seizure of power and subsequent reforms. Moreover, both el-Mallakh's and Nafi's books are very descriptive: they essentially present statistical material and historical description of the evolution of Qatar's economy, with little political detail as to what was occurring in the palace and bureaucracy and among the merchants in the period leading up to and after independence in 1971. While their statistical details are interesting per se and reinforce the major themes of the two books on the centrality of oil to Qatar's economic development in the 1960s and 1970s, neither are theoretically sophisticated apart from some very basic criticism of certain government policies such as on education, work force development, and the centrality of the state in capital formation. Although these works were published before some now-common theoretical approaches such as rentier-state theory were developed, they still had other explanations that could have been drawn upon and that arguably would have been of some validity, such as modernization theory, dependency theory, or leadership-centered approaches such as neopatrimonialism and sultanism.

There were, of course, broader histories of the Gulf, and at least one major work on the history of Qatar specifically, published around this time. In particular is Rosemarie Zahlan's *The Creation of Qatar,* published in 1979 and covering the longer-term history of the Qatar peninsula, from 1760 to the 1970s, especially the social and political dynamics of state formation and political development under the Al Thani dynasty.[12] Zahlan's book includes considerable reference to economic issues, including questions of how wealth was used by the Al Thani to consolidate power and manage political relationships, and of course the importance of oil in developing the Qatari economy in the decades leading to independence. To the extent that she introduces political theory, there is an implied modernization-theory approach to the book when Zahlan argues that the societal changes created by oil wealth are likely to redistribute power toward society at the expense of the royal family. As I will show, this has occurred only to a limited and controlled extent, mostly as the cause of regime cooptation of society rather than as a true reorientation or sharing of political power. Zahlan also predicted social tensions in Qatar as women gained new educational opportunities and sought greater career opportunities, and as Qataris traveled abroad and mixed with other societies more and more in the years subsequent to the publication of her book.[13] This, of course, started much later, although there remains little likelihood of serious social tension as a result, above all because of the staggering amount of wealth that has flowed into Qatar since the turn of the twenty-first century due to development and exploitation of the gas sector and the resulting dramatic expansion of the co-optive capacity of the state. Zahlan can hardly be criticized for failing to anticipate back in 1979 the profound changes that would come in the Hamad era.

Beyond this, few other works[14] were published until Jill Crystal's *Oil and Politics in the Gulf* in 1990.[15] Crystal's book has justifiably become one of the classic early works on rentier-state theory and the business-government relationship in the Gulf. As its title suggests, the book does not focus exclusively on Qatar—in fact, it gives more attention to Kuwait, the other case study in the book; however, it was the first work to include both a detailed economic history of Qatar and a theoretically sophisticated discussion of its political economy in the twentieth century. In the case of Qatar in particular, Crystal's specific argument is that the royal family has dominated the Qatari economy because of the weakness of the merchants in the pre-oil era, and then, after the exploitation of oil, because of the rentier dynamics that are so often attached to hydrocarbons. The merchants, she argued, were already weak in Qatar (but not in Kuwait) and had "renounced formal political influence in favor of a guarantee of economic survival: a trade of power for wealth."[16] The book was also an important piece for its other core point: that Qatar's political economy has been strongly defined by the size of and divisions within the royal family, and while Qatar thus has the institutions and allocative mechanisms that are to be found in other oil states, the emir's power is considerably more constrained in Qatar as a result of this royal factionalism and the limitations that it places on emiri absolutism and leverage over political institutions.[17] Later scholarship on Gulf political dynamics, especially rentierism, now makes Crystal's conclusions appear quite rudimentary; however, her work was the first to so critically examine Qatar's political economy, and it remains highly useful both as a history and for its insights into specific business-government dynamics under various emirs. Above all, its central arguments, on both rentierism and royal factionalism, remain valid and convincing, even after the rise of Hamad and despite the fact that he has managed to diminish some of the Al Thani family factionalism that long riddled the politics of Qatar.

The literature on Qatar, then, is patchy and most of it now quite old. Newer book-length works are limited to a couple of histories; a recent one, for example, is Habibur Rahman's,[18] although it is a broad history with little economic detail to it. Qatar does, of course, get mentions in other works on the Gulf more widely, but not in more detail than a single chapter or occasionally throughout more thematic works.[19] There are several journal articles on Qatar, but again not a large number.[20] The burst of work on Qatar in the late 1970s and early 1980s was probably a feature of that time: this was a decade or so after independence and a good time perhaps to consider the development and other challenges being faced by the new state, and it was also a time of new interest in the Gulf given the oil crisis of the mid-1970s, the 1978–1979 Iranian revolution, and then the outbreak of the 1980–1988 Iran-Iraq War. All of this created a first wave of literature on the Gulf subregion and the first major works on Qatar. More recently, interest in the Gulf has been revived by the Dubai experience with globalization and development, the 2003 Iraq War and the civil conflict that followed, tensions between Iran and the United States over the former's nuclear program, and of course by growing concerns about peak oil and energy security in the coming decades. I aim to contribute to this new wave of studies of the Gulf, adding to knowledge of Qatari politics specifically but also to the theoretical debates surrounding the political economy of oil states, and their non-oil sectors and initiatives, as well as the wider economic development strategies of the Gulf subregion.

Explaining Qatar's Political Economy

The central argument in this book is that, while Qatar shares the same or similar political and economic dynamics with other Gulf states in terms of the general impact of oil and gas on state-society relations and the resultant nature of the state as the central and allocative economic actor, it is also in many other ways unique, especially by virtue of its economic history; the nature of its royal family and especially since 1995 of the role played by Emir Hamad; and the specifics of its development strategy as a small but globalized state seeking to have a disproportionately visible international profile both economically and diplomatically. Moreover, as a second if related theme, Qatar's economy is an "energy-driven" one. It is no longer an oil economy in the sense of oil being a disproportionate part of its export income, and even with the expansion of the gas sector, there is considerable difficulty in labeling it a simple "gas economy" too, since it is so extensively vertically integrated along the oil and gas chain, and the economy so deliberately diversified into new sectors such as education, finance, tourism, transport, sports and leisure, and media. However, Qatar's economy remains driven by oil and gas. As this book will demonstrate, energy is central enough to Qatar's wealth and economic production that its political economy is still a highly rentier one, with a powerful, central allocative state. This is in part because the diversification of the economy has not occurred separately from the oil and gas sectors. Rather, energy has been used to support or subsidize other sectors, and increasingly, while other sectors are required to stand on their own feet, they do so in large part because they are linked into, and service, the energy sector. In other cases, the development of new sectors such as education and transport seek to build support sectors for the energy part of the economy, or because through careful state support such sectors potentially can be nurtured to stand on their own feet and generate employment opportunities in sectors other than the capital-intensive energy one. The argument, therefore, is that Qatar's economy is broad and dynamic, but ultimately the greater part of it is still the product of oil and gas.[21] It is too simplistic to consider Qatar a simple oil or gas shaikhdom, but equally crude and naive to treat it no differently than a diversified, extractive economy.

This links into the theoretical argument as well, wherein three interlocking arguments are made. The first is that the Qatari state-society relationship is rentier, but a specific type of rentier. The allocative power of the state, it is argued, is used as a co-optive mechanism by the state, and the regime's ability to remain in power and, in fact, to enjoy considerable support is the result of this co-optive spending of a substantial proportion of Qatar's oil and gas rents. Thus Qatar is a rentier state in terms of rents being used as a political *mechanism,* but rentier theory is far less adequate to the task of explaining the *structure* of the economy, which is also the product of Qatar's economic and political history, the Al Thani family's history and dynamics, and other dimensions of the state-society relationship. For instance, Qatar has a weak civil society, reflected by the absence of a strong religious elite and clergy, as well as in the limited size or cohesion of the business community as a political actor. Thus Qatar is described here as a "late rentier" state, for reasons that will be explained shortly. Second, and related to these historical dynamics, is the idea that Qatar's political economy can be characterized as representing a unique form of state capitalism, where the state is engaging in a neopatrimonial but very entrepreneurial form of state capitalism. In it, the royal family, on behalf of the state, becomes in effect a business meta-actor, with commercial activities a fundamental element of the state's and the Al Thani's political role and function, and with state capitalist dynamics and outcomes serving political ends as well. Third and finally, it is argued that Qatar is a microstate, and in particular an open, partially globalized, and activist microstate that is seeking, including through its economic strategy and policies, to build patronage with larger states and with foreign private sector actors, in the interests of both national security and the economic development and commercial opportunities that support the royal family's rule.

The theoretical explanations that are developed here have been shaped and informed for the most part by scholarship on other Gulf states, especially in light of the paucity of material on Qatar itself and given the pace of change in the emirate. The idea of "late rentierism" has been explored previously[22] and is related to the now long-established arguments of rentier-state theory, which seeks to explain state-society relations in states that generate a large proportion of government income from rents—that is, externally derived, unproductively earned payments such as royalties or other transfers for oil and gas exports, and other income such as fees and aid. At its most basic, rentier-state theory holds that, since the state receives this external income and distributes it to society, it is relieved of having to impose taxation, which in turn means that it does not have to offer concessions to society such as a democratic bargain or a development strategy. The theory was first developed in the 1980s, predominantly to explain the Gulf,[23] although later work on rentierism has developed the theory considerably, adding greater nuance and detail to it,[24] and expanding its ability to link to other theoretical approaches from history and international relations.[25]

Newer research challenges the more basic and structural assumptions behind early rentier-state theory, especially the idea that the state is autonomous from society. While it may be able to buy a degree of autonomy and aloofness, the state always faces an ultimate risk of revolution and thus, in needing to maintain at least a rudimentary level of legitimacy, is never truly autonomous from society. One good work on Saudi Arabia makes this point well in discussing how fluctuations in rent, fiscal and financial crises, changing power in the private sector, and discontent over socioeconomic conditions all give the lie to the claim of rentier-state autonomy from society.[26] Moreover, the 2011 Arab Spring—including the protests in Bahrain, also a state with a strong rentier dynamic, which nearly toppled the ruling Al Khalifa dynasty—adds another stark and recent reminder of the risk of uprising in rentier states.[27]

The idea of "late rentierism," therefore, accepts the fundamental arguments of rentier-state theory. Allocative states are able to buy toleration by society through the allocation of rental income, and at the same time buy the repressive apparatus necessary to control those who cannot be co-opted. The state has a degree of freedom from society; it can usually avoid making democratic concessions where rents are sufficiently large, and typically the political elite can operate as the government and in the name of society fairly much at will too. Through neopatrimonial networks and other informal mechanisms, the ruler and key elite will build ties to elites and use these to allocate wealth and opportunity, and in return to gain allegiance from these clients and obtain information and advice from them about wider dynamics that might impact the ruler's legitimacy or position. The state may have to be *responsive* to society to some extent, but is not democratically or otherwise accountable. All of this is true for Qatar, as it is for the GCC states to a large extent. However, late rentierism also seeks to refine these ideas to account for the more globalized, reformist regimes of the Gulf since the 1990s, but also for the fact that basic rentier levers remain central to the ability of Gulf monarchies to maintain power. The key difference is in the ultimate claims made by rentier-state theory versus those here about late rentierism. In the latter case, the argument is not that rentierism explains the entire nature and structure of the state but rather that rents provide a *mechanism* of control for rulers to maintain and massage their legitimacy. In this sense, late rentierism is different from the rentierism identified in the early rentier-state theory literature, including works on Qatar such as Crystal's, in seeing rentierism as mechanical, not structural. Furthermore, the nature of the changes introduced by Hamad requires a more sophisticated and refined rentier theory. The state has a very clear and long-term development strategy, economic policy, and foreign policy, none of which rentier theorists traditionally saw as a characteristic of the rentier state. This is because rents are merely a political tool, albeit an absolutely central one, and are not sufficient, in themselves, to explain the political structure overall.

Therefore the points that are presented and extrapolated upon in the chapters that follow detail how the state operates as an economic actor, how it both nurtures and controls (selected elements of) the indigenous and international business communities, and how it connects social reform, political change, and diplomacy to its economic development strategy and policies. In this way an argument that Qatar is a late rentier state is made, but also important and related to that argument is the idea that the Qatari state is "entrepreneurial state capitalist." What is most crucial here is that the state capitalism of Hamad's Qatar is very different from the earlier state capitalism fostered in the Arab republics after independence. Qatar promotes economic efficiency, profitability for the state, a state role in certain emerging or sensitive sectors, and a linkage of this capitalism to the state's political and diplomatic ambitions. It shares characteristics with the "new" state capitalism that Ian Bremmer has identified,[28] but is not the typical form of that either, as it is more benevolent and efficient than many of the cases cited by Bremmer. The argument instead is that the state is a business or commercial actor by its nature, and does not just set economic policy and assist with market development and correcting market failure, but also owns a large share of the means of production and seeks to make a risk-based return on its investments and to operate its assets efficiently and profitably. It often monopolizes the sectors in which it is most active or heavily invested—think not just of strategic sectors such as defense but of sectors such as telecommunications, air transportation, finance, and downstream oil and gas—or is highly regulatory if it allows private expansion into such sectors. Beyond these areas, however, the state is far more liberal: in areas where it is not active and is seeking international or local business engagement, it will introduce reforms to ease business development, lower transaction costs, and encourage competition. Such reform may include economic liberalization and marketization measures, but even then, such reforms remain tightly controlled. They never result in the state surrendering its dominance of the economy and thus do not constitute proper or literal neoliberal reform.

Qatar's entrepreneurial state capitalism is partly shared with that of other Gulf states, including most famously Dubai, but it is not the same, and the reforms in Qatar since 1995 cannot simply be categorized as the emirate following a "Dubai model" of development. There is a specific Dubai development approach, for example, which Martin Hvidt, the main theorist on the "Dubai model," has ably analyzed,[29] but he and others are on less firm ground when suggesting that this model is being or could be adopted by other Gulf states in lieu of rentierism.[30] Hvidt argues that there is "a shift from an allocation state model toward a more production-oriented economic model among the GCC countries,"[31] which as will be shown here in the case of Qatar is a conclusion that lacks sufficient nuance and specificity to state-by-state variations in political authority, allocative mechanisms, and development strategies in the Gulf. Qatar shares much with Dubai: a late-late development experience; an activist and (where politically suitable to the state) business-friendly policy toward the private sector; extreme labor market flexibility, including a reliance on foreign workers; and a strategy of branding the country. However, the two are also very different. Crucially, Qatar's development is underwritten by enormous gas reserves and income, which Dubai does not have in the same volume except through the patronage of Abu Dhabi—something it learned to great consternation during the global financial crisis, when its rollover of debt obligations had to be underwritten by Abu Dhabi to avoid Dubai defaulting.[32] The commercial histories of the two are completely different as well, with Dubai having over a century of open commercial links with the world, compared to Qatar's merchant class being small, weak, and largely apolitical. Indeed, Dubai has actively modeled its development since the 1980s on Singapore, but no serious argument could be mounted that there is a "Singapore model" that is somehow being adopted by Dubai; again, even if some economic strategies or tactics can be copied, the two states are otherwise too much at variance in crucial historical, political, and social ways.

Finally, it is argued here that Qatar's political economy and the dynamics of it under Hamad have been informed by its strategy and capabilities as a microstate. The term *microstate* has typically been used in the literature for a focus on developing states, and often on geographically and demographically smaller ones than Qatar;[33] however, J. E. Peterson and others have adopted the term in reference to Qatar. Peterson argues that Qatar has engaged in branding itself in large part as a security strategy, and this is certainly true. Branding raises not only the profile but also the very legitimacy of a microstate, as he has rightly argued.[34] This argument is further expanded here, however, into the political economy dimensions of Qatari microstatism. The argument certainly is in part that international branding acts as a form of security for the (very) small states; this is why Qatar both hosts the US Central Command (CENTCOM) and has a functioning relationship with Israel, and yet maintains a diverse and active diplomatic and especially economic relationship with states such as Iran. To an activist microstate, the best insurance against security threats or economic coercion is to ensure that all the major actors in a position to be a threat have a strong stake in not being so.

Beyond the security element, however, Qatar is also branding itself—actively and aggressively, even by the standards of other microstates and small states—as a way of developing itself into a global *commercial* brand. What is called here its "activist microstatism" is, in other words, an aspect of its entrepreneurial state capitalism too. It has sought, for example, to carve for itself a world-class niche as a host of sporting events—the 2006 Asian Games, the 2022 FIFA World Cup, other tournaments, possibly even a Summer Olympic Games—not predominantly as a security strategy but as a business development strategy. Concomitant with such events are new opportunities for the (state-owned) airline and for a tourism sector that the state is deliberately trying to develop around higher-end luxury and purpose-driven travel, and that of course provides opportunity to develop new facilities and infrastructure, which in turn provides a lift for the regime's support and legitimacy among the small population of Qatari nationals. Similarly, Al-Jazeera might not seem like a commercial enterprise—it famously failed to meet its profit-making targets in the early 2000s and has required credit from the emir several times since then[35]—and of course its reportage has upset most of Qatar's allies and friends (and others) at one time or another. However, the channel provides enormous reach into the Arab world. It is a popular channel, and its reports and opinions often set the tone for debates on certain issues around the region. This buys the Qatari state and royal family a degree of *popular* support elsewhere in the Arab world that would probably be impossible to achieve otherwise, and the regime escapes the worst consequences of offending friendly governments by maintaining a veneer of managerial and editorial independence from the broadcaster,[36] whatever the reality, and sends a message of liberalization to its own and other populations.[37] It thus forms part of the branding of the state as reformist, liberalist, and open to democratization, even though it is more likely to be engaging in a slight social liberalization and the creation of a veneer of political reform, rather than actual political liberalization of depth and substance. However, the regime also, not coincidentally, engages external actors commercially, as advertisers on Al-Jazeera, for example, or as employees, commentators, or others with a stake or interest in the channel. Branding is not only about security, in other words, but also—even mostly—about commerce and the economic interests of the entrepreneurial state.

About This Book

Qatar is a small, dynamic state seeking to punch above its weight. Its energy-driven economy and energy-supported economic strategies, in combination with the features of "late" rentierism, entrepreneurial state capitalism, and activist microstatism, provide the theoretical and analytical foundation of the book and the core of its argument. This approach is borne out by Qatar's development strategy, political economy dynamics, and foreign relations, especially the marked transformation of these since 1995 under Hamad. All of these issues are considered in the chapters that follow, with the emphasis on the political order and the dynamics of Qatar's political economy. In the process, issues of international relations, social change, and others are introduced and discussed, with the aim of exploring politics and the political economy in a comprehensive and integrated fashion. The goal is to enlighten the discussion of Qatar's political economy by looking beyond the narrow confines of political institutions, laws, economic actors and institutions, macroeconomic settings, and suchlike.

The study is also constrained by its emphasis on the contemporary period—that is, on Hamad's Qatar. Chapter 2 provides a historical overview, to provide the context for where Qatar and Hamad's regime started in 1995, and necessarily there are references to pre-1995 events or dynamics throughout the book. History is, after all, prologue to the present, and in the case of Qatar's economy and political system, historical circumstances and dynamics that have evolved or been put in place over long periods of time cannot be quickly or easily changed. Qatar and its political leadership are enmeshed in historically informed dynamics, as is the population, and there is, as a result, a considerable amount of historical context included herein. However, the stress is placed on Qatari political economy dynamics and the explanations for them in the period from around the mid-1990s until the early 2010s. Chapter 2, as the main historical and contextual chapter of the book, looks at the evolution of Qatar's political system and its political economy, from 1766, when members of the Bani Utba confederation settled in Qatar, to the rise of the Al Thani family, and into modern times and the influence of Ottoman and British control of the country. The chapter focuses on the twentieth century in particular, including the problems of intrafamily factionalism and squabbling among the Al Thani, and the problems of political continuity and stability that this presented, but also how it linked to various emirs' policies toward the British and the development of the oil sector. It takes the reader up to Hamad's seizure of power from his father in 1995. By that time, Qatar was a modern and developed economy, but it was far from the Qatar of today: Doha remained a comparatively secluded, insulated, and sleepy city, contrasting strongly with the trade, tourism, finance, and construction that was under way in Bahrain, Abu Dhabi, and especially Dubai, and that would make Dubai almost a household name only a few years later. Qatar in 1995 was still waiting to launch, and the chapter ends on that note, with the new emir, Hamad, beginning to very speedily change this.

Chapter 3 looks at politics in contemporary Qatar, including at how energy has impacted and shaped the political system and especially at how it has created, sustained, and shaped both the public and private sectors. In the former case, energy most obviously has allowed for the rentier, now late rentier, bargain that sustains the royal family and dictates the broad dynamics and climate of Qatar's polity. It is now increasingly transforming the regime into new, entrepreneurial state capitalism too. The role of the state in driving key state-owned enterprises, diversifying its political base, and fostering commercial linkages between merchants and the state are all focused on, from the role of the emir and the royal family at the summit of the system down to the impacts of energy-driven development on the political economy very broadly.

Chapter 4 is concerned with the central element of Qatar's economy—hydrocarbons—and is perhaps the most descriptive of the chapters. First oil and then, more spectacularly, gas have defined Qatar in recent decades. Oil helped begin its development, and gas in particular underwrote its transformation beginning in the 1990s. The double-digit growth figures of the following decade were a product of this gas enterprise, since they were mostly accounted for by new gas projects coming on-stream. The chapter looks at these dynamics: at the oil and gas assets of Qatar, its past and present exploitation of energy resources, its attempts to diversify downstream in the energy sector, and its plans for the future. They are at the core of political power in Qatar today.

Chapter 5 continues with the theme of the centrality of energy to Qatar's political economy, but looks at the additional question of how even wider economic and political dynamics are shaped by a relationship with oil, gas, and petrochemicals. Important here are sectors such as higher education, tourism, sports, construction, Islamic finance, and the like. These sectors are not part of the energy sector, of course, nor even very obviously linked into them, but they are of the size and nature that they are because of oil and gas income or the demand created by energy wealth. The dynamic here is described, perhaps a little generally, as energy-driven diversification. In some cases, it is argued, these sectors indeed exist for diversification and especially to create employment and new commercial opportunities, given the capital-intensity of the energy sector and the limited number of jobs it creates. They are also the result of energy, because, it is argued, energy provides the justification or the underpinning for them.

Chapters 3, 4, and 5 reinforce the arguments of the book in several ways by demonstrating the centrality of oil and gas to the economy, but also the political impacts of this energy centrality and how energy defines and shapes so much else of the economy, maintaining and enhancing Qatar's state capitalism as well. Chapters 6 and 7 are somewhat different, however, as they expand the discussion to also include the themes of microstatism and international relations and how these link to Qatar's political economy. Chapter 6 looks at the theme of national branding. Some of the cases considered here include Al-Jazeera television, the role of sports and major sporting events, and the development of a cultural sector. These all to some degree have outright economic aims, and to that extent they reinforce the arguments about late rentierism, entrepreneurial state capitalism, or both. However, they also represent Qatar's microstatism, especially the image the state creates in the act of branding itself, and the diplomatic, cultural, and social goals behind this strategy. These all feed into the economic, and in turn the domestic political, aims of the emir and the political elite.

Chapter 7 focuses on the same microstatist dynamic, but specific to Qatar's foreign policy and international relations. The argument in this chapter is that Qatar plays a diplomatic role out of all proportion to its size, economic power, or military capability because it is seeking not only to build its global image and reputation but also to gain economic security and new commercial opportunities from its foreign relations. This, in turn, strengthens the domestic political position of Hamad and the regime. At the basest level Qatar is building links with all the major regional and subregional actors to ensure that they have a stake in its stability and current economic trajectory; thus there exists a rudimentary goal to its foreign policy of enhancing security, as one would expect. However, Qatar has also taken a particular approach to its Arab neighbors, Iran, and emerging global powers such as China that suggests a strong economic aim behind its foreign policy. It is argued that, with these actors and its policies toward them, Doha is seeking economic stability and integration, new commercial opportunities, and maximum confidence of investors and others who are operating in the country.

Chapter 8 looks at the problems, challenges, and remaining questions surrounding Qatar's polity and political order, its economy, and its development strategy. The rise of Qatar has not been without complications or controversies. Explored here are several key issues, including the debates about the pace of economic change; the issue of Qatar's heavy reliance on foreign labor and the problems of the attempted "Qatarization" of the work force; questions of culture, especially of maintaining a Qatari identity in the face of globalization and when citizens are a minority of the population; the challenges from social changes, especially the dynamics of women and youth and their future roles in the political economy; the question of whether political liberalization needs to follow the economic changes of recent years; and the question of whether there is a "Qatar model" of development, which the chapter answers (conditionally) in the negative. In concluding the book, the chapter also reiterates the themes of energy centrality and a concomitant economic change and political stasis, and in the process reasserts the theoretical bases of late rentierism, entrepreneurial state capitalism, and activist microstatism.

Not only has Qatar itself undergone a striking change since 1990 but so too has its role and importance. Back in 1990, visitors to Qatar commonly departed with the sense that the country was comfortable but "boring." Today it is anything but boring. It is a global actor in diplomacy, media and culture, and the gas sector. It is an important regional actor, with a political system and political economy that is the envy of most of its neighbors and that is gaining increasing attention from scholars interested in the validity of old theories such as modernization and rentierism or looking for new ways of explaining a Gulf that is dramatically changing. Qatar, if still not a household name in the West, is no longer invisible to all but a few academics and oil executives. After its success in enduring the global financial crisis with few negative impacts, as it changes its economy and plays a greater international role, Qatar is not boring but in fact is one of the most arresting and vibrant states in the Middle East.

Notes

1. The Gulf Cooperation Council was formed in 1981 and consists of Saudi Arabia, Bahrain, Kuwait, Oman, Qatar, and the United Arab Emirates.

2. There are now several books on Dubai, of varying quality. One of the best is Davidson, *Dubai*. Others include Krane, *Dubai;* Barrett, *Dubai Dreams;* and Ali, *Dubai*.

3. In particular, Davidson, *Abu Dhabi;* but also Tatchell, *A Diamond in the Desert*.

4. There are actually an enormous number of works on Saudi Arabia, from very scholarly pieces on its modern history, politics, and economy to very sensationalist, mass market pieces, as well as pieces of both of these types on the dominant form of Sunni Islam in the kingdom, Wahhabism, which coincidentally the majority of Qatari nationals subscribe to as well. Specifically on the political economy of Saudi Arabia are, among others, Niblock and Malik, *The Political Economy of Saudi Arabia;* Aarts and Nonneman, *Saudi Arabia in the Balance;* Hertog, *Princes, Brokers, and Bureaucrats;* Lacey, *Inside the Kingdom;* and Champion, *The Paradoxical Kingdom*.

5. Again there are a range of books on the Gulf as a subregion, but recent ones with a focus on politics and political economy include Nugée and Subacchi, *The Gulf Region;* Seznec and Kirk, *Industrialization in the Gulf;* Legrenzi and Momani, *Shifting Geo-Economic Power of the Gulf;* and, of a slightly different style, Hanieh, *Capitalism and Class in the Gulf Arab States*. There are also politically and socially focused pieces with strong discussion of or relevance to political economy, such as Potter and Sick, *Security in the Persian Gulf;* Tétreault, Okruhlik, and Kapiszewski, *Political Change in the Gulf States;* and Foley, *The Arab Gulf States*. The fact remains that all of these books, and others not cited here, pay little attention to Qatar or other smaller GCC states, and focus their attention on Saudi Arabia and the UAE.

6. *BP Statistical Review of World Energy 2012,* http://www.bp.com/liveassets/bp_internet/globalbp/globalbp_uk_english/reports_and_publications/statistical_energy_review_2011/STAGING/local_assets/pdf/oil_section_2012.pdf.

7. Figures are from the historical data workbook attached to the *BP Statistical Review of World Energy 2011,* http://www.bp.com/sectionbodycopy.do?categoryId=7500&contentId=7068481. The North Dome/South Pars gas field is the largest in the world, holding an estimated 1,800 trillion cubic feet of natural gas condensate, some 1,260 trillion cubic feet of which is thought to be recoverable; of this, about 900 trillion cubic feet is within Qatar's North Dome.

8. Some examples—again not an exhaustive list—are Miles, *Al-Jazeera;* al-Nawawy and Iskandar, *Al-Jazeera: The Story of the Network;* and Zayani, *The Al Jazeera Phenomenon: Critical Perspectives on New Arab Media*.

9. Fromherz, *Qatar*.

10. el-Mallakh, *Qatar: Development of an Oil Economy*.

11. Nafi, *Economic and Social Development in Qatar*.

12. Zahlan, *The Creation of Qatar*. Rosemarie Zahlan is the author of multiple works on the history of the Gulf and in particular on the middle and lower Arab Gulf states.

13. See Zahlan, *The Creation of Qatar,* pp. 135–137.

14. The only other book-length work of any note is the anonymously authored *Economic and Social Infrastructures in the State of Qatar*. It provides some useful statistics and general overview material on various economic sectors in Qatar, but

is descriptive in the extreme and closest in style to a compendium rather than a critical piece of scholarship.

15. Crystal, *Oil and Politics in the Gulf.*

16. Ibid., p. 187.

17. Ibid., p. 112.

18. Rahman, *The Emergence of Qatar.*

19. There is a chapter on Qatari politics under Hamad in, for example, Tétreault, Okruhlik, and Kapiszewski, *Political Change in the Gulf States,* and considerable discussion of it in other works as noted earlier.

20. A few of the more recent examples include Bahry, "Elections in Qatar"; Rathmell and Schulze, "Political Reform in the Gulf"; Peterson, "Qatar and the World"; Mansour, "Public Policy and Privatization"; Dargin, "Qatar's Natural Gas"; Kamrava, "Royal Factionalism and Political Liberalization in Qatar"; and Berrebi, Martorell, and Tanner, "Qatar's Labor Markets at a Crucial Crossroad."

21. Author interview, Doha, January 2011.

22. Gray, "A Theory of 'Late Rentierism' in the Arab States of the Gulf."

23. The first use of the term and concept of *rentier state* was by Hussein Mahdavy, in writing about the political economy of pre-revolutionary Iran; see Mahdavy, "The Patterns and Problems of Economic Development in Rentier States." The two authors most associated with formation of the concept, however, are Giacomo Luciani and Hazem Beblawi, who in the late 1980s and early 1990s developed it further; see, for example, Beblawi, "The Rentier State in the Arab World"; and Luciani, "Allocation vs. Production States."

24. The literature in the late 1990s and the early 2000s developed rentier-state theory considerably from the early explanatory structures of Luciani, Beblawi, and others. One piece that used it extensively and developed considerable nuance around the concept was Knowles, *Jordan Since 1989*. Later sophisticated and contributing pieces include, among many, Chaudhry, *The Price of Wealth;* Moore, *Doing Business in the Middle East;* Niblock and Malik, *The Political Economy of Saudi Arabia;* and Hertog, *Princes, Brokers, and Bureaucrats.*

25. This point was made in Moore, "Rents and Late Development in the Arab World," pp. 8–11. Some works that do this—that bring together rentier-state theory and theories or approaches from history, international relations, or other disciplines—include, in the case of recent history, Chaudhry, *The Price of Wealth;* and in the case of international relations, Gause, *Oil Monarchies.*

26. Niblock and Malik, *The Political Economy of Saudi Arabia,* pp. 173–177.

27. See, for example, International Crisis Group, "Popular Protests in North Africa and the Middle East"; and Justin Gengler, "How Radical Are Bahrain's Shia?" *Foreign Affairs,* May 15, 2011, http://www.foreignaffairs.com/articles/67855/justin-gengler/how-radical-are-bahrains-shia?page=show.

28. Bremmer, *The End of the Free Market.*

29. Hvidt, "The Dubai Model." Martin Hvidt's central argument about Dubai as a model of "late-late" development (pp. 398–399) and his justification for this are not disputed here—indeed, they are spot-on—but rather the validity of the "Dubai model" as a catchall explanation for Qatar's or other GCC states' contemporary political economy is strongly contested.

30. Hvidt, "Economic and Institutional Reforms in the Arab Gulf Countries."

31. Ibid., pp. 101–102.

32. For details, see the collections of articles by *The Financial Times* (London) titled as "Dubai Financial Crisis" and archived and collected online at http://www.ft.com/indepth/dubai-financial-crisis.

33. Peterson, "Qatar and the World," pp. 733–735.

34. Ibid., pp. 746–748.

35. Miles, *Al-Jazeera,* p. 346.

36. Ibid., p. 347.

37. Rathmell and Schulze, "Political Reform in the Gulf," p. 53.

2

The Historical Context

The contemporary political system and economy of Qatar are the product, in large part but not exclusively, of its history and of the circumstances that have impacted the Qatar peninsula. Integral to the strength of the state nowadays relative to that of businesspeople, the clergy, tribal leaders, and others is the evolution of a political order in which wings of a large, often-fragmented royal family have often sought alliances externally, and a state-society relationship in which alternative power sources to the Al Thani emirs have been kept at bay through co-optation and divide-and-conquer tactics more than by coercion. Specifically, the influence of pre–oil era tribal leaders was countered by the Al Thani's relations with, in particular, the British. The clerics' power was minimized by the religious role of some key royals but also by the sparse population and relative poverty of the countryside, and the business community was neutralized by the very modest value of the country's foreign trade, which weakened the merchants as a class,[1] especially in contrast to other parts of the Gulf such as Bahrain and Kuwait. By the time that oil began being exploited in 1935 the Al Thani family was in control. Although the Al Thani were factionalized and internally unstable at times, the availability of rents thereafter guaranteed them a source of leverage and power and a new degree of durability.

This dynamic of a large royal family and a disorganized, then later co-opted, merchant class is at the core of this chapter. The evolution of state dominance of the business-government relationship, and the ultimate yielding by the business community to a rentier bargain with the Al Thani—essentially, access to rents and business opportunities in exchange for political acquiescence to the royal family—is the central theme of this chapter. It links to and explains the centrality of oil to political power in Qatar, the nature of Qatari state capitalism, and even to some extent the motivation and capability of Hamad in recent years to (quasi-)globalize the political economy and build Qatar's international image and brand name.

Several arguments unfold over the pages that follow. Above all, historical dynamics have allowed the Al Thani to neutralize the merchants as a potential source of political challenge, and because the merchant class has always been overwhelmingly domestic and not very engaged in international trade, they have been reliant for commercial opportunities on the royal family, and then on the state as it emerged. Such is the weakness of the business community, indeed, that the royal family itself became the dominant business actor. Along with a handful of key families, all interconnected with the royals or somehow linked into their patronage, the royals' economic power accounts in part for the state capitalism that developed in twentieth-century Qatar. That this royal power was even more enhanced by oil and then gas rents strengthens the fundamental characterization of Qatar's political economy as rentier (and under Hamad, late rentier), noting that Qatar's strong state capitalism is intensely interrelated with its rentierism, even if arguably, due to the nature of the business-government relationship, some sort of state capitalism would have emerged even in the absence of oil and gas.

Even with the business-government and oil-rent dynamics in place, however, the ultimate dominance of the Al Thani was not guaranteed until quite recently. Other factors were important in setting the political stage and ordering the economy over the past two centuries, especially in the latter half of the twentieth. Critical too have been the foreign impacts on Qatar, including the relationships that the Al Thani have relied upon for external support, especially the role of the British in boosting the Al Thani's position, first briefly in the early nineteenth century and then after a period of Ottoman possession and brief control by the Bahraini Al Khalifa dynasty, again from late in the nineteenth century and through much of the twentieth.

These historical themes, it will be argued, find their countenance in the political and economic dynamics of today. The royals, having established dominance in the commercial realm, remain entrenched at the top of it, while such a merchant class as there is derives enough of its wealth from the state not to challenge it politically. The entrepreneurial state capitalism and the activist, international microstatism and use of microstate branding as a form of economic and physical security are all, additionally, outgrowths of this past. The royals would not exist as features of Qatar's political economy—or would be much less likely to exist—were it not for Qatar's oil wealth, a history of major power protection, and the types of business community, social structures, and state-society relationship that have evolved over the past two centuries. The Qatar that Hamad seized power over in 1995 was not undeveloped, but nor did it possess the vibrant, activist state and political economy that it does today. Why Hamad seized power, and why he changed Qatar in the ways that he has, are in large part the result of historical settings creating the context for contemporary dynamics.

The Rise of the Al Thani Family

Although Qatar has been settled for millennia, its recorded history dates only to the mid-eighteenth century, and its modern history—the rule of the Al Thani and the development of a state system and the associated institutions—dates in effect only from the 1860s. Prior to 1766, the evidence suggests that the Al Thani were a strong local tribe first in the south and then in the area around Fuwayrit in the northeast of the peninsula, after having migrated, according to legend, from the Najd area of central Arabia in the late seventeenth or possibly the early eighteenth century. In the 1760s, however, they were one of many families controlling small settled areas on the Qatar peninsula, and there was little indication that they would ultimately rule Qatar as a nation-state a few generations later.

At this time, the population of the Qatar peninsula was small and mostly tribal, with small coastal populations engaged in fishing and pearling and with nomadic tribes who wandered the coast and sometimes the inland areas. There were only a handful of towns that were both sizable and permanent, including Fuwayrit, the largest; al-Huwayla, the main pearling area in the early 1700s, which was controlled by parts of the Bani Khalid clan; and al-Wakra and al-Bida', both on the central east coast and under the control of other groups. Other settlements were tiny and often temporary, constructed hastily around a source of water or in a promising feeding spot for livestock.[2] Tribes who ventured inland were highly transitory, often only moving into the interior of the peninsula briefly in winter and spring, when the modest rains at that time typically produced a brief and limited growth of flora. Such movements did not require formal land tenure or ownership, as the tribes claimed a traditional grazing right (*al-dira*). To the extent that politics existed outside of tribal groupings, it was only the handful of families who dominated a few settled areas who could exert much authority, and even then, their ability to raise taxes or build any real political institutions was severely constrained by the small populations and their poverty. Other actors who might possess legitimacy, such as the clergy, were similarly hobbled by geography and demography in expanding and formalizing their power, and the merchants, despite having previously been more important during the Umayyad and Abbasid periods, were by the 1700s extremely small in number and for the most part not engaged in foreign trade, certainly not to an extent that they could build any significant political base.

The area had been conquered repeatedly over the centuries, first incorporated into the Arab Islamic empires, then by the Portuguese from 1517 to 1538. While brief, this period of Portuguese control did witness a resurgence of trade in the Gulf, including on the Qatar peninsula, and the growing Iranian influence also reinforced this increased activity in the region, even if Qatar remained, compared to the coastlines of the upper and lower Gulf and Bahrain, a backwater. Over nearly three centuries following, the Qatar peninsula was either directly or indirectly controlled by Safavid Iran (three times), Oman (twice), the Ottomans a second time, and Bahrain twice. Despite this oscillation at the higher levels of politics, however, the evidence suggests that the tribes largely went about their business with little reference to politics beyond the peninsula. The Qatar peninsula certainly stood in contrast with Bahrain, Oman, and the areas on the main trade routes of the Arabian peninsula, which by the 1700s were significant local economic centers and sometimes political powers as well.

The year 1766 proved to be a turning point, when members of the Bani Utba confederation in Kuwait settled on the western coast of Qatar, establishing the town of al-Zubara. Prominent among the Bani Utba were members of the Al Khalifa house, which rules Bahrain to the present day. By virtue of providing various elements of the Bani Utba greater control over the pearling grounds of the Gulf, al-Zubara quickly, if briefly, became an important commercial and trading center. In 1783, as relations became increasingly strained between the Bani Utba and Iran and Oman, the main local powers at the time, the Bani Utba attacked and seized Bahrain.[3] Nearly all the Al Khalifa left al-Zubara shortly after the capture of Bahrain; Bahrain, after all, offered better towns and ports and, because of its advanced pearling industry, better business prospects.

This was to be crucial for Qatar's economic and political development. It led to a rapid decline in al-Zubara's trade, and thus in trade and economic prospects elsewhere in Qatar, as the Al Khalifa took much of the pearling industry with them to Bahrain. External threats to the peninsula remained—al-Zubara and al-Huwayla were caught up in the rise of Wahhabism on the Arabian peninsula, for example, and were attacked in 1795 by Saudi forces as a result—and yet the Al Khalifa left a profound power vacuum in their wake. No great figure or family arose to replace them, and none was able to exert proper control over the bulk of the country for the next half century or more. No external major power seized the country either: technically the Al Khalifa remained in charge, and they did retain a small presence at al-Zubara for some time, while the British were expanding in reach and influence in the Gulf but did not yet impose their tutelage over the Qatar peninsula. For a time, then, the area was under the varying control of several tribal shaikhs,[4] none of whom could be said to have a proper dominance or authority over the area as a whole.

When the British did begin to assert their power over Qatar, it was done through the Al Khalifa and Bahrain. In 1820 the British formalized their position in the Gulf with the first of several key local treaties, this one with the Al Khalifa, who in signing it and being recognized as the sovereign power over Bahrain were in effect signing it for and over the Qatar peninsula as well, much of which they still at least loosely controlled. The 1820 treaty was similar to most treaties that the British made in the region, in effect supporting the rule of a local figure and family and agreeing to underwrite that rule with British military power, but in exchange requiring that the local ruler maintain complete political and diplomatic fidelity with the British and agree not to cede territory to any other external power. Such an arrangement served the Al Khalifa well, as their rule just prior to 1820 was precarious, and the treaty gave them external support and the chance to build domestic alliances and bases. To the Qataris, however, this was all very remote: Jill Crystal tells the story of the British East India Company destroying Doha in 1821 as punishment for a violation of the treaty, but with the local population, even two years later when the British political resident visited, oblivious to the 1820 treaty—no local shaikh had signed it, after all—and thus completely ignorant as to why they had been attacked.[5]

Over more than a century from 1820 to 1930, the Qatari economy, apart from the basic herding and fishing done by many small tribal and town populations, was based around pearling. This did not necessarily bring growth or development to the bulk of the population, however, since it was seasonal and the foreign trade aspects of it were overwhelmingly handled by foreigners.[6] The settlements in Qatar remained modest in size and for much of this time very poor; al-Bida' was the center of pearl trading, but only had, by one account in the early 1860s, at most 6,000 people, while by the same account Doha was particularly poor at this stage and al-Wakra only somewhat more prosperous.[7] Rather unkindly, but perhaps not inaccurately, Michael Herb describes Qatar before 1949 as being "little more than a barren expanse of sand jutting out into the Gulf, its chief town, Doha, a dusty street lined with decrepit mud houses."[8] The central theme, however, is that of the near-absent business-government dynamic over this period. Whereas Kuwait and Bahrain were developing large and strong merchant classes with political interests and influence, Qatar was not. No large family could exert power across the peninsula as a whole: key figures in what would become the Al Thani dynasty by this time (probably in 1847) moved from the northeast down to Doha but still were not a national political force, even if they were beginning to build political alliances and links across family and tribal lines, through formal groupings, commerce, and marriages.[9] The rise of the Al Thani family came in the 1850s and especially the 1860s.[10] Its patriarch, Muhammad bin Thani al-Wadhiri, enhanced his power after he moved the family to Doha and consolidated his power through friendly ties with other tribes in the north and especially by making an alliance with Faysal bin Turki, the emir of the second Saudi state, who had visited Qatar in 1851. Muhammad's presence in Doha allowed him to build his wealth. His influence was such that he was now operating as de facto ruler of Qatar.

The formal start of the Al Thani dynasty can be dated to 1868.[11] (The subsequent line and transfers of power are outlined in Figure 2.1.) In 1867, the Bahraini leader sparked a war with Qatar by imprisoning Muhammad's son Qasim, who had been sent to negotiate over a tribal dispute. Muhammad demanded that Qasim be returned, but this led to a Bahraini attack on Doha, al-Bida', and al-Wakra, which in turn prompted a Qatari attack on Bahrain.[12] By this time the British were in effect in control of the littoral areas of the Gulf and were willing to support local elites such as the Bahraini rulers if they ultimately gave the British an overarching regional dominance, while at the same time Saudi power was waning, as demonstrated by their inability to resolve the dispute over the imprisonment of Qasim after Muhammad sought their intervention. The British thus could step in to impose a settlement in the conflict between the two rulers. Such a dynamic reinforces James Onley's argument that in the nineteenth century, London was not usually in the Gulf against the will of local leaders, even though it benefited from having a presence there, of course, but that many leaders sought out British protection.[13] The agreement, signed on September 12, 1868, included the appointment of a new ruler in Bahrain and Muhammad's recognition of him and agreement to cease hostilities, but it is most important because it in effect recognized Qatar as a separate and distinct political entity to Bahrain. It did not grant true independence to Qatar, which was still required to pay a tribute to Bahrain, but the fact that various tribes were allocated a share of this tribute and that Muhammad was

Figure 2.1 Abridged Genealogy of Qatar's Rulers Since 1868

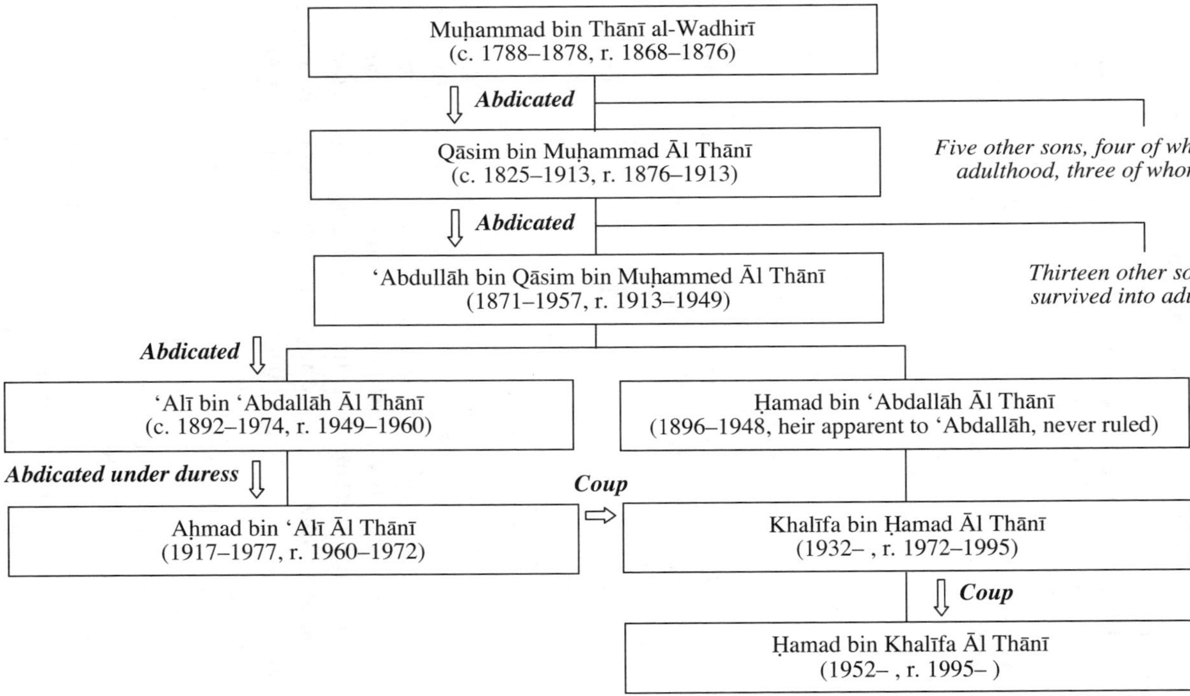

Sources: Derived from details in Crystal, *Oil and Politics in the Gulf,* p. xiv and throughout; Herb, *All in the Family,* pp. 112–126; and Anthony, *Arab States of the Lower Gulf,* p. 78.

to collect it suggests that the British now saw Muhammad as head of a distinct political entity and the most powerful local leader, granted with tribal affiliation, which is still the primary unit of political loyalty for the population.[14] The agreement brought stability to the Gulf littoral area and led to the consolidation, and greater urbanization and development, of the monarchical regimes that still rule the smaller upper and central Arab Gulf states to the present time.

Coinciding with the decline of Saudi power and the maritime and littoral strength of the British was the renewed interest of the Ottomans in the Gulf.[15] In 1871 the Qataris accepted Ottoman power, and in 1872 Ottoman troops arrived and were stationed in Qatar, even though the British, while not intervening against it, did not recognize this Ottoman claim of protectorship over Qatar. In 1876, Muhammad handed power to his eldest son, Qasim bin Muhammad Al Thani (r. 1876–1913), who is now considered the founder of the modern nation of Qatar by virtue of his role in successfully balancing the Ottomans against the British and developing the early Qatari polity and economy. Qasim maintained his position tenaciously and advanced and consolidated the Al Thani dynasty. As his power and local rule developed, he became increasingly unhappy about the Ottomans' interference in Qatar and their demands for tribute, and ultimately direct conflict occurred in 1893, when Qasim refused to host a visit to Doha by the Ottoman governor (*wali*) in Basra. This led to a military attack by the governor's forces on those of Qasim on March 26, 1893, which the Qatari forces successfully repelled. The Turks left Qatar but did not relinquish their claims of control over it, but Qasim's position and reputation as leader were established by the battle. On top of his military prowess, he was also now seen as a political leader and later as something of an elder political statesman when he began devolving greater powers to his brother and then his son. Their rule also led to some development of the infrastructure in Qatar. Qasim was the first leader to build roads between the major towns of Qatar and to establish the first basic schools. Qasim died in 1913, leaving a strong dynasty in place if still a modest economy, with power then shifting to his son Abdallah bin Qasim bin Muhammad Al Thani (r. 1913–1949).[16]

After the commencement of World War I, the Ottomans renounced their claims over Qatar and in 1916 the Anglo-Qatari Treaty brought the British in again as naval protector of Qatar. The country was technically considered independent under the treaty, although Britain's powers there were considerable. The British not only underwrote the maritime defense of Qatar but contributed also to its development in modest ways, including by building telegraph links and a postal service, and improving some other infrastructure. At the end of the war the British remained in the region as the dominant power, albeit against a growing nationalism and desire for independence around them. The British made a further agreement with Abdallah on May 5, 1935, related to the oil concessions under negotiation at the time, that extended London's defense of Qatar to the entire approaches, both maritime and land; the agreement was signed twelve days later.

The economy remained modest for most of Abdallah's reign and centered on pearling for several more decades. The state's revenues were integrally linked to pearling as well: what little relationship there was between leaders and merchants in the pre-oil era was the result of the ruler's need to raise money from the merchants through customs duties and pearl taxes.[17] There were only a few large merchant families in Qatar in the interwar period—the wealthiest were the al-Mana' and the Darwish—who had made their money from pearling, trading, and smuggling, and later by linking to the oil sector.[18] These wealthiest of merchants were able to gain monopolies or other favoritism from the ruler through social ties, loans, and other links, although the position of the families varied over time as they competed with each other. Qatar's merchants as a wider group, however, did not constitute a typical social or political force, much less any sort of formal actor in the political economy, and thus had very limited political power or influence.

The reliance on pearling proved catastrophic when, in the 1930s, the global pearling industry collapsed. The combination of the Great Depression, and then the Japanese cultured pearl coming widely onto the international market after about 1933, ruined Qatar's pearling sector. The 1930s witnessed the end of the income and development that had been financed in large part by pearling and external links to the economy, and over that decade and the 1940s the standard of living and population of Qatar both fell.[19] It was only the discovery of oil that offered some economic promise, but the exploitation of this did not begin until 1938, ceased from 1942 to 1947, and became truly central to the economy only in the late 1940s. Until then, Qatar remained poor and its business community feeble.

The Political Economy After Oil

The modern economic history of the Gulf has been largely dictated by oil, and Qatar is no different. Qatar actually features quite early in the oil history of the region, even though it was not until the 1940s that oil became really valuable to the Al Thani and the Qatari economy. The 1916 treaty, in common with other such agreements, had included constraints on Abdallah granting oil concessions to non-British parties, and so when his interest was tweaked in the possibility of oil reserves within his territory, he had to work with the British. Abdallah granted an exploratory option to the D'Arcy Exploration Company, part of the Anglo-Persian Oil Company (APOC) in 1926,[20] and the first oil survey was conducted shortly thereafter, without success. After the discovery of oil in Bahrain by the US firm Standard Oil Company of California (Socal), British interest increased again in Qatar, although still no one was certain what reserves would be found there. It was in the period from 1933 to 1935 that serious negotiations occurred between the British and Abdallah. Once the British had offered further protection guarantees and, in effect, linked them to the granting of an oil concession, Abdallah became keener on an agreement.[21] The concession was finally agreed on May 17, 1935. The terms included a seventy-five-year concession, with a payment to Abdallah of 400,000 rupees immediately and 150,000 rupees per annum.[22] In June 1935, Petroleum Development Qatar Limited (PDQL) was formed, which would later become the Qatar Petroleum Company (QPC) and then Qatar Petroleum (QP), which today is a state-owned oil company.[23] The ownership of the PDQL and then the QPC was 23.75 percent each by the Royal Dutch/Shell Group, the Compagnie Française des Pétroles, the British Petroleum Company, and the Near East Development Company, and 5 percent by the Gulbenkian Group.[24]

The income from the concession assisted Abdallah at a crucial time of economic recession, but little further oil income came to him until after World War II. The first well to become operational was Jabal Dukhan in October 1938, from which oil began flowing in commercial amounts the following year. However, the start of World War II brought production to a near halt, and a full halt took effect in 1942. This brought—yet again, following the collapse of pearling the decade before—significant economic problems to Qatar. Although Abdallah received payments of 300,000 rupees per annum plus additional support for some salaries during the suspension, this income was inadequate to his and the economy's needs.[25] Abdallah went into debt over this period, and the economy suffered strikingly as economic activity declined and people again moved temporarily to other parts of the Gulf looking for work. The economic situation was dire enough that food shortages became an issue at times in the 1940s.

Furthermore, this period coincided with Qatari-Bahraini tensions over sovereignty over al-Zubara. The Al Khalifa had never actually renounced control of the settlement after most of them left in 1783, and had long had some presence and political influence over the main tribe there. The town had fallen into disrepair, and then had been destroyed in 1873 and later resettled. A combination of economic deprivation in the 1930s and attempts by different sections of the Na'im tribe to separately seek patronage from the Al Thani and the Al Khalifa against other parts of the tribe brought the matter renewed political importance. After the Al Thani attacked a group from the Na'im in 1937, Bahrain imposed an embargo, which for several years combined with the other problems already mentioned to make the war years especially hard for the Qataris.

It was not until 1947 that oil flowed again, and while the royalties were very low when measured against the value of the product on world markets, sizable sums of money nonetheless again flowed to Abdallah's coffers. However, this proved a mixed blessing, and certainly did not bring stability. As Abdallah grew older, he had begun to groom his second, favored son, Hamad, to succeed him; however, Hamad died in 1948 while Abdallah was still alive. In the increasingly common theme of Qatari royal politics, a succession crisis ensued as Abdallah's eldest son, Ali, and Hamad's son, Khalifa, then still a teenager, both sought to succeed the emir. Various family members fell behind the two contenders, and at the same time demanded a greater share of oil income. As they became restless, even violent, the elderly Abdallah, presumably unwilling to deal with such squabbling any further, simply abdicated. In a public ceremony in Doha on August 20, 1949, Abdallah's eldest son, Ali bin Abdallah Al Thani, took power.[26] Ali's inheritance was not an enviable one, since his father had left with much of the national treasury but had not dealt with the family infighting.[27] An attempt had been made to deal with the succession problem by having Ali pledge, prior to his inauguration, that Hamad's son Khalifa would be heir-apparent. Despite this, Ali broke the deal in 1960 when he abdicated in favor of his own son Ahmad.

Two things saved Ali's political skin. One was the permanent British presence in Qatar, to which Abdallah had agreed under the pressure of the family's bickering in 1949. The British adopted a direct political role in Qatar in this period, appointing a political officer and an adviser—at Ali's request—and developing the first real bureaucratic institutions, even if they were little more than financial, taxation, and law enforcement bodies.[28] The British, of course, were motivated by the chance to gain leverage over the oil sector, but nonetheless their actions probably helped stabilize Qatar in the four years immediately after Ali's ascension to power. What also saved Ali politically was the enormous influx of oil wealth that began around the time he assumed power. Despite inflationary impacts,[29] this gave new patronage capacity to the emir. After the distribution of oil revenues had been agreed among Ali, the PDQL, and in effect the British, set sums were established for Ali and allowances were separately negotiated with the family. By 1954, Qatar had in place the basic elements of a proper accounting and financial system. The distribution of oil revenues had been amended in 1952 to an even split of profits between the Qatari government and the oil company: specifically, the Qatari government was guaranteed the higher of either the 1935 royalty figure or 50 percent of the profits, and a guarantee of a minimum of £1 million per annum regardless of production and profit levels.[30] The income that oil provided the state increased markedly each year until halting and then declining after 1958,[31] as shown in Table 2.1. Coincidentally, offshore oil, the concession for which had (controversially with the PDQL) been given to a foreign firm, Superior Oil, which sold it on to Shell, did not develop until after Ali's

Table 2.1 Qatari Oil Production and Export, 1949–1971 (million long tons)

	Production	Exports
1949	0.08	0.02
1950	1.62	1.54
1951	2.33	2.25
1952	3.25	3.22
1953	4.00	3.92
1954	4.70	4.55
1955	5.36	5.26
1956	5.78	5.67
1957	6.50	6.49
1958	8.09	8.06
1959	7.87	7.86
1960	8.08	7.98
1961	8.25	8.14
1962	8.67	8.62
1963	8.95	8.97
1964	9.98	9.93
1965	10.79	10.62
1966	13.63	13.69
1967	15.24	15.06
1968	16.02	16.03
1969	16.76	16.65
1970	17.10	17.12
1971	20.28	20.22

Source: Nafi, *Economic and Social Development in Qatar,* p. 61 (tab. 4.3).

Note: A long ton is 2,240 pounds, or 1,016 kilograms. It was used in Qatar, and in many of the British dominions, until the British began using metric measurements in the mid-1960s.

time, due to technical problems—as much as offshore royalties may have assisted Ali when the revenues from the oil company, by then renamed the Qatar Petroleum Company, began to fall.

The oil sector, not surprisingly, quickly came to dominate the economy. This was due not only to the influx of rental income and the development spending that such income permits the state but also to the fact that the business community still remained weak once oil output was expanding; if anything, the introduction of large amounts of oil income ensured that the co-optive means of the state, beginning under Ali's rule, discouraged business families from competing with or challenging the state. Apart from the QPC, which obviously had enormous power independent of Ali, domestic firms remained small and weak. Those that were established in the 1960s—and numerically a lot were—typically were set up to service the oil sector or the government sector, or as a result of new areas and amounts of state spending and to promote the circulation of new wealth in the economy.

At the same time, while spending was astronomical compared to the pre-oil period, infrastructure, the public sector, and state services still took time to deliver. Telecommunications arrived with the opening of an exchange in 1953, and a local power plant was built in 1957. Other infrastructure and government buildings began appearing in the 1950s as well, with an airport built in the 1950s to link the country and economy to this relatively new form of transport. Government departments and positions were also, not surprisingly, a facet of Ali's co-optation. Members of the Al Thani, as well as key shaikhs from other tribes whom Ali was seeking to placate, were given state-funded public sector roles, often senior ones. This co-optation, in fact, was the key reason why social and infrastructure spending in the 1950s was so incomplete: allowances to the family simply cost too much. The family controlled almost all aspects of government, apart from one minister (*wazir*), Abdallah Darwish, who for a time was very powerful in managing and coordinating some key state institutions until the royal family, many members of which despised him and his power, pushed him out (both out of office and out of Qatar) in 1956.[32]

The other dynamic at this time was socioeconomic change, and especially the emergence of social classes as the economy developed and expanded. In this early oil period, merchants became more numerous, even if no more powerful as a group. Yet in contrast, a working class did begin to emerge. Among the workers there was a sizable expatriate population, mostly Arab, but there was also a strong local working class, in many cases former pearl divers, nomads, or laborers who had moved into the oil sector or related firms. There were also slaves for a time—one estimate in

1951 put the number at around 3,000[33]—until Ali freed them in 1952, thereby building a new base of support.[34] Industrial problems were a regular feature of the Qatari political economy, especially against the oil company, and involved all types of workers (Qatari, expatriate, and freed slaves). Until a 1952 agreement with the oil company, labor was often backed by Ali, who was trying to keep pressure on the company. Over time, organized laborers, especially the local Qataris, increasingly emphasized their identity as a way of developing the bonds between them and enhancing their position; as Crystal notes, the "development of a Qatari consciousness"[35] was the single most important outcome of the strikes, although they also delivered economic and other changes by forcing Ali to decree commercial and employment preference for local Qataris. Labor troubles declined later in the 1950s, but over this time and into the early 1960s the legal and state structures were put in place to manage industrial relations better, and not long afterward, even greater oil wealth began to erode the Qatari working class and allow it to be replaced mostly with expatriate laborers.

Ultimately Ali's rule was underwhelming: it was a comparatively short eleven years, and was marked by spurts of development and by social change, but little of it the product of deliberate policy or intervention by Ali. The family was more powerful and demanding than ever, and this, coupled with Ali's declining health, led him to abdicate in 1960. As mentioned, he did not hand power to Khalifa as agreed when he assumed power but rather made his son Ahmad ruler. The contention over this was settled by Khalifa becoming formally titled crown prince and deputy ruler. This placated Khalifa, who in fact turned out to be quite a competent manager of state affairs. On the other hand, Ahmad proved incapable of handling the family. In fact, he increased their funding and access to government posts, a costly act that came at the expense of broader social spending. He also spent an enormous share of the oil wealth, some one-quarter, on himself.[36] There were changes and developments during this time, of course, as oil wealth continued to flow in, but these were modest: the bureaucracy expanded, and was somewhat reformed and partly Qatarized by Khalifa; a cement factory, a national fishing company, and a few other firms were formed; government land grants and loans were established for poorer Qataris; and a small, fifteen-member cabinet was formed, even though it never met.[37] Education was rolled out to a much wider number of students; Qatar went from possessing a single school with 240 students in 1951 to having 5,965 students in 1960 and over 52,000 by 1985.[38] Health standards and facilities improved equally sharply.[39] Housing became better and increasingly, after the early 1960s, state funded. Thus the Qatari political economy was becoming increasingly allocative, and the role of the royal family continued to expand, while that of the merchants as a group was constrained to only certain parts of the economy.[40]

Thus, again under Ahmad as under Ali, there were deep problems of poor and uninterested leadership and of a large, disruptive, and factionalized family, which impacted social and economic development. While Khalifa proved to be an able manager, there were persistent tensions between the two, sometimes with Khalifa seeking to undermine Ahmad's position and other times stemming from wider family fragmentation along the two branches of Abdallah's line that Ahmad and Khalifa represented. Ahmad, following the practice of Ali before him, tried to buy off key members of the family, through allowances and state jobs and later, in the case of Ahmad, by allowing them to branch into commerce, often protected with a monopoly or regulation against foreign competition.[41] Sometimes they pushed merchants out of the way, but more often they formed partnerships; these would bring the royal family deeper into the Qatari commercial realm but also consolidated their ties with merchants, beginning a theme, which still remains, of a symbiosis but royal dominance in the business-government relationship. It is crucial also to stress the size of the royal family here: Qatar's was and remains the second-largest royal family in the Gulf, after Saudi Arabia's, and the largest as a percentage of the population. It is, in effect, an extended grouping covering, with all the marriages and other links to it, perhaps as much as half the country's indigenous population. Keeping even the core houses of the family content, or at least somewhat stable, then, was no mean feat and yet was absolutely central to a ruler's ability to retain power.

Qatar's political system and economy were, by the late 1960s, becoming more akin to those of a state, if not an especially efficient or steady one. In 1968 independence loomed when Britain announced that it would withdraw from its military commitments east of Suez by 1971. This included its ties with Qatar: there was no longer a political resident in Qatar, but its ruler still relied on the backing that treaties and ties with Britain provided or implied. The initial thinking among the small Gulf states—Bahrain, Qatar, and the Trucial States (now the UAE)—was to form a federation. There was not to be agreement, however, about exactly where power would lie in such a federation. This worried the UAE's leaders, but also Qatar's, and Khalifa in particular strongly opposed any federation that would give Bahrain seniority or political precedence over Qatar. Ahmad publicly stated his support for the federation, but seems not to have genuinely wanted to sponsor it: he drafted a provisional constitution in April 1970 under which Qatar would be an independent state, not federated with the others, and in May 1970 Khalifa was appointed prime minister, in effect establishing a new and independent political process for the state. A council of ministers was formed at the start of 1971, and Qatar became independent on September 3, 1971.

When Qatar became independent, Ahmad was abroad in Switzerland.[42] It was Khalifa who made the public announcement of independence. Ahmad had lost the bulk of his support, both at a popular level and among key Al Thani figures. His absence was a reminder of his aloofness and probably damaged his popular legitimacy, but his lack of interest in ruling effectively had been crucial and illustrated an enduring problem in his rule. Moreover, both Britain and Saudi Arabia preferred Khalifa, not Ahmad, as leader. Relations between Khalifa and Ahmad were at a nadir at this time because of their differing positions over independence and, in 1972, by Ahmad's apparent attempt to make his son Abd al-Aziz heir-apparent and to again deny Khalifa the role.[43] On September 22, 1972, Khalifa removed Ahmad in a coup. He immediately shored up his position, dismissing key members of Ahmad's immediate family from central roles and replacing them with his own close family members.[44] Although most of the economic and industrial portfolios remained unchanged—these had been expanded in 1970 as preparations for independence were made—Khalifa's most significant changes, not surprisingly in terms of common coup-proofing practice in the Gulf, were in areas such as military command, foreign affairs, and the interior ministry.[45] It was under Khalifa that Qatar's politics and political economy would most dramatically change and transform—at least until his son Hamad seized power in 1995.

Qatar Under Khalifa, 1972–1995

Khalifa had gained enormous political and administrative experience and influence before he assumed power,[46] especially during Ahmad's latter years as ruler. He was deputy ruler as well as crown prince in Ahmad's final years in power, and among other roles he had been director of police and internal security, director of education, minister of finance and petroleum affairs, and prime minister.[47] Perhaps as a result of this experience, the changes that he implemented upon seizing power were substantial.[48] Among his earliest and most significant steps was to temper the power of the family and its drain on the state. He cut allowances to family members, spending the money instead on social development that would win him wider support and legitimacy. Yet he did not change the autocratic nature of the political order nor the centrality of the emir within it. In fact, in taking control of all public finances he in effect further blurred the boundary between the state's and the royal family's incomes from oil rents, but he managed public finances far more carefully and astutely than had his predecessors.[49]

Khalifa also sought to bypass the royal family politically as much as possible. He amended the provisional constitution, which Ahmad had not implemented and which remained in force until Hamad proposed a new one, ratified by plebiscite in 2003. Khalifa's amendments included the formation of a *majlis al-shura,* or consultative assembly. This was not in any sense real democratization: the assembly initially consisted of only twenty members, raised to thirty in 1975, but all appointed by the emir and with strict controls on their powers.[50] Since all the positions were appointed, as remains the case today, the mix of members allowed for a broader co-optation and consultation with societal elites than would a reliance on the family or on more informal consultation with specific figures. In fact, Khalifa appeared to deliberately maintain a broad assembly membership, representative of the constituencies that he needed to keep on his side: leaders of key tribes were the single largest group, followed closely by merchants and then by educated elites and regional representatives.[51] The assembly allowed Khalifa to consult both formally and informally with key individuals, but controversy or the public airing of disagreements or debates was avoided, with sessions being held in private and with the more contentious issues often resolved informally by Khalifa beforehand. Furthermore, in practice, membership had been for life, and on the death or resignation of a member of the assembly, the appointment would pass to a close family member, usually one of his sons. This served to ensure continuity in a particular group's representation and a long-term approach by them to their political relationships, both of which suited a clever and co-optive emir seeking to stabilize the wider polity beyond his family and, indeed, to build his support within these new constituencies. The assembly's structure also, of course, drew a clear line in what power the emir was willing to share: the *majlis* was able to review decrees, legislation, and budgets, and recommend amendments to the cabinet, but its agenda was largely set by what the government sent it, and it could never make demands on the emir or other Al Thani ruling elite nor vote no-confidence in such figures. Moreover, as already noted, Khalifa placed some key members of his immediate family into the most important and sensitive cabinet and bureaucratic posts, partly to clear out people loyal to his predecessor, but most of all to ensure trust and reliability among those most tightly linked into his neopatrimonial circle.

Khalifa also delivered a dramatic and extensive improvement in Qatar's economic and socioeconomic infrastructure, a far more thorough development of the country than either of his two predecessors had undertaken. In large part this was the product of the oil price increases during Khalifa's first decade in power due to the 1973–1974 "oil crisis" spike and then the increases again in 1979–1980[52] following the Iranian revolution and the commencement of the 1980–1988 Iran-Iraq War, both but especially the latter of which took sizable amounts of Iranian, Iraqi, and Kuwaiti oil off the international market. In Qatar, there was an immense injection of oil rent funds into the state's coffers beginning in 1974, which flowed through to state spending the following year, and massive increases in oil revenue and spending again in 1979, 1980, and 1981, all as shown in Table 2.2. These figures, even allowing for inflation and low non-oil productivity, are massive, and demonstrate the extent of spending, both nominal and relative to earlier periods, that the state undertook after 1974.

The other, related dynamics of the 1970s were the emergence of a more cohesive, development-based policy on hydrocarbons, and the expansion of Qatar's gas sector, as outlined in Table 2.3. The first of these, including the nationalization of the hydrocarbon sector, would lead to the second. Khalifa recognized the need for the state to manage its own interests in the sector and to maximize both its rent income and the vertical integration of the sector, so as to maximize the national benefits derived

Table 2.2 Qatari GDP, Oil Revenue, and State Spending, 1970–1982 (QR millions)

	GDP	Oil Revenue (percentage of GDP)	State Expenditure (percentage of GDP)
1970	1,313	1,099 (83.7)	505 (38.5)
1971	1,850	1,441 (77.9)	690 (37.3)
1972	2,172	1,673 (77.0)	959 (44.2)
1973	2,615	2,444 (93.5)	1,542 (59.0)
1974	7,895	7,811 (98.9)	1,931 (24.5)
1975	9,877	6,893 (70.0)	5,302 (53.7)
1976	13,017	8,470 (65.1)	5,809 (44.6)
1977	14,322	8,134 (56.8)	7,318 (51.1)
1978	15,709	8,955 (57.0)	6,473 (41.2)
1979	21,783	13,398 (61.5)	8,270 (38.0)
1980	28,631	19,728 (68.9)	10,937 (38.2)
1981	31,527	19,331 (61.3)	14,743 (46.8)
1982	27,652	14,840 (53.7)	12,619 (45.3)

Source: Gause, *Oil Monarchies*, p. 49 (tab. 2D). Copyright © 1994 by the Council on Foreign Relations Press. Reprinted with permission.

Table 2.3 Expansion of Onshore Gas Production and Utilization in Qatar, 1971–1981 (billion cubic feet)

	1971	1972	1973	1974	1975	1976	1977	1978	1979	1980	1981
Non-associated gas											
Production	—	—	—	—	—	—	—	24.8	64.3	80.0	94.4
Utilization	—	—	—	—	—	—	—	24.8	64.3	80.0	94.4
Utilization percentage	—	—	—	—	—	—	—	100	100	100	100
Associated gas											
Production	90.4	103.5	108.0	91.2	70.2	98.6	89.1	98.0	87.1	80.8	222.0[a]
Utilization	26.2	35.2	35.6	28.3	43.5	50.3	57.9	50.0	51.4	60.6	162.1
Utilization percentage	29	34	33	31	62	51	65	51	59	75	73

Source: Nafi, *Economic and Social Development in Qatar,* p. 68 (tab. 4.6).
Note: a. Includes offshore production.

from oil and gas. The oil sector was nationalized by Law no. 13 in 1972 and some subsequent decrees, which specifically noted the integration goals of nationalization: "The objectives of [the Qatar National Oil Company][53] shall be to engage in all phases of the oil industry in Qatar and abroad, including exploration and drilling for oil, natural gas . . . [and] production, refining, transport and storage of [oil and gas] and any of their derivatives and byproducts, as well as trading in, distribution, sale and export of these substances."[54] This came on top of the development of natural gas industries. After the creation of the Qatar Fertilizer Company (QAFCO) in 1969, the state increasingly emphasized the exploitation of gas and the manufacture of chemicals and fertilizers from it.[55] QAFCO started producing ammonia and urea in late 1973, and then in 1974 the Qatar Petrochemical Company (QAPCO) was established to manufacture ethylene and low-density polyethylene.[56] Further investment and joint ventures in gas, petrochemicals, and associated infrastructure in the 1970s and 1980s resulted in the dramatic development and expansion of the hydrocarbon sector beyond the basic crude oil production and associated activity that had dominated hydrocarbon production in the 1950s and 1960s.

The impacts of the spending boom in the 1970s were extensive and covered new infrastructure, better social services, greater welfarism, higher defense spending and defense modernization, a massive rise in the number of nationals employed by the state, and an increased reliance on foreign labor, especially for unskilled, semiskilled, and some very specific professional work.[57] The Qatari public service nearly tripled in size between 1971 and 1986,[58] reflecting ultimately quite a bloated bureaucracy, to be sure, but also, given its modest original size, a necessary expansion of public sector workers to deliver new and genuine social services and infrastructure. Throughout the 1970s and 1980s the educational system at all levels increased markedly in size and student numbers, while public health indicators and other social figures were similarly improved,[59] as Tables 2.4 and 2.5 show.

In the same period, there was an expansion of nonstate economic activity. The number of business establishments grew significantly, if not as massively as did the rents and socioeconomic indicators already mentioned, and this growth was quite broad in sectoral terms and steady throughout the 1970s. The exact figures are listed in Table 2.6. Two things, however, are important to note. The first is that this growth was largely the result of the influx of oil rents and the growth of firms to service the state and its socioeconomic spending. Second, this increase was also due to a boom in the construction sector as both government/commercial buildings and private dwellings were built to meet the growth of the public sector

Table 2.4 Expansion of Electricity and Water Production in Qatar, 1971–1980

	Electrical Power Production (million kilowatts per hour)	Desalinated Water Production (million gallons)
1971	351	1,174
1972	360	1,130
1973	419	2,440
1974	460	2,800
1975	625	3,500
1976	801	3,559
1977	1,011	4,544
1978	1,349	6,322
1979	1,986	7,738
1980	2,416	9,935

Source: Economic and Social Infrastructures in the State of Qatar, p. 50 (tab. 11).

Table 2.5 Expansion of Education in Qatar, 1960–1981 (number of students)

	1960–1961	1965–1966	1970–1971	1975–1976	1980–1981
Elementary					
Boys	3,722	6,682	7,949	11,150	13,911
Girls	1,942	4,550	6,530	10,252	12,891
Intermediate					
Boys	242	964	1,817	2,890	4,811
Girls	—	211	899	2,480	4,851
Secondary					
Boys	59	270	938	1,815	3,186
Girls	—	50+	398	1,355	2,960
Total	5,965	12,727	18,531	29,942	42,610

Source: Economic and Social Infrastructures in the State of Qatar, p. 81 (tab. 28).

and the rapidly growing size of the population (which nearly doubled in the 1970s alone).[60] Thus the fate of the private sector was dictated in large part by the state, spending by which was largely driven by externally derived rents. In a theme that recurs before and after this time, the state was the dominant driver of the economy, along with a few very wealthy businesspeople. Note, for example, that in the 1970s commercial credit and other forms of capital-raising were extremely limited outside of the government and trade sectors.[61] In effect, therefore, the basic nature of economic relations between the state and business remained unchanged, and

Table 2.6 Expansion of Trade, Industry, and Service Firms in Qatar, 1971–1980 (number of firms)

	1971	1972	1973	1974	1975	1976	1977	1978	1979	1980
Foodstuffs	1,864	1,520	1,789	1,818	1,952	1,910	1,982	2,116	2,280	2,476
Textiles and clothing	577	569	642	689	720	799	872	939	987	1,058
Fuel	22	22	24	25	27	26	26	26	31	33
Chemical products	112	118	126	137	145	153	170	194	224	263
Means of transportation	125	160	168	198	224	242	282	312	343	375
Electrical and nonelectrical products	390	380	416	520	541	667	814	954	1,075	1,188
Nonmetallic products	361	371	443	541	682	782	905	1,079	1,176	1,225
Metallic products	274	283	323	369	377	420	454	493	509	543
Exporting	25	26	30	38	42	44	44	47	51	52
Contracting and tendering	109	133	235	260	198	372	479	528	556	592
Services	806	841	859	885	915	958	1,003	1,058	1,219	1,351
Miscellaneous	166	177	189	198	210	236	251	297	336	377
Total	4,831	4,600	5,244	5,678	6,033	6,609	7,282	8,043	8,787	9,533

Source: Nafi, *Economic and Social Development in Qatar,* p. 14 (tab. 1.8).

despite the expansion in the private sector, business neither gained nor sought greater political power. If anything, the influx of rents encouraged merchants to continue to yield to the state, gaining access to business opportunities and state spending in exchange for surrendering any political aspirations they might otherwise have had.

At the political level, while Khalifa was quite successful in consolidating his position—in part because of the new rents flowing into the economy, but also because he spent this money more broadly and wisely than had his predecessors—there were also family issues with which he needed to contend. The withdrawal of some allowances to the family after he took power was only (partly) tolerated because of the new commercial opportunities that replaced them. At the more senior levels, throughout the 1970s and into the 1980s, Khalifa was engaged in a dispute with one of his brothers, Suhaym, over the issue of appointments and succession. Suhaym had reportedly been promised the role of crown prince by Khalifa in the lead-up to the 1972 coup. After Khalifa became emir, however, he apparently reneged on this promise, and later still supposedly reneged on another promise to make Suhaym prime minister. In yet another recurring theme of modern Qatari politics, Khalifa's appointment of his son Hamad as heir was a compromise, to keep the various wings of the family on his side. Khalifa would struggle with such family issues throughout his rule, and even if such dynamics were less overt than they had previously been, they were important nonetheless—Suhaym had reportedly been storing weapons and seeking Saudi backing against Khalifa before dying of natural causes in 1985.[62]

The 1980s followed a trajectory similar to that of post-1972 Qatar in terms of state expenditure and socioeconomic development. The main challenge of the decade, however, was the fluctuation in oil income; after the price increases in 1973–1974 and 1979–1981, oil prices fell beginning in 1985. Moreover, while Qatari oil production had not yet peaked, output did decline in the early 1980s and was low for the remainder of the decade, falling from an average of 421,000 barrels per day in 1981 to 316,000 in 1983, and only returning to above the 1981 figure a decade later, in 1991.[63] Compensating in part for both of these factors, however, was the expansion of natural gas production and petrochemical manufacturing, plus of course Qatar's enormous rents compared to the very small size of its (citizen) population. However, this did not stop the state from running a budget deficit throughout the second half of the 1980s, a result, for the most part, of the collapse of oil prices after 1984 and the related economic difficulties in the Gulf region.[64]

Nonetheless, the government followed other oil states in the Middle East at the time by instituting austerity measures and policy changes as oil income fell. Initially these were modest. The first charges for government services were introduced in 1983, and around the same time some 3,000 expatriates were cut from government employment after an initial drop in prices.[65] After an even more substantial drop in oil income in 1986, state spending was cut. Health staffing expenditure fell by around 10 percent and spending on major state-financed economic projects (including development of the North Dome gas field) was cut sharply.[66] This impacted Khalifa's support, both among the ordinary Qataris whom he had initially wooed and whose support for him had become a mark of his rule, and among some of the royal family and nonfamily political and business elites who were by this stage feeling the impact from lower state expenditure.[67] As in other oil states, the disadvantages of being a rentier state—particularly higher political risk at times of lower income—were becoming evident. Khalifa ultimately did not reduce the rentierism of the Qatari political economy. In fact, he would leave power having done the opposite, but higher hydrocarbon production levels after 1990 helped reverse the budgetary problems of the middle to late 1980s.

The other challenge for Qatar had long been its foreign relations, which while not in poor shape overall, still suffered from some tensions, especially with Bahrain, and from some wider negative impacts due to regional conflict and instability. After independence Qatar sought to remain cordial with the British, Iran, and Saudi Arabia. In a typical dilemma for a small state in a neighborhood with multiple new and competing states and weak security architecture, Qatar sought to balance ties with these actors. While reliance on them economically was necessary, Qatar's increasing prominence in global security, its broad trade and security ties, and its strategic sharing of gas contracts with various energy companies from around the world all served to keep it from becoming overreliant on any one state. Its ties with Iran were solid, built in part by multiple generations of Iranian-descended Qataris: despite the sectarian differences between this mostly Shiite population and the majority Sunni population of Qatar, the Iranian immigrant population was politically very docile, while trade links into the postindependence period further reinforced Iranian-Qatari ties and Qatar's generally favorable view of Iran.[68] As will be discussed in later chapters, while the 1978–1979 Iranian revolution strained this link somewhat, Qatar subsequently retained quite a solid relationship with Iran, especially in trade, which it maintained even as it built very close strategic links with the United States after 2002.

Likewise, Khalifa needed to maintain strong links with Saudi Arabia, the dominant military and economic power on the Arabian peninsula. Qatar had a border dispute with the Saudis for a time, with Riyadh laying claim to part of the territory in southern Qatar along the shared border, but this was resolved amicably enough in due course.[69] Relations between the royal families of the two states were kept cordial by a shared sense of religious identity, as a majority of the populations in both states are Wahhabi, but with Qatar far less socially strict than Saudi Arabia in recent decades, plus historically there have also been considerable tribal, trade, and other links between the two. More pragmatically, the Saudis have often played the role of intermediary and conciliator among the Arab Gulf states, including in Qatari-Bahraini tensions over sovereignty of al-Zubara and the Hawar Islands.

Bahrain did not relinquish its claim of control over al-Zubara, which had revived in the 1950s, although Qatar was able to maintain its control of the area after that time. The Hawar Islands are located to the south of Bahrain, close to the Qatari coast, and were long a point of dispute. There were tensions in 1982 over the islands, and again in 1986 over a reef near them. The issue lingered until Qatar took it to the International Court of Justice (ICJ), which in 2001 awarded Qatar sovereignty over al-Zubara and Bahrain sovereignty over the Hawar Islands.[70]

Qatar has therefore long had to manage its position as a small but wealthy state in an often-unstable subregion. The lesson from the 1980s and early 1990s, as Qatar was becoming more integrated into the political economy of the Gulf and into the global energy sector, was that this balancing can be very tricky to successfully manage. At the same time, as with other small Gulf states, Qatar has always been unable to achieve defense self-sufficiency—the sheer geostrategic imbalance between large and small states in the Gulf makes this obvious—while the rentier bargain with society requires the state to protect the population from external threat but not to make many demands on society to contribute to defense of the state. Thus Qatar sought in the 1970s and 1980s to develop its military capacity, especially qualitatively, and did make considerable improvements. The creation and development of the Gulf Cooperation Council (GCC) included military and security motivations as central drivers,[71] albeit with a defense of economic assets and interests at the core.[72] As such, a rapid-deployment force was not created until 1986,[73] and even then it was modest in size and capability compared with the enormous military power of Iran and Iraq. Furthermore, despite enhanced defense co-optation, the GCC, and not least of all small states like Qatar, would always be reliant on external stability and foreign relations to minimize the key threats faced by the Arab Gulf states and, worst case, to assist in their defense if the need arose.

Qatar was impacted by regional conflict and instability even where this had little to do with Qatar and little actual link to it. The 1978–1979 Iranian revolution, the 1980–1988 Iran-Iraq War, and the US involvement in the Gulf in 1987–1988 to protect Kuwaiti oil tankers were all important in this regard. These conflicts sent a message internationally that the Gulf was unstable, which inhibited Qatar's ability to build trade, investment, and other ties as it might otherwise have done. More concretely and practically, the costs of commerce increased as a result of these conflicts: shipping and insurance costs for international firms increased markedly, at a time when local investment by oil states was constrained due to lower oil income. Another lesson for Qatar was the August 2, 1990, Iraqi invasion of Kuwait and the subsequent 1990–1991 Gulf War. This demonstrated the vulnerability of small states, in this case Kuwait, but the lesson that regional dynamics can change quickly and lead to a military threat was there for Qatar as well. The previous assumption that Arab states do not conquer each other for territory or over border disputes was starkly disproven, while Kuwait's reliance on US political will and military power to liberate it from Iraq was an important further reminder of small-state security and defense vulnerability. It also demonstrated the limitations of relying on qualitative military capability when facing a genuine quantitative military threat, a lesson that jolted many Gulf leaders at the time.

It is important to acknowledge that Qatar changed under Khalifa, parts of its economy quite fundamentally, and many of the changes under Khalifa have in effect remained in place and been consolidated by Hamad since 1995. Khalifa can take the credit for the investment and integration along the oil and gas chain, which many rentier states failed to do, or did only much later. However, his attempts at economic diversification beyond the hydrocarbon sector were considerably less successful, and while new industries were established and private sector firms greatly increased in number during the Khalifa period, this did not alter the underlying rentier nature of the economy. In terms of the contribution of rents to gross domestic product or state revenue, Qatar in 2010 was still a rentier state as it had been in 1972, and only the characteristics of that rentierism have changed. In large part as a result of that rentierism, Khalifa's political economy was also, to stress again, state capitalist. While this is very different in its features from the state capitalism under Hamad, the centrality of the state, the incorporation and co-optation of business by the state, and the links of varying extents of most sectors to oil and gas were not primarily or fundamentally different in 2010 compared to the 1970s. As much as Qatar changed after 1995, in many ways Khalifa's rule established or reinforced the basic dynamics that would feature in Hamad's.

Hamad, the 1995 Coup, and the New Qatar

On June 27, 1995, Hamad bin Khalifa Al Thani seized power from his father while the latter was on vacation in Switzerland. Hamad had not only been heir-apparent since 1977 and minister of defense but also gained extensive experience in administration and politics in the two decades prior to his capture of power, especially after 1992 when he became responsible for a number of key government roles. Early on, Hamad had been firmly favored by his father, and although he retained his father's trust, the two increasingly disagreed on policy matters and Qatar's strategic direction. Increasingly, Hamad felt that his father was holding back from key reforms and acting too cautiously in some areas of economic and social policy, and the relationship between the two became more strained over several years leading up to the 1995 coup.[74] In the late 1980s and early 1990s, Hamad built up his position in the family and the cabinet, ensuring that supportive individuals were placed in key ministries and other roles, and gradually and discreetly constructed his own political base.[75] Despite some hesitations, the core elements of the family fell in line behind Hamad, and regional and international actors said little in criticism of the coup.

The 1995 coup contained elements that were both old and new. The old issue of family politics involving an aspirant to power seeking a critical mass of family support was the same with Hamad as it had been with previous plotters of such coups. The coup, as with earlier ones, was bloodless but not without controversy, as the departing Khalifa took a large pot of the treasury's assets with him—by some accounts US$3 billion or more[76]—and Hamad brought a lawsuit abroad against his father (later dropped after negotiations) to try to recover some of the funds. The coup also reflected a frustration, by both an aspirant to the leadership and sizable elements of the royal family, with Khalifa as an aging leader, who by some accounts was by then largely incapacitated by alcoholism.[77] When Hamad announced his first cabinet, a fortnight after the coup, it comprised significant reshuffling and changes but also, in keeping with the usual practice, included some thirteen Al Thani family members.

Somewhat unusually, Khalifa did not accept his forced retirement and the wealth that he had taken into it. For a time he moved around the Arab world trying to build international support for himself and against his son's coup,[78] but gained very little traction. About eight months after the coup, in February 1996, a countercoup was attempted, in which some of Khalifa's supporters among a tribal group whom he had recruited and armed during his rule sought to overthrow Hamad's new regime.[79] This failed, and Hamad's rule in the years after that proved safe from appropriation by his father or other relatives.

Important as these dynamics were, there also was much about Hamad that was new. The reforms that he promised and to a large extent subsequently undertook are significant and in many cases unique. Details on these follow, but among the more significant reforms and changes worth stressing here are the globalization of Qatari society and business; the creation of Al-Jazeera as the region's dominant media group; the drafting of a new constitution that was endorsed by referendum in 2003 and that includes substantial freedoms for individuals and society; the holding of local elections in 1999, the first in the GCC that allowed women to vote and to stand for office; and other economic and social changes. There was an expectation of considerable political change—only a small amount of which has occurred thus far—and of social change and modernization. Hamad was known to be accepting of technological and even social change, although the most dramatic changes have since been in the economy: after taking power Hamad basically "dispensed with ritual and began to run his almost bankrupt country like a corporation."[80] This quote says more than perhaps intended, because in reinvigorating the state and entrepreneurializing its capitalism, while maintaining the broad rentier dynamics that have been a feature of Qatar's political economy now for some two generations, Hamad has somewhat "corporatized" the state in terms of enhancing its scope, economic liberalism, and profitability. Moreover, branding Qatar as a microstate, even a model of development for other states to follow, is also a very "corporate" thing to do, but is consistent with the transformation that Hamad was seeking and that he continues to propound. Thus in many ways there is a continuity to Hamad's political economy. There was a new, "late" rentierism, but not an end to rentierism in itself; there was an entrepreneurial state capitalism instead of the previous model that had been more typical of the conservative oil states of the Gulf; and there was a more activist foreign policy that linked economic and security issues together in a deliberate attempt to protect and promote Qatar and its economy as a microstate. It is these dynamics and their post-1995 setting that form the central focus of this book and to which we now turn.

Notes

1. Crystal, *Oil and Politics in the Gulf,* p. 112.
2. Ibid., pp. 26–27.
3. Ibid., p. 27.
4. Ibid.
5. Ibid., p. 28. See also Qatar Ministry of Foreign Affairs, *Qatar,* p. 9; amended version online at http://www.heritageofqatar.org/assets/history/Complete_History_of_Qatar.pdf.
6. Crystal, *Oil and Politics in the Gulf,* p. 28.
7. Ibid., pp. 28–29.
8. Herb, *All in the Family,* p. 110.
9. Crystal, *Oil and Politics in the Gulf,* p. 29.

10. Much of what follows is taken from Zahlan, *The Creation of Qatar,* pp. 36–45; as well as from Crystal, *Oil and Politics in the Gulf,* pp. 29–33.

11. Zahlan, *The Making of the Modern Gulf States,* p. 100.

12. These battles were quite fierce. Much of Doha was destroyed in the Bahraini attack of 1867, for example, while some sixty ships were destroyed and a thousand military personnel were killed in the 1868 Qatari naval battle with Bahrain.

13. This addresses a key question in the study of Gulf history very deftly and convincingly, though doubtless will not conclude it. See Onley, "The Politics of Protection in the Gulf"; and Onley, "Britain and the Gulf Shaikhdoms."

14. Crystal, *Oil and Politics in the Gulf,* pp. 30–31.

15. The details here are taken from Anscombe, "The Ottoman Role in the Gulf," pp. 265–267.

16. Abdallah was Qasim's fourth of twelve sons, not his eldest, but was preferred and groomed for power by Qasim. Abdallah faced considerable opposition from some of his brothers, and struggled to control parts of the countryside at times. Further, the Saudis courted other members of the royal family and tried to weaken Abdallah's position, probably so as to gain Saudi protection over Qatar. Such in-family fighting would prove a sign of similar and even deeper future problems among the royal family. Zahlan, *The Making of the Modern Gulf States,* p. 102.

17. Crystal, *Oil and Politics in the Gulf,* p. 133.

18. Ibid.

19. Ibid., pp. 116–118.

20. Ibid., p. 116.

21. Ibid.

22. Ibid.

23. On the PDQL and QPC, see Nafi, *Economic and Social Development in Qatar,* especially pp. 48–52. On Qatar Petroleum, see its most recent annual report, available online at http://www.qp.com.qa/en/homepage/mediacentre/publications/10-2015054360.aspx.

24. Nafi, *Economic and Social Development in Qatar,* p. 49. The Compagnie Française des Pétroles is now, after several name changes and mergers, Total SA, and the Gulbenkian Group is now Partex Oil and Gas.

25. Crystal, *Oil and Politics in the Gulf,* p. 117.

26. Zahlan, *The Making of the Modern Gulf States,* pp. 102–103; Herb, *All in the Family,* pp. 110–111.

27. Herb, *All in the Family,* pp. 110–111.

28. Crystal, *Oil and Politics in the Gulf,* p. 122.

29. Ibid., p. 119.

30. Except in the case of a *force majeure* interruption to production, in which case the government was still guaranteed a payment of £750,000. Nafi, *Economic and Social Development in Qatar,* p. 49.

31. Crystal, *Oil and Politics in the Gulf,* p. 132.

32. Herb, *All in the Family,* p. 111.

33. Crystal, *Oil and Politics in the Gulf,* p. 140.

34. Ibid., p. 139.

35. Ibid., p. 145.

36. Zahlan, *The Making of the Modern Gulf States,* p. 103.
37. Herb, *All in the Family,* p. 114.
38. Crystal, *Oil and Politics in the Gulf,* p. 146.
39. Ibid.
40. Ibid., p. 149.
41. Ibid., p. 147.
42. Herb, *All in the Family,* p. 114.
43. Crystal, *Oil and Politics in the Gulf,* p. 155.
44. Herb, *All in the Family,* pp. 116, 118.
45. See the detail in fig. 5.4 in Herb, *All in the Family,* p. 117, and the accompanying description on pp. 116, 118.
46. Anthony, *Arab States of the Lower Gulf,* p. 79.
47. Ibid.
48. On these steps, see Crystal, *Oil and Politics in the Gulf,* pp. 155–164.
49. Rathmell and Schulze, "Political Reform in the Gulf," p. 59.
50. Peterson, *The Arab Gulf States,* pp. 86–87.
51. Ibid., p. 87.
52. Beblawi, *The Arab Gulf Economy in a Turbulent Age,* pp. 3–5.
53. Renamed the Qatar General Petroleum Corporation (QGPC) by Law no. 10, decreed in 1974.
54. From Decree-Law no. 13 of 1972, art. 4, quoted in Nafi, *Economic and Social Development in Qatar,* p. 56.
55. Nafi, *Economic and Social Development in Qatar,* p. 54.
56. Ibid., pp. 54–55.
57. For details, see Gause, *Oil Monarchies,* pp. 58–70.
58. Ibid., p. 63.
59. Ibid., pp. 60–67.
60. Nafi, *Economic and Social Development in Qatar,* p. 5.
61. On issues of commercial credit, see the discussion and tab. 2.5 in Nafi, *Economic and Social Development in Qatar,* pp. 33–35.
62. Herb, *All in the Family,* p. 116.
63. Figures are from the historical data workbook attached to the *BP Statistical Review of World Energy 2011,* http://www.bp.com/sectionbodycopy.do?categoryId=7500&contentId=7068481.
64. Specific budgetary positions can be seen in Qatar Statistics Authority, *Annual Statistical Abstract 1989,* pp. 339–340; and Qatar Statistics Authority, *Annual Statistical Abstract 1992,* pp. 366–367.
65. Crystal, *Oil and Politics in the Gulf,* p. 161.
66. Ibid.
67. Ibid.
68. Anthony, *Arab States of the Lower Gulf,* pp. 89–90.
69. Ibid., p. 89.
70. For discussion of the decision, see Tanaka, "Reflections on Maritime Delimitation in the Qatar/Bahrain Case." The ICJ decision itself (*Case Concerning Maritime Delimitation and Territorial Questions between Qatar and Bahrain* [*Qatar* v. *Bahrain*], March 16, 2001), is available online at http://www.icj-cij.org/docket/files/87/7027.pdf.

71. Kechichian, “The Gulf Cooperation Council.”

72. Ibid., p. 853.

73. Kahwaji, “Gulf Cooperation Council Threat Perceptions and Deterrence Objectives,” p. 518.

74. Herb, *All in the Family,* pp. 118–119; “Qatar’s Leader Makes His Mark,” *Middle East Economic Digest,* May 5, 1996; “*MEED* Special Report on Qatar: An Ambitious Amir Takes the Helm,” *Middle East Economic Digest,* August 28, 1995.

75. Herb, *All in the Family,* pp. 117–119.

76. “Qatar: Government Announces Cases Against Former Amir,” *Middle East Economic Digest,* September 30, 1996.

77. Herb, *All in the Family,* p. 119.

78. “Former Amir of Qatar Bids to Regain Power,” *Middle East Economic Digest,* January 8, 1996; “*MEED* Special Report on Qatar: Creating Facts Worthy of Fiction,” *Middle East Economic Digest,* August 26, 1996.

79. Herb, *All in the Family,* p. 119.

80. “Hamad bin Khalifa al-Thani Profile: Sheikh Who Bought the Pharaoh’s Bazaar,” *Sunday Times* (London), May 16, 2010.

3

The Political Order

The previous chapter was about the evolution of politics and the economy in Qatar in the two centuries or so leading up to Emir Hamad's seizure of power in 1995. This chapter is about the pattern of his rule. To that end it covers both political and economic dynamics, with the latter usually discussed in terms of their role in creating an "energy-driven" economy and thus in sustaining the political order: the allocative, support-building, and legitimacy-building dynamics bestowed by oil and gas are substantial, and the actors created and sustained by them are central in explaining political power in present-day Qatar. That Qatar's is an "energy-driven" economy suggests that it is a very allocative state, which is indeed the case, but particular actors and the relationships between them are of greatest importance. The highest level of political decisionmaking in Qatar ultimately comes down to a few key people—the emir, his wife, the prime minister, and the crown prince, for the most part—and this chapter explores their roles. However, there is also a discussion of wider dynamics, especially how these core few elites link to key state institutions, merchant families, and ultimately wider social forces, which is an important if secondary issue in understanding how power is derived and wielded. Broader political dynamics, such as the roles of other institutions and actors, nongovernmental groups, and external actors, are important but are explored separately in later chapters.

An "Energy-Driven" Economy: The State as Chauffeur

The central aim of this chapter is to reinforce two themes. The first is of Qatar being, to a considerable extent, a family enterprise, albeit a much more sophisticated and benevolent one than most and not simply a state seized by a sultanistic or oligarchical control of public resources by a family dynasty. The second goal is to explain elements of Qatar's extensive neopatrimonial political and institutional system and how this relates to its late rentier structure; in so doing it will explore the meaning and implications of Qatar's political economy as being "energy driven." Specifically, it addresses several questions. The first is that of exactly how much influence members of the Al Thani dynasty possess compared with both Shaikh Hamad and the institutions and bureaucracy of the contemporary state. Here Qatar shares some similarities with other Gulf monarchies, but by virtue of the size and role of its royal family, some significant differences as well. The second emphasis herein is on the role of state-owned firms in the political economy. In twenty-first-century Qatar, such firms give the lie to the idea of such enterprises being inherently inefficient, politically corrupted behemoths. They are, instead, tools of profit generation and thus state revenue and sources of economic diversification, but they perform such functions not simply for the political sake of it or opportunistically but as a deliberate strategy of regime survival and legitimacy-building, and elite consolidation. The third issue is about the strategies in place to sustain the political order, specifically those seeking to expand the sources of state revenue and to reduce, to the extent possible, the risk that a reliance on rents will be a weakness when the world ultimately transitions to a post-oil economy and then eventually a post-hydrocarbon one. This is a core element of state-owned firms, of course, but is also a driver of Qatar's attempts at developing its human capital and diversifying its economic structure, both of which are central arguments later in the book. The neopatrimonial character of Qatar's business-government relationship is important here, however, as the private sector is starting to gain greater attention and a little more autonomy from the state in part for the sake of economic diversification and employment generation. In this vein, the chapter also examines how other elite actors link to the state, especially powerful indigenous businesspeople and multinational firms, as the contributions of these to the economy carry political corollaries as well.

The discussion here sheds further light on the late rentier and entrepreneurial state capitalism arguments. Where the previous chapter focused on the sources of state revenue and thus on the capacity for rentier dynamics to function, this chapter moves the discussion into the more interesting stage of how that rentierism takes place. In particular, it considers the allocative mechanisms possessed by the state, and not only how some of these distribute funds to society—a simple profile of key economic ministries would be rather dull—but also how other political institutions, in deriving from or sustaining rents (and often both), are as integral to Qatar's late rentierism strategy and processes as are Qatar Petroleum (QP), the Ministry of Energy and Industry, or the Ministry of Economy and Finance. In defending this approach, linkages to the other two theoretical pillars—entrepreneurial state capitalism and activist microstatism—are also necessary. The first, entrepreneurial state capitalism, is a feature of late rentierism, where the state gives itself a quite *dirigiste,* yet also very market-based and in many ways business-friendly, role. The state does this, as will be shown, both as a way to compensate for some of the weaknesses and threats inherent in very passive or static attitudes toward rents, and as a way to plan for a future when the original rents that first built or sustained the state are no longer flowing into the coffers or are not large enough to ensure the political status quo. Therefore, to call Qatar's political economy "energy driven" is not completely adequate. In effect, energy is the *engine* and the state is the *driver*—or actually the chauffeur, it might be argued—for the economy and socioeconomic development. Oil, gas, and energy-related activity permeates the economy in multiple ways, and in providing the means by which politics is able to operate in the ways that it does, or indeed must necessarily exist as it does, allows the (resulting) political system to function.

The Qatari energy policy for several decades had been quite an intelligent one, in that it has maximized the value and diversification opportunities that are extracted from the sector, and has not relied on simple rents alone. This is explored more fully in the next chapter. However, Qatar's political economy is not immune from some of the features and risks of the "oil curse." Oil and gas extraction, and even to a lesser extent the downstream energy and associated activities, are capital-intensive. They create some extremely well-paying jobs for Qataris, but only for a relatively small number of them. There is a need to find sustainable employment opportunities elsewhere for the overwhelming bulk of the population, and a policy of artificially constructing jobs by diverting some rents to a large public sector or to subsidizing redundant labor in state-owned firms is not workable in the long term. Qatar also faces challenges from a youth population whose perspectives differ somewhat from those of their parents. They are more globalized than their parents and do not remember the preboom (that is, pre-1990s) period, something that is both a positive and a negative for them and for intergenerational relations. These are the same youth who are hobbled by persistent problems with education and the policy settings around and impacting employment. For the state, tackling these issues is not only about acting intelligently and responsibly, and in so doing building up some authority and legitimacy—and for that matter, new sources of funding or support—but also a central element to the survival strategy of the political elite. The 2011 Arab Spring reminded the Qatari elite that profound popular anger existed against the political order in many Arab states, and although Qatar was one of the most stable states during the uprisings and Hamad's regime among the most tolerated by its population, the risk of revolutionary change remained present. There is much at stake in the energy-driven political economy, therefore, and there are multiple facets to it.

The Royal Family

The royal family is at the center of Qatar's politics, not simply because of the autocratic pattern of emiri rule, and the size and reach of the family into society, but also because so many government departments, other political institutions, and civil society bodies are headed by royals or have them somewhere near the summit of the organization. Moreover, business is highly penetrated by Al Thani family members, and so major state-owned and private firms both regularly feature royals as chief executive officers (CEOs) or board members, and public funds are distributed, through joint ventures through both state-owned and private firms, to individual members of the family and members of other key commercial families and tribes. Qatar is run very differently from how it was back in the mid–twentieth century, when up to a quarter of rents at one stage were being dispersed directly to the royal family as handouts, but a fundamental fact remains that Qatar is, if not a family business literally, then nonetheless a political economy dominated by the Al Thani family and its key allies. The family still wields power and gains wealth through state mechanisms, even if many of the processes of this have changed over time.

At the summit of the system, of course, is the emir, Hamad, who as ruler of the highly (but "soft") autocratic system enjoys considerable influence across a family that, while cumbersomely large and factionalized, has a very outsized political and financial capacity relative to society. What has been different under Hamad is that he has brought to the palace a particular image of what the country ought to be like, and of the socioeconomic changes and reforms required to meet that vision. Hamad's reformist focus once he seized power in 1995 should not have surprised observers, even if the extent of those reforms—at least the socioeconomic ones, if less so the delivery of promised political reforms—has been quite astonishing. In the years leading up to 1995, Hamad had gained considerable experience within government and had a wide impact across development planning; the management of the oil and gas sector; as a defense minister, especially prominent during the 1990–1991 Gulf War; with events and other initiatives that enhanced the country's international image; and in initiatives to augment national identity.[1] For several years, in effect, he was the day-to-day manager of the affairs of state. He developed an image in the 1980s and especially the first half of the 1990s as a very active figure with "a reputation for getting things done."[2] In a political system that under Khalifa was still much more conservative and shy than it is now, this reputation was deliberately earned and nurtured, and signaled the type of leader that Hamad would be.

While Hamad's coup against his father was very low key, the reforms that he introduced very quickly upon assuming power, and the further ones promised by him, have been anything but. In a similar vein to the rulers of Bahrain and Jordan, where new, young monarchs took power in 1999, there was a sense with Hamad that he was the first of the successor generation—a collection of young leaders who assumed power in the late 1990s and early 2000s as reformers and political liberalizers who were very different from their fathers and ready to adjust the polity and society to the "post–Cold War realities" they suddenly faced.[3] Hamad has been the driver of profound economic and social changes since 1995, even if, like for the other young monarchs, reform of the political system has been far less substantial than promised or anticipated.

The list of reforms that Hamad did introduce, however, is extensive. In the economic realm, his first move—in fact the first decree he issued as emir—was the creation of the Doha securities market.[4] This suggested a commitment to the development of the private sector and perhaps privatization of some state-owned firms too. Reinforcing the entrepreneurial state capitalism thesis, however, is the fact that reform has delivered an enormous amount of foreign investment and new sources of capital to the private sector, but there has been virtually no large-scale privatization since the market's launch.[5] Hamad also enhanced business confidence in his rule with a carefully crafted first budget, with bold new projects often funded by specific capital-raising. His overtures toward the Gulf Cooperation Council (GCC) in his early years, his resolution of some border issues with neighboring states, and his seeming commitment to stronger intra-GCC economic relations have all sent a similar message. He also appointed an heir-apparent very quickly, a sound political move given the family squabbling over succession that could otherwise have emerged. At first, this was his eldest son, Misha'al, whose appointment as heir-apparent was perhaps pushed on him by the family in its desire to return the succession line to the eldest son.[6] His probable first choice, Shaikh Jassim bin Hamad bin Khalifa Al Thani, served in the role of heir-apparent from 1996 until 2003, and was a Sandhurst-educated, business-friendly figure with an interest in the oil and gas sector[7]—a perfect crown prince for a period of transition and consolidation by Hamad.

In the political and social realms, Hamad introduced some political reform, albeit of a more limited scope than social or economic liberalization. He created elected municipal officers for the twenty-nine-seat Central Municipal Council (CMC), an advisory body to the Ministry of Municipal Affairs and Agriculture. When the poll for the CMC was held in 1999 it included universal adult suffrage and allowed women to also run for office. But none of the women candidates won a seat, and arguably women's suffrage was allowed not so much for democratization but both as a show to Western allies, especially the United States, and also given the rivalry with Kuwait, which has its own, very activist, parliament.[8] Uniquely in the Gulf at that time, Hamad announced an end to media censorship. He then abolished the Ministry of Information, which had been responsible for media censorship as well as setting standards for the media and journalists and had also operated its own state-run television and radio services.[9] He also announced his support for women's education and improved opportunities for women, again something that few Gulf leaders at the time were publicly pronouncing on. Finally, and perhaps most famously, he created Al-Jazeera television as a technically autonomous but state-supported media channel, an experiment in state-media relations that ultimately altered the media landscape of the Arab world.[10]

However, his political reforms have had their (quite strict) limits. The CMC held subsequent polls in 2003, 2007, and 2011, and as of 1996, Chamber of Commerce members were allowed to elect their own board for the first time.[11] However an expected wider legislative liberalization has not emerged. Qataris voted in April 2003 to approve a new constitution, with a supporting vote of 96.6 percent, which allowed for the separation of executive, legislative, and judicial power and provided for the popular election of thirty of the forty-five members of the legislature.[12] However, the elections for these thirty members did not follow, despite regular assurances that they would take place. It was not until late 2011 that polls were promised for 2013, perhaps as a result of the Arab Spring and a consequent need for Hamad to reiterate a commitment to political reform.[13] The term of the existing appointed Consultative Assembly was extended in June 2010 for a further three years. Observers argue over exactly how genuine the emir is in pursuing democratization, but agree to a greater extent that extensive political liberalization and electoral politics have not developed because reform was above all a method of political consolidation by Hamad and a way to win over international audiences, especially the United States.[14]

If not quite as powerful as Hamad, almost as high profile has been his wife Shaikha Muza bint Nasir al-Missnid. The second but favorite of his three wives, she has been a prominent force for social and other change in Qatar, and a socioeconomic actor in her own right. She comes from a politically important family. Her father, Nasir bin Abdallah al-Missnid, is often described as a political opponent of Hamad's father, Khalifa. More accurately, Khalifa had willingly or not had to exile Nasir when he refused to surrender a local person who had sought his protection after a dispute with the British.[15] Thus, Shaikha Muza spent some of her youth abroad while the family was in exile, before returning to Qatar in her teens to attend Qatar University. It was at this time, at eighteen years of age, that she married then–crown prince Hamad.

Shaikha Muza has been especially prominent in promoting and supporting education and social development. She has been chair of the Qatar Foundation[16] since its establishment in 1995, through which she has pursued a lot of these goals. The Qatar Foundation is a nonprofit body, nominally privately run but closely linked to the state because of its creation by the emir and its close elite and financial links to the government. It has three pillars—education, science and research, and community development—although it is perhaps best known for its educational initiatives, especially its higher education campus, Education City, although important too have been educational and youth enterprises such as the Qatar Academy and the Qatar Leadership Academy. Education City has gained enormous attention for the novelty of its approach, its openness to female students, and indeed some controversies within Qatar about whether its social dynamics are conservative enough for the country, especially given the interactions between male and female students at the universities on the campus.[17] However, it has created fresh opportunities not least of all for women but also for some men whose parents may have been keen on them obtaining a Western university education but were not willing to let the children travel abroad.[18] The Qatar Foundation also financially supports research through the Qatar National Research Fund and the Qatar Science and Technology Park, among others.

The shaikha's position at the summit of the Qatar Foundation, and her support of many of these initiatives, gives her considerable power. It also signals her as an important political economy actor beyond simply her role as the emir's spouse, important though the palace role is as well. Unlike the emir's other two wives, Muza is both active and visible; she is a public figure. She is also a representative—and a fairly popular one—for the political and development goals of her husband and in mounting publicity for them. In interviews she talks in glowing terms about her husband, but always explicitly tags her own actions as something she is undertaking jointly with him.[19] In her pronouncements in support of education, for example, she usually links it back to critical thinking, the development of a more diverse economy, and the creation of employment opportunities for young people. She is important, too, of course, in supporting his initiatives, including his active diplomatic role and his attempts to engage more dynamically than did previous emirs with the Qatari population. In this she is less unusual, since Arab leaders increasingly have visible and popular wives involved in some element of politics or in social initiatives, but Muza is an especially driven, dynamic figure. She is particularly important in ensuring a link between the emir and his reformist goals, and in heading a government-established and government-nurtured nonprofit that provides an arm's-length but politically advantageous way for the state to spend energy rents on social development, including some quite significant and occasionally contentious initiatives.

Other members of the royal family carry significant influence as well, in both the political and commercial realms, and sometimes both. After Misha'al there have been two subsequent crown princes, both of them sons of Muza: Jassim bin Hamad bin Khalifa (crown prince in the period 1996–2003), as mentioned, and then Tamim bin Hamad bin Khalifa after 2003. Both are widely held in high esteem by those who have worked closely with them, are considered bright, and are presumed to be capable of being very good emirs if they should reach the throne. Tamim has subsequently been given considerable opportunity to build his experience and profile, including as chair of the board of directors for the 2022 World Cup; in Qatari diplomatic initiatives over Libya during the 2011 rebellion and North Atlantic Treaty Organization (NATO) air strikes there; and in working on and launching Qatar's 2011–2016 national development strategy. Hamad clearly trusts him to enough of an extent to grant him such political prominence and clout. This is notable because the change in crown prince in 2003 reportedly was the result of Jassim seeking greater powers.[20] That should have been a rather imprudent request given that Hamad's ability to move against his own father in 1995 was developed by building up his power base and contacts in the family and state institutions. Jassim may have genuinely felt sidelined from the center of decisionmaking, as some rumors had it. Whatever its source, it is most likely that such a request prompted Hamad to push Jassim to renounce his rights to the throne because Hamad saw him as a longer-term threat.

It is a reminder that even though at a certain level the Al Thani family divisions have been brought under greater control by Hamad, and the ability of family members to mount a coup against him has become extremely constrained, the threat of such a move still exists. Even in 2011, long after Hamad's seizure of power and consolidation of his rule, a coup attempt was made, and was a further reminder that internal opposition to Hamad remains. The 2011 coup attempt was orchestrated within the military but coincided with a statement by key figures in some major families, including sixteen Al Thani family members, who complained of the high profile of Shaikha Muza, called for greater adherence to tradition in the country and more conservative leadership at home and in foreign relations, and expressed support for the emir's brother, Abd al-Aziz bin Khalifa, in exile in France, as an alternative emir.[21]

Beyond Hamad's immediate family, a wider number of the Al Thani are important actors in the political system and the political economy. The Al Thani dynasty has innumerable family branches (*buyut,* the plural of *bayt,* meaning "house"), four of which are especially high profile and descended from Muhammad bin Thani al-Wadhiri: the Qasim, Ahmad, Jabr, and Thamir. The emirs since Muhammad have come from the Qasim line, but even within that house there have been differences, as some emirs have favored certain wives or sons and, as noted earlier, it has been contentious with some royals, even within the Qasim *bayt,* that the line of succession has not remained with the eldest son of a ruler's first wife. Hamad strengthened the political position of his own house and line by amending the constitution by decree in 1996 to specify that succession would be from the emir to "one of his sons," where previously the stipulation had been than any male from the Al Thani dynasty could become emir.[22] The new permanent constitution, approved by referendum in 2003, included the same succession rule in Article 8, which reads in part: "The rule of the State is hereditary in the family of Al Thani and in the line of the male descendants of Hamad Bin Khalifa Bin Hamad Bin Abdullah Bin Jassim. The rule shall be inherited by the son named as Heir Apparent by the Emir."[23]

The Qasim *bayt* is the most prominent in Qatari politics. In his first cabinet, announced in July 1995, Hamad included thirteen members of the Al Thani family, eight of them from the Qasim *bayt,* counting the emir who holds the defense portfolio. Not that other houses of the family were completely absent. The chief of the Emiri Diwan (i.e., the palace), Muhammad bin Fahd, appointed at ministerial rank as of Hamad's 1995 cabinet, was from another line, as were the minister of agriculture and municipal affairs and the minister of justice (both from the Ahmad *bayt*), and the prime minister and minister of foreign affairs, a double portfolio held by Hamad bin Jassim bin Jabr (from the Jabr *bayt*). Later cabinets included a similar fraction from the Al Thani and typically spread somewhat across the houses of the dynasty but with a disproportionate number from Hamad's house. The main criterion for retaining a cabinet position, along with competence, is loyalty to the emir and the continuity of his rule.

Other important political roles are held by members of other houses of the Al Thani.[24] A few prominent but illustrative examples are worth mentioning. Within the Qasim *bayt,* there are five branches, or *bani,*[25] including the Thani, which has supplied several figures prominent in finance and state investment, but most famous of all, perhaps, Hamad bin Thamir bin Muhammad bin Thani Al Thani, the chairman of Al-Jazeera and of its parent company and owner of the other state media company in Qatar, the Qatar Media Corporation. Other *bani* include the Muhammad, from which the chairman of the Qatar Chamber of Commerce and Industry, Khalifa bin Qasim bin Muhammad, and the chairman and managing director of Qatar Navigation (the main shipping operator), Ali bin Qasim bin Muhammad, both come; and the Fahd, from which the governor of the Qatar central bank, Abdallah bin Saud bin Fahd,[26] and some other key family business figures come. Beyond the Qasim *bayt,* other *buyut* provide some key Al Thani businesspeople too. In the Ahmad *bayt* this includes multiple Al Thani merchants and investors in Qatari firms and local branches of multinational ones, plus the governor of Doha city. The Jabr *bayt* possesses several other important figures, of which by far the most powerful—arguably the second most powerful person in Qatar after the emir—is the prime minister.

In effect a great many Al Thani figures—at least those who are in favor with the emir and with the core political elites or not opposed to them—cross the boundary between politics and business and are prominent in both. The consummate example of this is the prime minister and minister of foreign affairs, Hamad bin Jassim bin Jabr. As mentioned, he is a member of the Jabr house and is far from being part of Hamad's immediate family; he and Emir Hamad are second cousins twice removed. Despite this, and despite also having been minister of foreign affairs under Khalifa after 1992, he retained his portfolio, and subsequently expanded it, under Hamad, and he is one of Hamad's closest allies and most trusted confidants. He is assumed to have been the power broker in the coup that brought Hamad to power and in suppressing the attempted countercoup by Khalifa in 1996.[27] He retained his foreign affairs portfolio after Hamad came to power, and subsequently was appointed first–deputy prime minister in 2003, and then prime minister in 2007. In formal Qatari politics, he is probably more powerful than all but the emir. He is also seen as a key supporter, and behind the scenes possibly as a driver, of many of the reforms that Qatar has undertaken since 1995, especially in foreign policy, although the opacity surrounding his exact influence on Hamad makes it difficult to be certain of the extent of his influence over other policy areas such as economic and social reform.[28] That said, he certainly shares the energy and rhetoric of the emir and the same public enthusiasm toward the reforms.[29]

Hamad bin Jassim is also active in the economy, especially as the CEO of the Qatar Investment Authority (QIA), Qatar's sovereign wealth fund, which was established only recently (in 2005) to manage the state's wealth and reinvest surplus energy rents and other income at home but especially abroad. It is now very valuable, worth some US$115 billion or more by late 2012. The prime minister, in his role as CEO of the QIA, is thought to handle some US$20 billion of new investments each year. Coincidentally, the chair of the QIA is the crown prince, Tamim, and several other members of the Al Thani family—granted, with commercial or financial experience—sit on the board as well. The prime minister, beyond his formal political role and that in the QIA, is also extremely wealthy in his own right. This combination of a public role and private wealth is of course common (and commonly sought) in the Gulf by such senior figures but is rarely achieved to the same extent as Hamad bin Jassim has managed. At various times, either directly or through his family, he has held investments in Qatar Airways; Al-Fardan, one of Qatar's largest trading firms; Qatari Diar Real Estate Investment; The Pearl, an artificial island real estate project; as well as hotels, the media, and foreign banks.[30] His family is also prominently involved in business; one of his sons, Shaikh Qasim bin Hamad Al Thani, is chair of the Qatar Islamic Bank and director of the Qatar Insurance Company (QIC).

The Al Thani businessmen are important because they are central to Qatar's late rentierism and especially to its style of entrepreneurial state capitalism. The most powerful of the Al Thani figures, especially those in state-owned firms, on boards, and heading or linked into state-led initiatives, are serving to a large extent at the pleasure of the emir. Obviously, some are in these positions as a way to placate them or their corner of the family, in which case the emir's room to maneuver against them is limited, but two things are worth noting. First, their involvement in the affairs of state or its business interests links them to the state and gives them a stake in it, often in the reforms that Hamad is driving. Second, the entrepreneurial aspect of entrepreneurial state capitalism is important. There is still an expectation of financial and service performance of those appointed to office and the firms or initiatives they are heading, and this expectation varies very little whether the appointee is an Al Thani or not. Some members of the family have reputations for being change averse or ineffectual, but this is routine in the institutions of the Gulf. What marks out Qatar is how many of its key figures have the opposite reputation, renowned not just for their political connections and position in the Al Thani family but for their technical proficiency or leadership skill. This and the dynamic, reformist, and moderately risk-accepting mood of Qatar's state capitalism are in large part what make it an *entrepreneurial* state capitalism.

What, then, can be gleaned from this, and specifically, what do family structure, politics, and commercial interests say about Qatar's political economy? Three themes arise. The first is the overarching power of the emir himself. This is not surprising at the usual political level and is little different compared to the power of rulers in many other Gulf monarchies, but Qatar varies slightly because of the relatively large size and influence of the royal family and the relatively weak power of the merchants and other societal actors relative to the royal family and especially its political elite. Second, family size and stability—in the past, often *in*stability—have continued to dictate at least some elements of the current political economy.[31] Even as the threat of a successful coup against Hamad seems to become increasingly remote (if still remaining present), family stability and mood still dictate the national political situation and climate to some extent. Arguably, family issues have prompted Hamad to put members of the family into various state and quasi-state positions, including commercial ones—the more favored members into the most powerful or dynamic positions, of course, and others into more minor positions, some even of the "make-work" variety. For those he trusts, however, including the prime minister, others in his inner circle, and some key figures closest to his *bani* and *bayt,* state positions can be politically and financially rewarding. This links to the final point, namely, that while Qatar has developed increasingly efficient and dynamic institutions of state, these organizations and firms still remain weak as rational-legal institutions within the political economy compared to the more opaque, informal dynamics of interpersonal elite and intra- and interfamily linkages. There are benefits to this, of course, since, for example, the family is cumbersomely large yet linked into society far more effectively (and is much more widely popular) than, say, the Al Khalifa dynasty in Bahrain, which presides over a much poorer and more unhappy population, a majority of it Shiite, than does the Al Thani.

State Mechanisms and State-Owned Firms

Beyond the family dynamics that inform and shape Qatar's rentierism and state capitalism, another crucial dynamic is that of state-owned firms. For the most part they represent the new, entrepreneurial form of state capitalism, and act in two ways that can be construed as political. The first is the most obvious: that state legitimacy and popular perspectives on leaders are built to some extent on the image of the state as a service provider. State firms, like ministries and other institutions, therefore need to be somewhat efficient if the leadership is to maintain domestically, and Qatar is to maintain internationally, an image of being relatively uncorrupt and effective. This image serves the emir and elite well. It is perhaps Hamad's greatest claim to efficient leadership and is increasingly part of the family's claim to rule legitimately as well. State bodies must therefore not only dispense rents and the benefits they provide—cheap energy, free schooling and nearly free higher education, world-class medical care, and the like—but they must do so, and be seen to do so, efficiently, effectively, and at least somewhat fairly.

State-owned firms are also integral to both late rentierism and entrepreneurial state capitalism because they provide a new stream of rentlike income to the state. Rents have been invested in these firms over time, and the state obtains an increasing proportion of its revenue from the profits that are returned to it as a shareholder. State-owned firms are a rentier tool, in other words, because even though the firms themselves are engaging in productive and often-competitive activity in the pursuit of a profit, the state, when receiving profits back as dividends or suchlike, is obtaining this income in a rentier fashion, because of its holdings rather than through a taxation bargain with society, and of course because the income is the result of the state investing some of its earlier original rental income. More of this follows in the case of the QIA and spells out its "late rentier" function as custodian and investor of energy rents.

However, Qatar's state capitalism is not of the same politicization as the republican Arab states' much less efficient version. Instead it follows closely the efficient state-owned firm style analyzed by Steffen Hertog.[32] Hertog argues that successful, profitable, state-owned firms come from a political economy that has not experienced "a populist-mobilizational history of economic development" and where "substantial decisional autonomy" exists between the regime leadership and societal forces and interest groups.[33] Qatar fits this model perfectly, given the historical weaknesses of merchants and their incapacity for forming into a politically influential group, and of course the strength of the Al Thani both in the relative political power they possess compared to other actors and increasingly, since the late twentieth century, in their strength in commerce as well. They have neither a populist development mandate (nor a history of having attempted one) nor a reliance to any great extent on the business community or any other group to consolidate and legitimize their power. It has probably been advantageous that Qatar's rent-driven economic boom has occurred so late compared to other Gulf states, as this has meant that government ministries and state-owned firms have evolved with tighter royal control over them and with less expectation that they will be directly co-optive toward society. While Qatar has had substantial amounts of oil income since the mid–twentieth century, it was a much more reclusive state and modest economy than others such as Saudi Arabia during the oil booms of the mid-1970s and the late 1970s and early 1980s. The point here is not that some inefficiencies or indolence are not to be found in these enterprises—of course they are—but rather that these institutions do not exist primarily for nonfinancial political purposes. There can still be political dynamics behind or underlying state-owned firms, but their primary raisons d'être are service provision to society and at the same time profit for the state, and the royal family, which dominates the state, is accorded a higher priority than in many other rentier states.

Where politics intervenes in state-owned firms, it tends to have little impact on efficiency or financial performance anyway. It is, of course, a neopatrimonial tool for the emir and for those close to him, including most prominently some family members. Hamad's close family members alone (i.e., members of the Qasim *bani*) in 2009 were represented on nearly half of the forty-three firms listed on the Qatar Exchange (the stock market).[34] The emir's eldest son to Shaikha Muza, Qasim, is highly active as a chairman or board member of multiple listed but partly state-owned firms.[35] In itself this demonstrates both the commercial reach of the emir and key royals and a neopatrimonialism that is very typical of the small, wealthy rentier states of the Gulf. However, it also suggests the capacity for the state to push such firms toward greater efficiency and entrepreneurialism while at the same time not intervening in the firms excessively for political gain but at financial expense.

This indeed appears to be the strategy for another reason, namely the preponderance of key public service firms on the Qatar Exchange, but with mixed state and private shareholding. The exchange was established as the Doha Securities Market (DSM) in 1997. It has expanded into a very dynamic, if still somewhat narrowly focused, exchange. As of 2005, foreign nationals have usually been able to own up to 25 percent of the tradable shares in a listed firm.[36] Local large private sector firms have begun to use the Qatar Exchange more effectively to raise new capital, especially as it operates as efficiently as most emerging exchanges, even though it is still categorized as a "frontier" market, in large part because of the small capitalization and the low levels of foreign ownership (in most firms, foreign shareholder ownership is well below the 25 percent maximum).[37]

Still, especially as a result of its 2009 partnership with the New York Stock Exchange's Euronext, it is transforming into a high-quality market.

However, the Qatar Exchange serves another purpose. It lists major firms that traditionally were state owned and that remain partly so even after their listing. This is important because it highlights the mechanisms by which the regime ensures that firms are efficient and profitable, while the state also guarantees its ongoing interest in and link to them, including (often) control over strategic direction through its ability to control these firms' boards or to occupy many of the positions on them. There are multiple examples, including firms that Qataris deal with on a daily or otherwise regular basis. The two largest firms on the Qatar Exchange by market capitalization (of free-floated shares) are the Qatar National Bank (QNB) and Industries Qatar, which together account for around one-third of the Qatar Exchange Index. Both are intimately linked to the state, as are a range of other top listed firms, as shown in Table 3.1. The QNB was established by Emiri Decree no. 7 in 1964 as a Qatar-owned bank—previously the sector was completely foreign owned, apart from some informal lending—and is in effect 50 percent state owned, since half its shares are held by the state-owned sovereign wealth fund, the QIA. This is notable because, among other reasons, the QNB dominates the Qatari banking sector: around 40 percent of all banking sector assets in Qatar were in the QNB's hands in 2010, making it easily the economy's largest bank. Industries Qatar is also in effect state owned, with only 30 percent of its shares traded and the other 70 percent held by the fully state-owned and intimately state-linked Qatar Petroleum.

At the top of the list in Table 3.1 are various other firms with strong state interests retained in them despite some shares freely floating. By 2011, in effect only about 22 percent of shares in Qatar Telecom (Qtel) were being actively traded by private individuals and small firms; the majority were under state or state-owned firms' ownership: the state directly owned 55 percent of the Qtel's shares, while other Qatari state entities owned 13 percent and the Abu Dhabi Investment Authority (ADIA), the Abu Dhabi regime's main sovereign wealth fund, owned another 10 percent.[38] Similarly, Barwa Real Estate, one of the highest-profile real estate firms in Qatar, is partly owned by Qatari Diar, which is a real estate development and investment firm owned by the QIA. Many of the banks, both conventional and Islamic, also have the state or a state body as one of the minority owners, although this is also an outcome of the global financial crisis, during which the state stepped in to ensure confidence in the banks and the financial sector by investing new funds into many of them, typically buying 10–20 percent of their shares and taking

Table 3.1 State Capitalism at Work: State Ownership in Key Qatar Exchange Index–Listed Firms, 2011

Symbol	Company	Free-Floated Shares (millions)	Market Capitalization (QR billions)	Weight[a] (%)	State Ownership (%)
QNBK	Qatar National Bank (QNB)	317.86	45.84	21.37	QIA 50
IQCD	Industries Qatar	165.00	24.22	11.29	Qatar Petroleum (state owned) 70
MARK	Masraf al-Rayan	749.10	17.75	8.28	Qatar Holdings 10.1, other state 7.2
QIBK	Qatar Islamic Bank	194.66	15.73	7.33	QIA 10
CBQK	Commercial Bank of Qatar	189.50	13.85	6.46	QIA 9.1, QNB 3, QIC 2
QTEL	Qatar Telecom (Qtel)	79.18	12.95	6.04	State 55, QIA 10
BRES	Barwa Real Estate	388.72	12.36	5.76	Qatari Diar (QIA owned) 45
QEWS	Qatar Electricity and Water	78.80	11.58	5.40	State ~ 43
QGTS	Qatar Gas T'port (Nakilat)	553.10	10.14	4.73	State and various semistate 50
DHBK	Doha Bank	155.71	8.39	3.91	QIA 20
KCBK	Al-Khalij Commercial Bank	359.40	6.43	2.99	Qatari Diar 17.24, Qatar Holdings 10, state pension fund 5.36, state health and education fund 5, Qatar Foundation 4.56
QIIK	Qatar International Islamic Bank	119.33	5.63	2.62	QIA 20
QATI	Qatar Insurance (QIC)	63.81	5.30	2.47	State 12
QNCD	Qatar National Cement	27.87	3.19	1.49	State 43
GISS	Gulf International Services	94.61	2.81	1.31	Qatar Petroleum 30
VFQS	Vodafone Qatar	338.16	2.71	1.26	Qatar Foundation ~ 27, other state 10
NLCS	National Leasing	32.23	1.28	0.60	Milaha 5.34, National Cement Co. 2.67, Qatar International Islamic Bank 2.67
Total			200.16		

Sources: Shares, capitalization, and weighting are from the "QE Index" page of the Qatar Exchange website, http://www.qe.com.qa/pps/qe/qe+english+portal/Pages/About+QE/QE+Index. Ownership details are from company websites and annual reports, with some derived from Gulbrandsen, "Bridging the Gulf, p. 82.

Note: a. As of mid-2011. Weight refers to the percentage share of the entire market, not just of the firms listed here.

over some of their riskier projects, especially in real estate. There are other examples, as listed in the table.

Further, even where state ownership in a firm is modest, many firms trace their origins to the state, often to an emiri decision to establish or support them. The Qatar Islamic Bank (QIB) is one such example. It was established in 1982 as a shareholding company, but by emiri decree (no. 45 of 1982) and under the existing regulatory framework of the central bank.[39] It was the product of a deliberate decision by then-emir Khalifa to bring Islamic (sometimes called "sharia-compliant") banking to Qatar. In a somewhat similar way, Barwa Real Estate was incorporated in late 2005, and began operations on January 19, 2006, under instructions issued in 2003 by the Ministry of Economy and Commerce; that is, it was founded by a government ministry, albeit as a publicly listed firm. Finally, even firms without large state shareholdings still have members of the royal family involved with them, either because of their business skills, contacts, or both. Those firms with strong state investment have greater royal family involvement, of course—the QNB in 2010 had three Al Thani family members on its ten-member board—but another example is Al-Khaliji Commercial Bank. Al-Khaliji is privately owned, and its CEO is a South African expatriate, but its chairman is a prominent Al Thani businessman, Shaikh Hamad bin Faysal bin Thani Al Thani. His other roles have included previously being a member of the politically powerful Supreme Council for Economic Affairs and Investment—the body, chaired by the emir, that sets the country's strategic economic direction and development strategy—and he also holds multiple other board appointments.[40]

All of this demonstrates the state capitalism at the core of the Qatari system, given the size of the state's holdings in various firms, often state-owned and publicly listed hybrid firms. It is an entrepreneurial type of state capitalism, however, as these firms are for the most part free from day-to-day state intervention in their management and decisionmaking.[41] They are expected to be dynamic and profitable enterprises and not merely vehicles for the promotion of economic nationalism (although they dabble in the rhetoric of that, but only mildly and occasionally) or employment generation. Whatever the differences between these firms and the more traditional state-owned ones, they are, along with others that are fully state owned and not listed at all, at the core of the state capitalism dynamic, because they are expected to contribute to the overall strategic direction of the country and the economy—in that sense, they are not fully autonomous in deciding their own strategic direction—and because they reinforce the centrality of the state in the political economy. There is no presumption, as there is in more market-driven or neoliberal systems, that the state will, out of ideology, refrain from involving itself in firms unless forced to do so by market failure.

The indirect state role in the economy is probably even deeper than suggested by the ownership of major listed firms, since key individuals, not least of all Al Thani family members, are abundant on the boards of these firms. Among Hamad's sons, Qasim is on the board of the Qatar Islamic Bank and Qinvest, an Islamic investment banking firm, and a member of the boards of the Qatar Insurance Company and Qatar Navigation.[42] The prime minister, Hamad bin Jassim, is even more powerful. As noted, he is involved with key state financial bodies such as the QIA, and is also chairman of Qatari Diar and on the board of Qatar Energy and Water.[43] This is illustrative of why firms with strong QIA investment, such as the QNB, the Qatar Islamic Bank, Qtel, Barwa Real Estate, and others, and for that matter those in which Qatar Petroleum is a major shareholder, such as Industries Qatar and Gulf International Services, are linked strongly into the state capitalist dynamic. The QIA and Qatar Petroleum have very close relationships with the state, both structurally, say through their legal mandate and obligations, but also through less direct mechanisms such as board memberships and family connections. The QIA is fully state owned and quite opaquely but tightly controlled by key figures in the regime, while Qatar Petroleum, of course, being state owned and so absolutely central to the state's revenue, is perhaps the state-owned firm most core to the regime's survival and to the success of its development strategy.

The Business Families, Tribes, and Social Linkages

All of this demonstrates the tremendous financial power of the Al Thani family and the few powerful nonroyals linked closely with them. These are the central actors of the Qatari political economy—many works on the economies and politics of the Gulf shaikhdoms, including some of the major works on Qatar, are state- and elite-focused for this reason. Yet it would be remiss not to consider the roles of other actors that link into the late rentier or entrepreneurial state capitalism dynamics of the political economy.

Within elite politics, there are other actors who cross the boundary between the political and commercial realms who have not yet been discussed in much detail but are important. Some are people who are close to the emir and the Al Thani family through tribal linkages, such as the al-Mahmud family, who derive from the same Tamim *bani* confederacy as the Al Thani. The al-Mahmud have made their name in both politics and business,[44] for example Ahmad bin Abdallah al-Mahmud as a minister of foreign affairs after 1995, and who became increasingly high profile after the early 2000s because of his additional appointment as a deputy prime minister and minister of cabinet affairs, and because he has been active in other roles such as on the board of regents at Qatar University. Of note also has been his daughter Shaikha bint Ahmad al-Mahmud, who served as education minister from 2003 to 2009 and was Qatar's first female cabinet member, and other family members prominent in business such as Ibrahim bin Abdallah al-Mahmud (a director at the Qatar Insurance Company) and Mansur Ibrahim al-Mahmud (head of risk management at the QIA and a director at the Qatar National Bank, Qatari Diar, and Hassad Food).[45] There are numerous other family members in other roles in politics, diplomacy, and business,[46] including for example the journalist Abd al-Aziz Ibrahim al-Mahmud.[47]

Another famous family is the al-Attiyya, perhaps the most powerful family outside of the Al Thani. Like the al-Mahmud, they come from the Tamim *bani* and thus share a tribal linkage to the emir and his family. Indeed, Emir Hamad is the son of a wife his father took from the al-Attiyya family, and the three previous emirs have all taken an al-Attiyya wife.[48] Thus the family members are almost ubiquitous in Qatari politics and business and among the ranks of the officialdom. They include Abdallah bin Hamad al-Attiyya, previously mentioned as the deputy prime minister, head of the Emiri Diwan, and chairman of Qatar Petroleum, and also Abd al-Rahman bin Hamad al-Attiyya, the Doha-born secretary-general of the GCC from 2002 to 2011 but also having extensive commercial experience and interests. The family has even produced the famous rally driver Nasir al-Attiyya. There are numerous others who are active in business, including in the Al-Attiyah Group, a family-owned firm conglomerated in 1978, with some 6,000 employees as of 2010, and engaged in a range of sectors including manufacturing, leasing, project support, hospitality, construction, and retailing.[49]

The closeness of the Al Thani and the al-Attiyya is extensive and enduring, especially through marriage, but is especially strong under the current emir given his lineage and his close friendship with key figures such as Abdallah al-Attiyya. This is a reminder and reiteration of the importance of proven trust to a client's prospects under Hamad's neopatrimonialism, while the wider al-Attiyya business interests attest to the state capitalism linkages fostered by the political system in which the emir controls much of the largesse and the opportunities attached to it.

Other families more focused on business are prominent and possess political and other influence. One with a large, diversified family firm is the Jayda family, which controls the Jaidah Group.[50] The firm began in 1898, importing basics such as foodstuffs from South Asia and Iran, but as the economy developed, so too did the firm. It expanded and became more sophisticated in its operations, and gained a particular boost from servicing the expansion of the oil sector in the 1950s.[51] Its interests include automotives (it has close ties to General Motors and is the sole distributor in Qatar for Chevrolet); heavy equipment and machinery; industrial supplies and tools; energy sector supplies and components; and technology for education, medicine, and defense. Other similar firms are the Al-Mannai Group, how headed by Khalid Ahmad al-Mannai, the son of the founder of the firm,[52] the Aljaber Group, the Alfardan Group, and the Almana Group (owned by the al-Mana‘ family, mentioned in Chapter 2, one of Qatar's early major merchant families).

These groups link into the state because of their use of royal connections to gain favorable business conditions, or because of their reliance on state contracts, or both. To the extent that businesspeople coordinate and collaborate to exert political pressure and act as a class, they do so through two groupings, the Qatari Chamber of Commerce and Industry (QCCI) and the Qatari Businessmen Association (QBA). The QCCI dates back to 1963, while the QBA was formed by emiri decree in 2002. In effect, the two are in a form of soft competition with each other. The QCCI, recall, represented an early experiment in democratization by the new Emir Hamad, who in 1996 allowed members of the chamber to elect their own board, when previously they had been appointed by the emir. The QBA is seen by many as a counterweight organization to the QCCI and one deliberately established as such by the emir; to others, it simply represents a competing body through which the informal mechanisms of business promotion and networking can occur. The former is a classic divide-and-conquer tactic adopted by rentiers, and so as an explanation is quite plausible. Yet both views are probably overstated to some extent. There is certainly an element of competition between the two, whether Hamad intended this to develop or not, yet both groups' boards are populated with both Al Thani family members and well-connected merchants. The QCCI board is chaired by Shaikh Khalifa bin Qasim bin Muhammad Al Thani and has on its board some figures from large merchant families such as the al-Mannai and the al-Kuwari. The QBA, however, is more closely linked to the Al Thani. Its chairman, Faysal bin Qasim Al Thani, is a very wealthy businessman who employs some 3,000 people across more than thirty firms,[53] plus the board also includes three other prominent Al Thani family members and heads or senior figures from well-connected families such as the al-Fardan and al-Mana‘. Whether intended or not, the QBA has the reputation of being better connected with the royal family, perhaps because it is seen as a more "exclusive" or elite body.[54]

This may also be the product of the royal family cultivating some of the more senior business figures or of the (controlled) wealth of these families serving the emir and key royals well, and in this informal way—and arguably a much more important way—businesspeople link to and influence the state and the political elite. Some families such as the al-Mannai and al-Mana' are long established. The al-Mannai consist now of several *buyut* of varying degrees of influence, but some wings remain influential because of both family history and current links to royal family members.[55] The al-Mana', likewise, are influential. At the highest family level the al-Mana' are split between the Hamad and Umr *buyut,* and these often compete with each other, but senior figures in the family such as Saud al-Mana' are very close to Emir Hamad and thus seen as very powerful.[56] The Abd al-Ghani family, which has distribution rights in Qatar for Toyota, was for some time seen as having exploited its Toyota monopoly to profiteer, and was widely viewed, rightly or wrongly, as being able to do this because of royal patronage. The story is often told of how the family nearly lost the Toyota contract because of problems with pricing and customer complaints in the late 2000s, and the unsubstantiated claim often made that political support had helped them maintain their monopoly, including when Toyota threatened to seek out a new partner in Qatar.[57]

Another family, the al-Fardan, are important and unusual in being of Emirati origin and Shiite.[58] Some Qatari businesspeople claim that the regime is seeking to build support or a positive image with local Shiites through families such as the al-Fardan, although given the seemingly limited political power and social influence of the family, this may simply represent the fact that the al-Fardan are not especially popular among some Qatari businesspeople and are seen by many as reclusive and miserly.[59] At one level such business families are a key group through which the goals of economic diversification must be pursued, and having their support is important in neutralizing a potential source of opposition from emerging, one potentially with its own sources of income and wealth.

The political elite's relationships with key business families is important because it allows the emir and his inner circle to tap into wider societal forces that otherwise are kept peripheral from, or given only a marginal role in, formal political institutions. This includes not only other business actors—though the state's relationship with Qatar's small private sector is increasingly important, to be sure—but also other groups such as key family figures and tribes. Tribes and extended family structures are strong in Qatar not only because they provide social and commercial opportunity—social status and business opportunities are typically correlated with a person's family background, given the centrality of lineage in Qatari society[60]—but also because such social groupings build group identity and solidarity through them. Family and tribal networks are thus of literal value as well as being social units that preserve and transmit collective memories. Moreover, as Allen Fromherz notes, tribalism has not been diminished by the social and economic changes in Qatar in recent decades and indeed has probably increased in importance because of such changes: they mark out Qataris in a society where they are now a clear minority, and through transmitted traditions help reassure Qataris that their distinct identity is surviving, even thriving, across generations and in the face of change.[61]

Lineage is also important for families that have their own historical narratives that they feel have been usurped or forgotten as the Al Thani have stressed their own history as a way of legitimizing and cementing their power, especially given the royal family's propensity to correlate their own rise with the emergence of the nation-state.[62] Perhaps because of their co-optive capacity, or simply because they cannot counter the strong narratives in other families, the Al Thani elite seem unconcerned by the endurance of such narratives, although in the past they have given financial concessions to key families to avoid confrontation, or have marginalized other families, such as the al-Na'im, who have genuinely strong internal structures and the potential to challenge the Al Thani if granted access to substantial institutional power or resources.

International Business Actors

Finally, an increasingly important set of formal political actors are multinational firms, especially those that enter into joint ventures with the large state-owned firms. These of course have a completely different structure of relationship with the state and senior political figures. To some extent relationships are still built on interpersonal linkages, but much less commonly than among indigenous business figures and the political elite. Most often multinationals are chosen for their particular expertise on a project, and in many cases also on their willingness to bring project investment or other funding with them. Some observers assume that the joint venture approach by the state through Qatar Petroleum has deliberate foreign policy goals, and specifically that it seeks a breadth of engagement with the international energy sector so as to guarantee that the states where these major energy firms are headquartered will be supportive or sympathetic toward

Qatar.[63] Such a strategy is impossible to prove but makes some sense in light of Qatar's branding and foreign relations strategies, as will be discussed shortly.

Regardless, a strong link with multinational firms and a willingness to encourage foreign investment makes sense, given that an integral part of the state's development strategy involves responding positively to globalization and the easing of restrictions on international trade and international communication, even if key figures, from the emir down, have been at pains to remind Qataris and foreigners alike of the importance of retaining and protecting the Qatari culture and identity at the same time. Investment also suits the regime's attempts to integrate the local economy with the global economy, and to build a world-class set of state-owned firms and private sector. Emir Hamad hinted at these types of considerations, and at the same time Qatar's energy-driven economy, in a 2010 interview with *The Financial Times:* "We are trying to build industries around hydrocarbons, like aluminum, petrochemicals and others. Even around these industries, we are going to build another chain of small factories. We are concentrating more on light and medium industries. We are trying to attract companies from outside to invest here in Qatar, whether with the Qatar Investment Authority or with the private sector."[64]

The role of multinational firms is strengthened by the policy of investment abroad, as well as the active attraction of foreign investment into Qatar.[65] To some extent Qatar benefited from the difficulties faced by Dubai over 2008–2010 as the global financial crisis emerged,[66] and then the 2011 Arab Spring added further to Qatar's appeal given that it seemed virtually immune from the upheaval that struck a number of other Arab states.[67] However, its diversification strategy and deliberate attempts at improvements in business processes were important factors too in developing its trade and investment appeal in the 2000s. In particular, as its economy took off in the mid-2000s, demand for new consumer goods, construction, and services boomed as well, furthered by state-sponsored initiatives toward socioeconomic development, and the opportunities from the *Qatar National Vision 2030* policies of a more diversified economy and a focus on human development initiatives.[68] Separately, Qatar has also boosted its attractiveness by improving the mechanisms and processes attached to business, such as cutting red tape and making the investment environment more attractive through both macroeconomic reforms and changes at the more mundane level of administrative procedures.

Last, at a more abstract level, multinational firms are important for the outward show and image of change and development that they bring, both by their presence in the country and through the ability of the state to legitimize them as benefiting technology transfer and skills transmission. Even given that Qatarization has been halfhearted and of little effectiveness, multinationals are still important in suggesting and symbolizing change and economic modernization, and in Qatar multinational firms do not, for the most part, have the negative, exploitative connotations that they often possess in states with a radical or revolutionary history. Certainly, in the development of the gas and petrochemical sectors, multinational firms have provided Qatar Petroleum and the state with both expertise and ability to spread risk, and there has been little opposition to their roles. In other sectors, such as higher education, international universities have provided a sense of quality that has been used both to ensure the prestige of Education City and to provide a form of competition for Qatar University. In other sectors, such as banking and finance, international firms have been more tightly controlled but still send a message from the state to the international business community that the economy is internationalized and open to competition.

These various dynamics, and the practical and symbolic roles that international firms play in Qatar's economy and politics, reappear and are further explored later, including in the next chapter, which provides a discussion of the most important sector to Qatar's economy and to the survival of the regime and its key clients—the hydrocarbon sector—and then in the following chapters on economic diversification as well.

Notes

1. "Qatar: Profile—Shaikh Hamad bin Khalifa Al Thani," *Middle East Economic Digest,* August 28, 1995; "*MEED* Special Report on Qatar: An Ambitious Amir Takes the Helm," *Middle East Economic Digest,* August 28, 1995.
2. "*MEED* Special Report on Qatar: An Ambitious Amir Takes the Helm."
3. Curtiss, "Qatar's New Ruler Breaks the GCC Policy Mold."
4. "*MEED* Special Report on Qatar: An Ambitious Amir Takes the Helm."
5. Mansour, "Public Policy and Privatization."
6. The minister of foreign affairs, who made the first statement on Misha'al's appointment, made this claim. See "Qatar's New Amir Hastens Change," *Middle East Economic Digest,* July 17, 1995.
7. "Shaikh Hamad bin Khalifa Al Thani: Move to a Gas Economy," *Middle East Economic Digest,* November 3, 1997.
8. On the CMC and the elections, and the environment in which they occurred, see Lambert, "Political Reform in Qatar."
9. Curtiss, "The Arabian Gulf in 1997."
10. On Al-Jazeera, see Miles, *Al-Jazeera;* and Zayani, *The Al Jazeera Phenomenon.*

11. Crystal, "Political Reform in Qatar," p. 120.

12. Neil Ford, "A Trailblazer for Democracy?" *The Middle East,* January 2004, p. 21.

13. Author interview, Doha, April 2012.

14. On this contrast, compare Crystal, "Political Reform in Qatar," and Kamrava, "Royal Factionalism and Political Liberalization in Qatar." A similar but wider point about political process manipulation in much of the Gulf—less so in Kuwait than in the other states, as argued—is made in Mitchell, "Political and Socioeconomic Transformation in the GCC."

15. Author interview, Doha, October 2011.

16. Its full name is the Qatar Foundation for Education, Science, and Community Development. For more details, see its website, http://www.qf.org.qa.

17. "In Oil-Rich Mideast, Shades of the Ivy League," *New York Times,* February 11, 2008.

18. Ibid.

19. A point made in "Backstory: Qatar Reformed by a Modern Marriage," *Christian Science Monitor,* March 6, 2007.

20. "Qatar—Sheikh Hamad bin Khalifa Al Thani," *Middle East Economic Digest,* September 22, 2003.

21. The attempted coup was not insignificant: the opposition letter reportedly was signed by sixty-six people, sixteen of them Al Thani, and some sixty military officers were arrested afterward. Coming as the coup attempt did during the outburst of the 2011 Arab Spring, the letter's authors may have felt more able to publicly criticize the emir and his wife (although their comments about her were very blunt). "Report: Qatar Emir Foils Coup Attempt Amid Growing Tensions," *Middle East Economic Digest,* March 1, 2011.

22. Herb, *All in the Family,* p. 126.

23. Text and translation by the Qatar Ministry of Foreign Affairs, on its webpage "The Constitution" at http://english.mofa.gov.qa/details.cfm?id=80. Note that "Jassim" is an alternative transliteration of "Qasim" used elsewhere in this book.

24. What follows is taken from details in Gulbrandsen, "Bridging the Gulf"; from the extensive Al Thani family tree online at http://www.althanitree.com (in Arabic); from Internet searches of individual Qatari institutions to ascertain leadership positions and board memberships as applicable; and from author interviews, Doha, October 2011.

25. The term *bani* literally means "sons [of]," but in this usage denotes an extended family line within a larger *bayt.*

26. Abdallah bin Saud bin Fahd is also chairman of the Qatar Development Bank (http://www.qdb.com.qa/management.html) and on the board of the Qatar Investment Authority, according to the SWF Institute (http://www.swfinstitute.org/swfs/qatar-investment-authority) and Gulbrandsen, "Bridging the Gulf," p. 80.

27. Tom Owen, "Qatar Leads the Way," *The Middle East,* September 2000, p. 6.

28. Ibid.

29. Ibid.

30. Ibid., p. 7.

31. This point has been made widely, but a recent piece that stresses it and makes the argument soundly is Kamrava, "Royal Factionalism and Political Liberalization in Qatar."

32. Hertog, "Defying the Resource Curse."

33. Ibid., p. 263.

34. Gulbrandsen, "Bridging the Gulf," pp. 18–19.

35. Ibid., p. 18.

36. These were the result of amendments on April 3, 2005, to parts of Law no. 13 of 2000; see the Qatar Exchange website, at http://www.qe.com.qa/pps/qe/qe%20english%20portal/Pages/About%20QE/About%20QE.

37. Santhosh V. Perumal, "Foreign Ownership Levels Below Allowed Limits for Most Listed Firms," *Gulf Times*, July 6, 2011, http://www.gulf-times.com/site/topics/printArticle.asp?cu_no=2&item_no=445275&version=1&template_id=57&parent_id=56.

38. The company is quite open about this state linkage, despite (or perhaps because of) the competition that now exists in the telecommunications sector in Qatar. Its fact sheet for the first quarter of 2011 (http://www.qtel.qa/idc/groups/public/documents/document/ir_qtel_fact_sheet.pdf) states that it has "strategic backing by the Qatari government (directly and indirectly)" and graphs its ownership clearly.

39. For details, see the "Key Facts" page of the QIB website, at http://qib.com.qa/english/site/topics/static228e228e.html?cu_no=1&lng=0&template_id=321&temp_type=42&parent_id=300.

40. On him, and other members of the board, see the "Our Board" page on the bank's website, at http://www.alkhaliji.com/AboutUs/TheBoardThatSupports_en_gb.asp.

41. Author interviews, Doha, October 2011 and April 2012.

42. Gulbrandsen, "Bridging the Gulf," pp. 18–19.

43. Ibid., p. 17.

44. Ibid., pp. 20–21.

45. From the profile "List of Experts: Mansoor al-Mahmoud" on the website of the Belfer Center for Science and International Affairs, Harvard University, at http://belfercenter.ksg.harvard.edu/experts/2356/mansoor_almahmoud.html.

46. Gulbrandsen, "Bridging the Gulf," p. 21.

47. See the brief biographical background on him on the Wharton School (University of Pennsylvania) website, on the "Wharton Global Alumni Forum 2009" page, at http://www.whartondubai09.com/bio-mahd.html.

48. Gulbrandsen, "Bridging the Gulf," p. 23.

49. See the Al-Attiyah Group website, http://www.al-attiyah.com/about%20us.htm.

50. The firm uses the transliteration "Jaidah Group"; see its website, http://www.jaidah.com.qa.

51. Crystal, *Oil and Politics in the Gulf,* 151.

52. See the website http://www.qataribusinessmen.org/Support/KHALID.htm. Also author interview, Doha, October 2011.

53. See http://www.qataribusinessmen.org/Support/SH.FAISAL.htm.

54. Author interviews, Doha, October 2011.

55. Ibid.

56. Ibid.

57. It should be stressed, however, that much of the detail in these stories varies, although they are still important to the discussion here as indicators of the influence that such families are *assumed,* rightly or wrongly, to possess. Author interviews, Doha, October 2011.

58. It is often claimed that the al-Fardan are Iranian in origin, but this is not the case, even though they are Shiite.

59. Author interview, Doha, October 2011.

60. Fromherz, *Qatar,* especially pp. 6–8, 17–21.

61. Ibid., p. 8. During an interview in Doha in October 2011, a Qatari interlocutor made a comment to me along these lines, arguing almost contradictorily both that lineage is a bulwark against what would otherwise be overwhelming Al Thani dominance of the political economy and yet that elite linkages between the Al Thani and other families are a chance to guarantee a "fair" share (although perhaps he was alluding to wanting more than a "fair" share?) of national wealth such as energy income.

62. Fromherz, *Qatar,* pp. 18–20.

63. Author interview, Doha, January 2011. Also noted in Ulrichsen, *Insecure Gulf,* p. 102.

64. "Interview Transcript: Qatar's Sheikh Hamad," October 24, 2010, http://www.ft.com/cms/s/0/9163abca-df97-11df-bed9-00144feabdc0.html#axzz1UWReOddR.

65. "Qatar's Global Spree Shows No Signs of Slowing," *The Independent* (London), October 31, 2010.

66. "Focus Shifts from Dubai," *Middle East Economic Digest,* January 28, 2011.

67. "Investors on the Edge," *Middle East Economic Digest,* February 25, 2011.

68. See Qatar General Secretariat for Development Planning, *Qatar National Vision 2030.*

4

Oil, Gas, and Rents

Impressive as Qatar's development has been since the mid-1990s, it is fundamentally the result of hydrocarbons. Were it not for oil and now increasingly natural gas, the resources that have funded and underwritten Qatar's economy would be only a fraction of what they are. In the mid-twentieth century it was oil that dominated the economy, and as discussed in the previous chapter, this dictated much about its political economy. Initially it created British interest in the area in the interwar and post–World War II periods, and also expanded the power of the emir as of the 1950s, including vis-à-vis the influential but demanding and divided royal family. It also limited the capacity for alternative sources of power to emerge, hobbling the ability of merchants and tribal groups in particular to develop sources of financial power independent from the state. Oil in the 1950s and 1960s served to consolidate the emir's power by giving him new and increasing co-optive capacity, as well as the beginnings of a coercive capacity too. In this period and beyond, through Khalifa's rule as well, Qatar was a typical rentier state. Later, starting as early as 1969 but a feature more of the 1990s and after, natural gas grew to become Qatar's key hydrocarbon and the key source of rent in its political economy: the rapid development of Qatar's liquefied natural gas (LNG) capabilities meant that as of 2009, gas exports became more valuable than oil exports to the economy.[1] Qatar has also marked itself as one of the more strategic energy-dominated economies by its early and effective expansion and integration of its energy activities. It makes money not only from the simple rents that accrue from crude oil and natural gas royalties but also by extensive mid-stream and downstream activities, including petrochemicals and refining, and by its investment in and encouragement of development in separate sectors that supply or otherwise link to oil and gas.

This chapter is about hydrocarbons, which despite the changes in and diversification of the Qatari economy in the past couple of decades or so, remain at the very center of the political economy. They have constituted the single largest component—in fact, the majority—of its gross domestic product (GDP) and overwhelmingly dominate state revenue, both directly and through returns on state investments originally paid for from oil and gas income. In looking at the oil, gas, and petrochemical industries in Qatar, there are three aims to the chapter. The first is to look at the sector itself, to consider Qatar's energy assets, production capacity and potential, efforts at integration, and the factors that have influenced, and continue to impact, the energy sector. The second goal is to reinforce the book's theoretical assertions. Specifically, the energy sector is at the very core of Qatar's rentierism, including the "late" rentierism of the Hamad period and the particular state capitalism that has been a central feature of the political economy since the start of the oil era and especially the more entrepreneurial and dynamic state capitalism that has been its specific feature since the mid-1990s. Finally, in outlining and explaining the dynamics of energy, this chapter lays the groundwork for the argument that Qatar's wider political economy is "energy-driven," an argument that is central to understanding the exact natures of rentierism, entrepreneurial state capitalism, and microstatism that explain contemporary Qatar. But the chapter also shows that Qatar is more than a simple oil or gas state living luxuriously but straightforwardly off its rents, and instead that it has developed a much wider political economy, one that is increasingly integrated, connected to other sectors, and international in its linkages. Ultimately, while Qatar possesses more than just an oil and gas economy, it remains very much an energy-driven economy nonetheless.

Qatar's Energy Resources and Political Economy

So central are hydrocarbons to Qatar's economy and to state revenue that the Qatari economy can be broadly divided into the oil and gas sector and the non–oil and gas sector. Depending on prices, especially for oil, the two parts of the economy were of approximately the same value, or hydrocardons the greater, throughout the period from 2000 to 2011, even though in 2009 the non–oil and gas sector was, briefly, the more valuable of the two when energy prices plummeted. Despite this trend toward greater diversity in its economic base and production, Qatar is still dominated by oil and gas and its GDP is very much influenced by global energy prices. This is likely to continue for the foreseeable future, for two reasons. First, the current and projected production levels of both oil and gas suggest that, unless there is a massive shift in its non–oil and gas economy, the size of the oil and gas components of the economy will remain large and valuable enough to be central to it for decades to come. Second, there is an enormous amount of energy reserves—at estimated rates of exploitation, some 55–60 years of oil production and around 200 years of gas production—meaning that Qatar is projected to be among the last of any states, in the Gulf or globally, to stop receiving hydrocarbon rents.

Oil exports, and energy more generally, have dominated the economy since at least the 1950s, as discussed in Chapter 2. It was noted there that the exploitation of oil, while it commenced rather unevenly and was delayed during the middle to late 1940s, quickly dominated Qatar's GDP and exports. While reserve figures always need to be treated with some caution, notable has been the expansion of oil production since the late 1990s, such that overall production increased from an average low of 315,000 barrels per day in 1985 to over 1 million barrels per day in 2005, and then to well over 1.5 million barrels per day in 2010 and 1.7 million in 2011. Table 4.1 illustrates this fluctuation since the early 1970s, showing the declines in production through the 1980s and the two major increases in the second half of the 1990s and again after 2004, respectively.

The rise of the gas sector has been even more dramatic, as shown in Table 4.2. Qatar has, of course, long been a gas producer, usually exploiting associated gas during the oil production process. This changed dramatically after about 2008, as gas increasingly took center stage. The exploitation of North Dome gas expanded dramatically as Qatar, through international joint ventures, developed its LNG export capacity sharply, with the final major development projects for the gas sector all online in the early 2010s. Once its contracted export volumes maximize around the year 2014, gas exports will be far more valuable than those of oil and in the global gas sector Qatar will be among the largest and most powerful gas suppliers in the world. By 2010 it had already become the world's fifth largest gas producer after the United States, Russia, Canada, and Iran.[2] Given the lower carbon dioxide emissions from gas and improvements in technology, international demand for gas is likely to grow in the 2010s and 2020s, making Qatar all the more important as a gas superpower.

Despite the enormous increases in hydrocarbon production and export after 2004 or so, oil and gas production, as a share of Qatari GDP, actually trended slightly downward in the period 2005–2010. This is due to several

Table 4.1 Qatar's Oil Reserves and Production, 1972–2011

	1972	1973	1974	1975	1976	1977	1978	1979	1980	1981
Production (thousand barrels per day)	482	570	518	437	487	435	484	506	476	421
	1982	**1983**	**1984**	**1985**	**1986**	**1987**	**1988**	**1989**	**1990**	**1991**
Reserves (billion barrels)	3.4	3.3	4.5	4.5	4.5	4.5	4.5	4.5	3.0	3.0
Production (thousand barrels per day)	325	316	353	315	355	315	360	403	434	420
	1992	**1993**	**1994**	**1995**	**1996**	**1997**	**1998**	**1999**	**2000**	**2001**
Reserves (billion barrels)	3.1	3.1	3.5	3.7	3.7	12.5	13.5	13.1	16.9	16.8
Production (thousand barrels per day)	495	460	451	461	568	692	701	723	757	754
	2002	**2003**	**2004**	**2005**	**2006**	**2007**	**2008**	**2009**	**2010**	**2011**
Reserves (billion barrels)	27.6	27.0	26.9	27.9	27.4	27.3	26.8	25.9	25.9	24.7
Production (thousand barrels per day)	764	879	992	1,028	1,110	1,197	1,378	1,345	1,569	1,723

Source: Derived from statistics in the historical data workbook attached to the *BP Statistical Review of World Energy 2012*, http://www.bp.com/sectiongenericarticle800.do?categoryId=9037130&contentId=7068669.

Table 4.2 Qatar's Gas Production, 1972–2011 (billion cubic feet per day)

	1972	1973	1974	1975	1976	1977	1978	1979	1980	1981
Production	0.1	0.2	0.1	0.2	0.1	0.2	0.1	0.4	0.5	0.4
	1982	1983	1984	1985	1986	1987	1988	1989	1990	1991
Production	0.5	0.5	0.6	0.5	0.6	0.5	0.6	0.6	0.6	0.7
	1992	1993	1994	1995	1996	1997	1998	1999	2000	2001
Production	1.2	1.3	1.3	1.3	1.3	1.7	1.9	2.1	2.3	2.6
	2002	2003	2004	2005	2006	2007	2008	2009	2010	2011
Production	2.9	3.0	3.8	4.4	4.9	6.1	7.4	8.6	11.3	14.2

Source: Derived from statistics in the historical data workbook attached to the *BP Statistical Review of World Energy 2012*, http://www.bp.com/sectiongenericarticle800.do?categoryId=9037130&contentId=7068669.

dynamics. One was the Qatari government's policy of economic diversification, despite the problems experienced in developing an economy more autonomous from rents. As with most oil exporters and rentiers, the regime realized that whatever benefits accrue in terms of state revenues, oil and gas create relatively few jobs and often have negative impacts on other parts of the political economy, especially inflationary and currency impacts, of course, as proponents of the "oil curse" would argue, but also political challenges associated with rentierism and the expectations of the population toward their political leadership. The Qatari government, as a result, deliberately sought to develop and diversify the non–oil and gas economy. The second dynamic is that much oil and gas rent is circulated through the non–oil and gas economy by associated spending, the investment of surplus rents by the state and wealthy individuals, and of course rent-based state expenditure. Finally, like other wealthy Gulf states, Qatar has a small indigenous population and a large expatriate work force: the number of people holding Qatari nationality among the almost 1.7 million living there is by most estimates no more than 300,000. This has provided enormous flexibility and speed in developing the economy, including a capability to quickly develop the non–oil and gas economy. Rather than having to train and develop an indigenous population across all areas and skills, large numbers of people—the overwhelming majority of the work force—can be brought in, already trained and experienced, on short notice. The cost of this approach, and the fact that rents pay nearly all such expatriate salaries and costs, is another reason why Qatar is an energy-driven economy, even in sectors of the economy that appear very distinct from oil and gas.

As a result of all of these dynamics, the oil and gas sector as a percentage of GDP has declined only marginally, from 60.4 percent of GDP in 2000 to a little above 57.7 percent in 2011, albeit with flucations in between as shown in Table 4.3. The table also shows that, as a result of such figures, Qatar remains a very stark example of a rentier state and, by implication from the economic structures behind these figures, a strongly state capitalist political economy as well. This is a continuation of the situation that emerged in the 1950s and above all the 1960s, as already discussed, in which oil, and to a much lesser extent gas, dominated GDP, state revenue, and state expenditure, and permitted the state to impose very minimal taxes or charges on the population and, through a combination of pacifying merchants with rents and elbowing aside those who resisted, to own a disproportionate share of the means of production.

Scholars of oil states and especially of rentier-state theory have long debated at precisely what point an economy or a state becomes rentier. Is

Table 4.3 Qatari Rentierism: The Oil and Gas Sectors as a Share of GDP, 2000–2011

	2000	2001	2002	2003	2004[a]	2005	2006	2007	2008	2009	2010	2011
Revenue from oil and gas sectors	39,065	36,812	40,717	50,551	67,533	92,071	130,203	166,642	215,053	165,325	235,500	364,458
Percentage change from previous year	89.2	–5.8	10.6	25.2	33.6	46.3	41.4	28.0	29.1	–23.1	42.4	54.8
Revenue from other sectors	25,581	27,767	31,016	35,367	40,124	62,493	90,005	127,291	187,940	192,535	223,025	267,151
Percentage change from previous year	4.6	8.5	11.7	14.0	13.5	18.8	39.4	41.4	47.6	2.4	15.8	19.8
Total GDP	64,646	64,579	71,733	85,918	107,657	154,564	220,208	293,933	402,993	357,860	458,525	631,609
Percentage change from previous year	43.3	–0.1	11.1	19.8	25.3	33.8	40.6	33.5	37.1	–11.2	28.1	37.7
Revenue from oil and gas sectors as percentage of GDP	60.4	57.0	56.8	58.8	62.7	59.6	59.1	56.7	53.4	46.2	51.4	57.7

Sources: Derived from statistics in QNB Capital, *Qatar Economic Review,* various years; Qatar National Bank, "Facts and Figures," 2012, http://www.qnb.com.qa/qnbcapital/inner.jsp?page=QNBQatarFactsAndFiguresConv&pagetype=documents&lang=en; and author's calculations.

Notes: Revenue in QR millions in current prices.

a. Estimated by QNB Capital in the 2005 and 2006 editions of the *Qatar Economic Review.*

it when rents reach a certain percentage of GDP, as many earlier rentier theorists argued? Many have suggested 30 percent of state revenues as a benchmark for qualifying as a rentier state, others 40 percent, and within the literature there is also an expectation that state expenditure will be a larger than usual share of GDP as well.[3] Regardless, in the case of Qatar, it easily qualifies as a rentier state on such grounds: oil and gas incomes constituted a majority of GDP in all but one year of the 2000s, accounting for between 46 and 62 percent of GDP, and in terms of state revenue varied from about 50 to 70 percent over approximately the same period.[4] The specific figures for state revenue sources over this period are shown in Table 4.4. These figures are comparable with those of the most rentier of the small Gulf states, and thus there can be little contention about Qatar's underlying status as a rentier state unless one challenges the entire rentier approach.

This reinforces the assertion that Qatar is a rentier state, but especially that it is a "late" rentier state,[5] with a more sophisticated and vertically integrated energy sector than many other rentiers and with a state that is more activist and economically engaged than what traditional rentier theorists would argue. The original rentier arguments of Giacomo Luciani, Hazem Beblawi, and others,[6] for example, precluded the typical rentier state from engaging in a development policy or even an economic policy, apart from an expenditure policy or allocative approach. This, of course, is no longer valid, if ever it was. Qatar has not just an economic and development policy, but also a sophisticated set of strategies and policies with specific socioeconomic goals in mind. The idea that the rentier state neither needs nor seeks an economic or development role ignores both the social linkages of its elites and, more pragmatically, the fact that even the wealthiest of rentiers can face social pressure, even the threat of revolution, if they are seen as too distant from society. This also relates to the other problematic aspect of early rentier literature, that the state is autonomous from society. While rents may buy the state some greater independence from society than otherwise, the political risks if society feels marginalized or betrayed by the state remain. Thus the Qatari regime has a certain aloofness and liberty from society, but it ignores it at its grave peril. Moreover, the royal family and the political elite are *of* the society and intimately linked to it. Through the extended royal family, tribal linkages, and patronage networks out to merchants, social actors and forces, and others, the Qatari state cannot be separated from the actors and individuals that constitute its political order. Arguably it has been especially active in pursuing economic diversification and development for these reasons.

Table 4.4 Qatari Government Finances as Evidence for Rentier-State Characterization, 2004–2011 (QR millions)

	2004–2005	2005–2006	2006–2007	2007–2008	2008–2009	2009–2010	2010–2011[a]
Total hydrocarbon revenue	36,319	46,381	55,429	70,748	80,009	82,807	99,538
Oil revenue	33,192	40,235	48,181	60,050	61,245	61,742	69,333
Gas Revenue	3,127	6,146	7,248	10,698	18,764	21,065	30,205
Other revenue	18,745	19,304	30,634	47,042	60,984	86,288	81,561
Total revenue	55,064	65,685	86,063	117,790	140,993	169,095	181,099
Hydrocarbon revenue as percentage of total state revenue	66.0	70.6	64.4	60.1	56.7	49.0	55.0

Sources: International Monetary Fund, "Qatar: 2010 Article IV Consultation," Country Report no. 11/64, p. 26 (tab. 2a); International Monetary Fund, "Qatar: Statistical Appendix," Country Report No. 10/62, p. 10 (tab. 13).

Note: a. Preliminary.

The Scope and Future of the Oil Sector

The oil sector and much of the gas and petrochemical sectors as well are managed through Qatar's state-owned national oil company, Qatar Petroleum (QP). Qatar Petroleum is absolutely central to the finances of the state, and while there is considerable managerial autonomy given to the firm, there can be no illusions about its strong linkages into the upper levels of the political system: its chairman and managing director, Abdallah bin Hamad al-Attiyya, is also the deputy prime minister, and from 1999 to 2011 was also the minister of energy and industry. Muhammad Salih Abdallah al-Sada, who replaced al-Attiyya as minister of energy and industry in January 2011, had worked for QP for twenty-three years and for RasGas, which is 70 percent owned by QP, before joining the ministry.

Qatar Petroleum's interests are broad and substantial across the entire energy sector, in Qatar especially but also abroad. It is typical of the new type of state-owned enterprise (SOE) in the Gulf, one that is professionally autonomous, efficient, well-managed, and profitable. Such firms break the older stereotype of an SOE as politicized, bloated, bureaucratic, and subsidized; such SOEs persist elsewhere, of course, but the oil and gas SOEs of the Gulf Cooperation Council (GCC) are of the new, efficient sort, as are most of its SOEs in other sectors. Firms such as QP have capabilities and competencies on par with those of any of the international oil companies such as Shell and British Petroleum. Qatar manages its energy resources and the exploitation of them through Qatar Petroleum, including QP's subsidiaries and joint ventures. These activities cover all the stages of the oil and gas sectors, and include exploration and extraction (both onshore and offshore), refining, the sale of oil, gas, refined liquids, and petrochemicals, and associated work such as LNG processing, the manufacturing of fuel additives, and insurance. Oil production is done both directly by QP and with international firms under specific agreements covering defined areas. This is not to say that there are not problems with the firm: it has somewhat of a reputation with contractors for being slow or late in delivering projects, and for being at times bureaucratic or inefficient.[7]

In terms of oil production, Qatar Petroleum produces from one large onshore field and two large offshore ones. The onshore field, Dukhan, is located roughly along the western coast, and runs north-south with a bend slightly eastward at its southern end. QP uses multiple wells to produce from the onshore field. Dukhan is Qatar's oldest field (oil was discovered there in 1938), and it has the highest production capacity of the oil fields, some 335,000 barrels per day, although recent production has sometimes been below that level, for example at 254,000 barrels per day in 2009.[8]

Dukhan is thought to have reserves of at least 2 billion barrels, which would give it productive life until around 2032 at current production levels or about 2027 at its full production capacity.[9] The Dukhan oil is especially high quality, a light crude with a gravity of 40 degrees and a sulfur content of about 1.2 percent.[10]

The offshore fields managed directly by QP are Maydan Mahzam and Bul Hanine. Maydan Mahzam, located about 150 kilometers east-northeast of Doha, started production in 1965 and as of 2010 was producing 30,300 barrels per day. Bul Hanine is to the southeast of Maydan Mahzam and is larger; it began production in 1972 and as of 2010 was producing 54,000 barrels per day.[11] The oil from these two fields is also light crude, although of slightly lower gravity (32–33 degrees) and higher sulfur content (about 2.2 percent) than that produced at Dukhan.[12]

Qatar Petroleum also owns and manages an enormous amount of exploration and production-related oil infrastructure. This includes, for example, Halul Island, which is the storage facility and export terminal for Qatar's offshore oil.[13] The island can store some 5 million barrels of oil in eleven tanks, and also has pumping stations and the infrastructure and facilities for the staff based there. QP also owns and manages Mesaieed Industrial City (MIC), a 17–square kilometer facility that commenced operations in 1996 supporting gas processing, petrochemical activities (such as production of fertilizers and methanol), and oil refining. On top of these, of course, QP operates multiple other facilities and infrastructure.

Qatar Petroleum, like some other national oil companies in the Gulf, is seeking to expand its international activities by investing and operating abroad. In 2007 it established a stand-alone arm, Qatar Petroleum International (QPI), designed to expand its oil interests and diversify across markets and into new international downstream oil and other projects.[14] QPI also reflects a clever strategy by the parent firm and the Qatari government to expand QP's international presence and link it with economies that in future will likely have strong energy relationships with Qatar. This is likely to have a positive impact on QP's image and bottom line, but also is part of the microstatism that characterizes Qatar's approach to international economic relations and diplomacy: as discussed in later chapters, it is a deliberate strategy to develop relationships with key states and to see to it that they have an interest in Qatar's stability and security.

Foreign links in Qatar's domestic energy sector are important too. Output at the three QP production fields constitutes only a minority share of Qatar's total oil production, typically about 40 percent; operations by international firms account for the remainder. QP has divided Qatar's onshore and offshore areas into twenty-two hydrocarbon blocks. QP then manages the exploration and development of the blocks that it is not exploiting itself through agreements with international oil companies. These are either exploration and production-sharing agreements, or development and production-sharing agreements. Under the former, the contracting firm is given the rights to explore for oil in a particular block; if oil is found, the contractor can then develop it. Following the discovery of oil, under a development and production-sharing agreement, the contractor's role is either to develop the area for production or sometimes to further develop or exploit an existing or mature field.[15]

A development and production-sharing agreement covers production at the highest-yielding field in Qatar, Al-Shaheen, which produces 297,000 barrels of oil per day.[16] Al-Shaheen, located in Block 5 in the North Dome, was discovered by the Danish firm Maersk Oil in 1992. Maersk then commenced production at the field in 1994, having invested the hefty sum of about US$2 billion in the field, in part because of the operational complexity of drilling it. In 2001 a further agreement between QP and Maersk's local arm, Maersk Oil Qatar, further increased the field's production, and an exploration and production-sharing agreement was signed in 2005 to allow the firm to search further areas in Block 5 near Al-Shaheen. The operations at Al-Shaheen are large and complex. Maersk operates 131 production and water injection wells at the field plus platforms and pipelines, and engages in complex extraction that involves horizontal drilling and water injection. Such methods are increasingly likely to be necessary as Qatar's oil fields mature and oil becomes more difficult to extract and wetter.[17] The site also produces associated gas, some of which is exported. Enhancements to the field in 2005 brought capacity closer to the goal of 525,000 barrels of oil per day.[18] There are several other international ventures beyond Al-Shaheen, although for the most part output from them is considerably smaller. These ventures include Idd al-Shargi (with Occidental Petroleum), Al-Khalij (with TotalFinaElf), Al-Rayyan (with Occidental), and others. Table 4.5 shows production for Qatari oil fields, not including condensates and suchlike.

What is the future of Qatar's oil sector? The decline in its relative size compared to the gas and petrochemical sectors might suggest a fairly modest future, but it is important to note how much production increased from 1997 onward and again after about 2005. This means that while in future decades gas will occupy an evermore prominent place in the Qatari economy, and presumably the minds of political leaders, oil will remain very important. Regardless, the Qatari economy is in a better position as a result of the increase in the size of the gas sector relative to oil, for two reasons: first, the unpredictability of oil prices and their propensity to fluctuate; and

Table 4.5 Qatari Oil Field Production, mid-2012 (barrels per day)

Oil Field	Operator	Production
Al-Shaheen	Maersk Oil	300,000
Dukhan	Qatar Petroleum	230,000
Idd al-Shargi	Occidental	90,000
Bul Hanine	Qatar Petroleum	45,000
Maydan Mahzam	Qatar Petroleum	25,000
Al-Khalij	TotalFinaElf	25,000
Al-Rayyan	Occidental	8,000
Al-Karkara	Qatar Petroleum Development	5,000
El-Bunduq	Bunduq Oil Company	5,000
Total		733,000

Source: Qatar National Bank, *Qatar Economic Insight 2012*, pp. 18–19.

second, because Qatar's oil reserves are comparatively modest—its oil production is likely to peak soon and then begin declining. On the first point, previous oil price slumps were severe: during the 1985–1986 price slump, Khalifa cut spending markedly and urgently, including investment spending, and was seen to have "panicked."[19] In the late 1990s, there was less panic, but it was a trying period because gas exports were yet to become sizable, and so oil still predominated as a state revenue source: in the late 1990s oil constituted some 70 percent of state revenue[20]—in other words, it constituted a larger share of state revenue than would oil and gas combined a decade later. In the 1990s the state was able both to pause some spending, especially on capital projects, and to borrow,[21] and as a result minimize the austerity required before prices rose again in the early 2000s.

In these respects Qatar is not a typical oil state, important though oil is to the state's coffers and to macroeconomic results. Gas is typically managed on longer-term and more stable supply contracts, and the Qatari economy is more diversified today than in the 1990s or especially the 1980s. This bodes well for Qatar overcoming any future decline in oil income. Oil created and has long financed the rentierism and state capitalism that have characterized the political economy, but increasingly this role is now shifting to gas.

The Centrality of Gas

Natural gas was first slated for development by the state in 1969, and despite output being very modest for a long time, it was only from about

2004 onward that Qatar's natural gas output began to increase massively. The other dynamic of Qatari natural gas is the sheer size of its reserves—almost exclusively the result of the North Dome field—and the likelihood that even with economic diversification, the state will rely heavily on gas to some extent into the twenty-second century. It was also the coming online of gas that most accounted for Qatar gaining the headline-grabbing double-digit GDP growth rates that it did in 2008 and again in 2010 and 2011.

The North Dome field is the largest nonassociated gas field in the world; measured in its oil-equivalent reserves, it is in fact the largest proven hydrocarbon reserve in the world as of 2012. The field crosses the maritime boundary between Qatar and Iran, and so the northern part of the field, under Iranian waters, is called South Pars by the Iranians, and the southern part, under the northern tip of the Qatar peninsula and projecting out into Qatar's territorial waters, is known as the North Dome (or often the North Field). As of 2012 the North Dome's proven recoverable reserves stand at around 903 trillion cubic feet, or 13.7 percent of the world total, plus there is a further 360 trillion cubic feet of recoverable reserves in South Pars. At the production levels slated for 2014, North Dome will remain productive for a remarkable 176 years.[22] The field was constructed from two separate gas-bearing formations and now contains mostly natural gas condensate, but also small oil fields; the Al-Shaheen oil field, mentioned earlier, is in the northern part of the North Dome, for example.

The North Dome was discovered by Shell in 1971. Initially it lay largely unexploited, however, as a result of almost no international interest to either invest or buy gas on long-term contracts at that time. The very small production from the field in the 1970s and 1980s consisted of associated gas for domestic use.[23] It was in the 1980s that the decision was made to begin exploiting the North Dome, and to do so in phases and through Qatar Petroleum LNG joint ventures with international firms; thus, from the outset, the gas sector was managed differently—more internationally and collaboratively—compared to the oil sector, and with an emphasis on the use of technology to focus on gas exports. This approach has been emphasized by Hamad, who had responsibility for Qatar's oil and gas development as of 1992, and he drove this approach before he took power and encouraged its continuance after.[24] This has been a feature of much of Qatar's large projects, whether in energy or other sectors, since the early 1990s: some public sector funding, but also private sector investment and technology transfer as well, brought together into a Qatari government-controlled but commercially run joint venture. Much of this funding was raised through very successful international loans and bonds issues.[25]

In developing its gas production, Qatar Petroleum established two major phased projects, Qatargas and RasGas. The initial stage of Qatargas (Qatargas 1), contracted in 1984, was the first such agreement. It included two streams. The first was an upstream joint venture (onshore receiving of offshore gas), with QP holding 65 percent of the equity and the rest being held by international firms: TotalFinaElf (20 percent), ExxonMobil (10 percent), and Mitsui and Marubeni (2.5 percent each).[26] The second was a downstream joint venture, involving construction and operation of an LNG processing plant, where the equity was divided only slightly differently: QP 65 percent, TotalFinaElf 10 percent, ExxonMobil 10 percent, and Mitsui and Marubeni 7.5 percent each.[27] The first sales agreements under Qatargas 1 were signed in 1992, and the first shipments, to Japan, occurred in 1996. In the years immediately after that, Qatargas 1's production capacity was expanded.

Three further joint ventures under the Qatargas name were subsequently agreed.[28] Qatargas 2 was a joint venture, signed in June 2002 between QP and ExxonMobil, to add two further trains to the Qatargas project, which expanded capacity to add new exports to the United Kingdom to Qatargas operations. Initially QP held 70 percent of the equity and ExxonMobil 30 percent, but the French firm Total acquired a minority stake (16.7 percent) in Train 5 in 2005. Qatargas 3 was signed in July 2003 and involved an agreement with ConocoPhillips for a sixth train; equity was split 68.5 percent to QP, 30 percent to ConocoPhillips, and 1.5 percent to Mitsui. Finally, Qatargas 4 was launched in 2005 with an agreement by QP and Shell to construct a further train to liquefy gas for export to Europe and Asia, with equity divided 70 percent to QP and 30 percent to Shell. Qatargas 3 came online in 2010, and Qatargas 4 in 2011.[29]

Qatargas 2 came online in 2009,[30] and that year exported 14.1 million tons of liquefied natural gas through three trains, with the fourth coming online in 2009 as well, and with the majority of the LNG going to Japan (about 7.7 million tons), some to the United Kingdom (3.6 million tons) and Spain (2.7 million tons), and the tiny remainder being sold elsewhere on the spot.[31] This increase in output when Qatargas 2 came online, coupled with higher average prices from 2008 to 2010, account for the massive influx of new gas wealth into Qatar in this period, although it is also important to note that Qatar's high public debt is the result in part of borrowing for these major, long-term projects. Higher production in the 2010s, through the later Qatargas joint ventures mentioned earlier, will add considerable new capacity, and so meet export contracts that total 40 million tons by 2014.[32] The exact details of the LGN export contracts, and the joint ventures under which they were agreed, are outlined in Table 4.6. Gas

Table 4.6 Qatari Liquefied Natural Gas Export Contracts, 2005–2015 (million tons per annum)

Supplier	Purchaser	Export Destination	2005	2006	2007	2008	2009	2010	2011	2012	2013	2014	2015
Qatargas 1	(multiple firms)	Japan	6.3	6.4	6.6	6.6	6.6	6.6	6.7	6.7	6.7	6.7	6.7
RasGas 1	KOGAS	Korea	8.8	8.8	8.8	8.7	7.0	7.0	7.0	7.0	7.0	7.0	7.0
RasGas 2	Petronet	India	3.8	5.0	5.0	5.0	5.6	7.5	7.5	7.5	7.5	7.5	7.5
RasGas 2	Edison Gas	Italy	—	—	—	—	4.7	4.7	4.7	4.7	4.7	4.7	4.7
Qatargas 1	Gas Natural	Spain	2.2	2.6	2.9	2.9	2.9	2.9	2.9	2.9	2.9	2.9	2.9
Qatargas 1	British Petroleum	Spain	0.7	0.5	—	—	—	—	—	—	—	—	—
RasGas 2	Endesa Generacion	Spain	0.6	0.8	0.8	0.8	0.8	0.8	0.8	0.8	0.8	0.8	0.8
RasGas 2	Fluxys LNG	Belgium	—	—	2.6	3.4	3.4	3.4	3.4	3.4	3.4	3.4	3.4
RasGas 2	Distrigas	Belgium	—	—	—	2.1	2.1	2.1	2.1	2.1	2.1	2.1	2.1
RasGas 2	CPC	Taiwan	—	—	—	1.2	2.5	3.0	3.0	3.0	3.0	3.0	3.0
Qatargas 2	ExxonMobil	United Kingdom	—	—	—	—	4.0	6.5	7.6	8.0	8.0	8.0	8.0
Qatargas 2	Total and ExxonMobil	France, United Kingdom, and United States	—	—	—	—	3.0	6.5	7.6	8.0	8.0	8.0	8.0
Qatargas 3	ConocoPhilips	United States	—	—	—	—	—	—	6.0	7.0	7.5	7.7	7.7
RasGas 3	ExxonMobil	United States	—	—	—	—	2.1	8.5	8.5	8.5	8.5	8.5	8.5
Qatargas 4	Shell	United States	—	—	—	—	—	1.5	5.3	4.5	1.0	1.8	1.8
Qatargas 4	Marubeni	Japan	—	—	—	—	—	—	0.9	0.9	0.9	0.9	0.9
Qatargas 4	PGNiG	Poland	—	—	—	—	—	—	—	—	—	1.0	1.0
Qatargas 4	CNOOC	China	—	—	—	—	—	—	—	—	3.0	3.0	3.0
Total			22.4	24.1	26.7	30.7	44.7	61.0	74.0	75.0	75.0	77.0	77.0

Source: QNB Capital, *Qatar Economic Review 2010*, p. 18.

production is also crucial to petrochemical and other downstream operations, where gas is used as a feedstock. This gives gas a further importance to the economy as a pathway to (partial) diversification of the economy, at least from basic hydrocarbon extraction and processing to more sophisticated manufacturing.

The other major joint venture firm is the Ras Laffan Liquefied Natural Gas Company, or RasGas 1.[33] This was founded in 1993 as a major grassroots facility for LNG production and related work. The equity was also majority-held by QP, at 63 percent, with partners that included ExxonMobil (25 percent), Koras (5 percent), Itochu Corporation (4 percent), and LNG Japan Corporation (3 percent). Production began from the first train in 1999 and the second in 2000, each producing around 2.5 million tons of LNG per annum initially,[34] now closer to 3.3–3.4 million.[35] RasGas originally supplied most of its production to South Korea, and that was an initial goal of the firm; in 2000, for example, South Korea received 3.5 million tons out of a total production of 3.9 million tons, but by 2009, out of a production of 23 million tons, South Korea received 7 million, India 6.2, Belgium 4.5, and multiple others the remainder.[36]

This also illustrates the speed with which LNG production by RasGas has increased. RasGas quickly developed the capacity to outproduce Qatargas, overtaking it in production in 2005,[37] and it also manufactures associated products such as solid sulfur, its capacity for which in 2010 was about 200 tons per day. Table 4.7 shows the production, both recent and contracted, for Qatargas and RasGas.

Further RasGas initiatives followed, beginning with RasGas 2 in 2001.[38] This was driven by QP, specifically by the government, as it was based on an emiri decree of March 26, 2001. It retained the 70-to-30 percent QP-ExxonMobil ownership structure. It expanded the production capacity of the firm by adding three new LNG trains; construction of the three trains was performed by an international consortium.[39] This new production was slated for the Indian market, and production began from Trains 3, 4, and 5 in 2004, 2005, and 2006 respectively. This was followed by RasGas 3, which was the result of a long-term supply contract with the United States being agreed in 2005, to start in 2010, and requiring new production capacity. RasGas 3 was a massive downstream and shipping project, needing some US$14 billion in investment, including two new trains (Trains 6 and 7). Again the construction work was outsourced: energy, procurement, and construction of the trains went to a joint venture of Chiyoda Corporation (Japanese) and Technip (French), and a similar offshore contract to a US firm, J. Ray McDermott Middle East. Trains 6 and 7 came online in 2009 and 2010 respectively.[40]

Table 4.7 Qatargas and RasGas Production and Contracts, 2005–2014 (million tons per annum)

	Qatargas	RasGas
Actual		
2005	9.9	12.3
2006	9.5	15.6
2007	9.4	18.0
2008	9.7	20.7
2009	14.1	23.0
Contracted		
2010	24.0	27.0
2011	37.0	37.0
2012	38.0	37.0
2013	38.0	37.0
2014	40.0	37.0

Source: QNB Capital, *Qatar Economic Review 2010*, tabs. 3.6 and 3.8.

There are several other gas ventures worth noting. One of the best known, perhaps better known even than Qatargas and RasGas because of its regional international dimension, is the Dolphin Project. This is a project that developed a gas export pipeline from Qatar to the United Arab Emirates (UAE). The idea sprang from an initiative, led by Qatar, at the November 1989 GCC summit to develop a GCC-wide integrated gas pipeline network, with the North Dome at the center of the web.[41] The project began, in its very early years, as a multinational initiative, but by the mid-1990s had been abandoned in effect by all but Qatar and the UAE, as had possible extensions of the pipeline to South Asia and Israel,[42] given issues among GCC member states at the time (political differences and likely gas competition, especially). However, strong interest in seeing the project to completion by Qatar, as the gas supplier, and the UAE, given its future gas needs and the strong interest by the Emirati government's UAE Offsets Group (UOG), kept these two states involved cooperatively.

The Dolphin Project is a US$7 billion project, split evenly between offshore development and onshore downstream and pipeline development. It involves the development of new gas wells and platforms in the North Dome, lines to the processing plant at Ras Laffan Industrial City, gas processing at Ras Laffan, and offshore pipelines to Taweelah in the UAE and gas receiving facilities there. Oman is also linked to the project through an effort, technically separate from Dolphin, to link Dolphin to an extension of the pipeline beyond Taweelah. The Dolphin Project and its operations are the responsibility of Dolphin Energy, a joint venture firm that was established by the UOG to manage the project on its behalf. Dolphin Energy, based in Abu Dhabi, is owned by the Abu Dhabi sovereign wealth fund Mubadala Development Company (51 percent) and the US firm Occidental and France's Total (24.5 percent each). The joint venture firm is the operator of all phases of Dolphin.[43] A second phase of the Dolphin Project is planned and involves expanded piping of gas to the UAE and other developments in the UAE.

Dolphin is an interesting and quite contentious development because of its international relations context. It is telling that the project began with much fanfare and optimism, but quickly the bulk of participating states withdrew. Some observers[44] still see it as a pathway to closer GCC integration, and it does indeed have political and financial incentives in it for such longer-term outcomes, but for now its potential remains limited to the Qatar-UAE dimension, with extension of the pipeline beyond Qatar and the UAE (and by extension Oman) remaining in theory a future goal. Also crucial, however, is the spread of gas contracts to international buyers and the deliberate involvement of multiple and different international partners in Qatar Petroleum's joint ventures. According to at least one expert who is intimate with Qatari gas policy, this breadth of external involvement was a deliberate attempt by Qatar to build its international linkages and increase the number of firms and states with an interest in its long-term stability, thereby demonstrating and strengthening an explicit link between its energy and foreign policies.[45] Even if the diplomatic and security benefits of Dolphin are sometimes overplayed by observers, the security importance to Qatar of the internationalization of its energy is, conversely, often not stressed sufficiently.

There are multiple other gas initiatives in Qatar, again led by or managed for the Qatari government by QP. These include the Al-Khalij gas project, agreed in 2000, again between QP and ExxonMobil, but focusing on gas for domestic consumption and in effect linked to RasGas 2. A second area of development is QP's natural gas processing capacity; a basic natural gas liquids (NGL) plant was built in 1974 and a second in 1980, but these focused on processing associated gas and were simple compared with later projects to improve, expand, and increase the sophistication of these plants.[46] QP is also investing heavily in new technology, especially a gas-to-liquid (GTL) capability, so that gas can be exported more easily and made more marketable by being in a final liquid product.[47] The Oryx GTL plant—the world's largest GTL plant—began operations in 2007. Oryx is a 51-to-49 percent joint venture between QP and the South African firm Sasol Synfuels International, which takes gas from the Al-Khalij project and manufactures high-grade fuels from the feedstock. The other GTL project is Pearl GTL, with Shell, which came on-stream in 2011, and which uses a separate technology of Shell's for GTL manufacturing.

All of these projects, on top of other associated gas-processing and gas-related infrastructure and support systems, account for the tremendous increase in gas and petrochemical production by Qatar in the twenty-first century. Gas exports alone are impressive in how rapidly they have expanded. This drive is due to a number of key figures supporting and pushing for the development of the sector, including the emir himself, who was especially keen on intelligently developing the gas sector,[48] and who was integral in setting the goal, reached in December 2010, for Qatar to sell 77 million tons of gas per year. Other figures have been integral too. One, already mentioned, is Abdallah bin Hamad al-Attiyya, who as minister of energy and industry from 1999 to 2011 drove Qatar's ambitious energy development, especially the expansion of its gas sector. Behind al-Attiyya's thinking was the need for diversity in the energy sector, which was key to avoiding the problems of the energy "curse," such as unpredictable and abrupt fluctuations in the underlying commodity price and an overreliance on one source of export earnings. In this vein he spoke to the strategy of a gas "basket": "We don't want to be only an LNG producer, a GTL producer, a petrochemical producer or a piped gas supplier. We have to create a basket of all four. This is the way to spread the risk and to avoid fluctuations in prices."[49] Similarly, al-Attiyya noted the strategy of diversity in the export orientation of the gas sector, saying: "Our LNG map is now Asia, Europe and the US. We believe that a diversified market is very important to create balance."[50] That Qatar's export destinations have expanded since al-Attiyya said this in 2003, from predominantly Japan to later include South Korea, India, the United States, Britain, and others, is demonstrative of this policy. It also highlights, again, Qatar's very close linking of foreign policy and energy policy.[51] Another example of this linkage is the relationship between Qatar and Iran, which while driven by energy connections, has gradually broadened.[52] Finally, there are key figures in Qatargas, RasGas, and elsewhere who have been important in the development of the energy sector; these include Faisal al-Suwaidi, who as chief executive officer of Qatargas from 1997 to 2010 was integral in driving the company's production expansion and diversifying its export destinations.[53]

At the same time, this expansion of the gas sector, especially LNG capacity, has not been without problems. As noted earlier in the context of dealing with QP on oil outsourcing, contractors have complained about problems with some of these projects and have run into financial difficulties with them as joint venture partners. Famously, the Japanese firm Chiyoda ran into financial problems with Qatargas 3 and 4, especially with subcontracting. While this was not the result of the Qatari government directly, it was due in large part to the impacts of its policies; as the *Middle East Economic Digest* noted in 2009: "The roots of the problem lie in the dynamics of the Gulf construction sector over the past four years. Doha's strategy of building several LNG megaprojects simultaneously pushed up construction costs, and the situation was aggravated by its preference for striking lump-sum turnkey contracts, placing the bulk of the risk on the contractor rather than the sponsor."[54] Other firms had similar experiences from the 2006–2008 boom in Qatar, and an upside of surviving the global financial crisis of 2008–2009 so easily, as Qatar did, is that this problem was only reduced, not eliminated.[55] At around the same time, Chiyoda and the French firm Technip made claims on Qatargas for compensation payments to cover expected costs, which Qatargas initially scoffed at but ultimately reached agreement on.[56] Moreover, shortly thereafter—beginning in 2010 but especially as of 2011—contractors faced new challenges as the overall amount and value of work declined as major projects were finalized,[57] and with a moratorium on new projects in the North Dome, first announced in 2005 because of Qatar's fear of overproducing, expected to be in place until at least 2014.[58] This is not to say that Qatar is held in poor esteem by investors, but problems, often the result of government policy, have impacted the development of the energy sector nonetheless.

Qatar's future, given all of these dynamics, is now fully and inextricably linked to gas and its related subsectors. It is now the single-largest source of state revenue, likely to grow increasingly more important than oil. Furthermore, while oil and gas have overall since 2000 been gradually declining in their share of contribution to GDP, in combination they remain the majority, if just, of GDP and certainly the most important sectors of Qatar's economy. Moreover, the North Dome is an enormous field—a "super field"—not far from the coast or major centers, in the seabed in relatively shallow water,[59] and Qatar's reserves are nearly all in this one location. If this changes, it will be only gradually and only if the international energy environment changes markedly as well.

Qatar is aware of some risks attached to its gas sector that, particularly in combination, constitute a long-term set of potential issues. One is the rise in resource nationalism, something that Doha has explicitly sought to avoid with its own energy sector but that is increasingly heard as an issue in the United States and elsewhere. What may give this greater realism is the rise of unconventional gas, especially improvements in the ability of producers to extract shale gas, which has already suggested to US policy-makers the prospect of returning to gas self-sufficiency.[60] This is likely to change the global politics of energy as states and regions—especially the United States and Europe—that had expected to become increasingly reliant on gas imports instead develop self-sufficiency, or at least greater production capacity of their own. If this were to suppress prices for a lengthy period of time, it could impact the Qatari economy; as one scholar noted, between new competition from suppliers to the Asian markets and the likely changes in production in the United States and possibly Europe, suppliers such as Qatar could be acutely impacted in terms of gas prices and ultimately their income from LNG exports.[61]

Likewise, unconventional gas will potentially reduce the power of natural gas suppliers, including Qatar, which along with Russia, Iran, Canada, Australia, Norway, and others had expected gradually increasing demand and prices for their gas in the coming decades, as energy demand overall increased, but especially demand for gas as a cheap and comparatively clean source of energy.[62] Neither this nor the changes in unconventional extraction are certain—unconventional gas has brought enormous environmental controversy with it, as well as reliance on high average prices for its financial viability—but such dynamics are very possible and would impact Qatar's political economy markedly if they occurred.

Petrochemicals and Energy Integration

Part of Qatar's push for diversification—and arguably an intelligent move toward greater insurance against a plummet in crude oil or gas prices—has been its emphasis on investing in and extracting value from vertical integration; that is, from petrochemicals and from industries associated with oil and gas such as refining, shipping, and insurance. Much of this is linked to gas first and foremost, as gas provides the feedstock for many petrochemicals, but refining, shipping, and insurance have all been a focus as well. As mentioned, this pursuit of broader energy-related diversification has been long-established policy, but its emphasis has increased under Hamad. It is also, as argued at the outset of the chapter, an integral feature of the late rentier state, of which Qatar is a perfect example, and of entrepreneurial state capitalism, of which Qatar exhibits a very pure case. Yet again, Qatar Petroleum has been at the forefront of integration and diversification, reinforcing the state capitalist aspect of its role, but other firms apart from QP have been important too. Several initiatives and firms are therefore worth mentioning as background on the sector and to reinforce the theoretical points about late rentierism and entrepreneurial state capitalism.

One of the largest and most impressive examples of a firm deriving from gas is the Qatar Fertilizer Company (QAFCO).[63] This is a joint venture between the Norwegian firm Yara International, which owns a 25 percent stake in QAFCO, and Industries Qatar, which owns the other 75 percent, and which is itself 70 percent owned by QP and 30 percent by Qatari shareholders. It dates back to 1969, formed by emiri decree to produce urea and ammonia. Its operations and capacity have expanded markedly over the intervening decades, through six main development phases: QAFCO-1 in 1973, QAFCO-2 in 1978, QAFCO-3 in 1997, QAFCO-4 in 2004, QAFCO-5 in 2011, and QAFCO-6, which was completed in late 2012. Each of these phases included a train for both urea and ammonia. Such has been the development of the firm that by 2009 it was the largest fertilizer producer in the Middle East[64] and by 2010 the largest onsite producer of both urea and ammonia in the world.[65] Much of its ammonia is sold to India, Jordan, and South Korea, and its urea to the United States, Thailand, Australia, and others.[66]

Another key gas-related firm is the Qatar Petrochemical Company (QAPCO), a joint venture owned 80 percent by Industries Qatar and 20 percent by Total Petrochemicals. It was established in 1974 and first began operations in 1981, using associated ethane gas from oil production. Although it struggled with problems of supply in its early years, and then again during the 1997–1998 Asian financial crisis, by 1999 and especially into the following decade it had established itself as a producer of several chemicals, including ethylene, low-density polyethylene, and sulfur.[67] In 2009 it was manufacturing 800,000 tons, 400,000 tons, and 46,000 tons of each of these respectively.[68] Like QAFCO, QAPCO has been clever in quickly developing (for most of its products) a sufficiently broad range of export destinations such that regional-specific economic or other problems are no longer fundamental threats to the business; by the late 1990s the two firms were fairly well established, building their reputations, and diversifying their customer bases.[69] This was a considerable improvement on the situation just prior to the Asian financial crisis, when QAFCO relied on Asian markets for 80–90 percent of its export sales and QAPCO for about 65 percent.[70]

There are yet further examples, especially as the petrochemical sector was further expanded in the early years of the 2000s. One firm is the Qatar Fuel Additives Company (QAFAC), 50 percent owned by Industries Qatar with the remainder of the equity held by several other firms. It was established in 1991, but experienced some problems in its early years in reaching agreement among the joint venture partners, and in particular it nearly collapsed in 1996 when a key partner, Total, withdrew from the venture.[71] Having overcome the initial problems, however, it subsequently established itself as a key producer and exporter of methyl tertiary butyl ether (MTBE)[72] and methanol, with production beginning in Mesaieed in 1999, and its exports of methanol in particular expanding significantly in the subsequent decade. Another firm is Qatar Chemical Company (Q-CHEM), established in 1999. It is owned 51 percent by QP and 49 percent by Chevron Philips Chemical Company, and began producing high-density polyethylene and various other chemicals from ethane and butane at a plant in Mesaieed in 2004. An extension of the firm, Q-CHEM II, was agreed in 2005 and completed five years later. Q-CHEM II greatly expanded high-density polyethylene production facilities at the Mesaieed plant and added further production of other petrochemicals.

Qatari petrochemical production, therefore, is broad, covering all the three main types of petrochemicals—olefins, aromatics, and synthesis gas[73]—as well as related activities. The petrochemical sector has received increasing focus in recent years, given the emphasis on diversification and on maximizing the economic advantages of Qatar's hydrocarbon reserves. The emphasis on the petrochemical sector is not diminishing, moreover, since it, along with other downstream activity, is a key focus of QP's 2010–2014 planning and is likely to be equally or more important beyond that time too. The global financial crisis had some impact, for example in encouraging the firm in some cases to consider breaking projects into separately financed and managed subprojects rather than, as previously, seeking joint venture partners and funding for a single enormous project in one package.[74]

Finally, and briefly, it is worth noting the considerable other downstream activity, and oil and gas infrastructure and support, in which Qatar Petroleum in particular is engaged. This includes various other joint ventures not already mentioned, such as in oil and condensate refining, gas production and delivery for domestic consumption, and other activities.[75] One example is Ras Laffan Industrial City. The downstream aspects of Qatargas, RasGas, parts of Dolphin, and the GTL projects are all based at or strongly linked with Ras Laffan, located about 80 kilometers north of Doha. It is worth mentioning this since Ras Laffan is, in itself, a major development project of QP and one of the largest LNG facilities in the world. Apart from the downstream projects mentioned, it is also host to the Laffan oil refinery; water and power plants; the Ras Laffan port, one of the largest LNG exporting ports in the world; and other facilities. Some of these are discussed in the following chapter, where the position and role of state-owned firms in Qatar's political economy are discussed.

Rents Reinvested: Qatar's Sovereign Wealth Fund

In recent years, Qatar has reinvested a proportion of its rents into a sovereign wealth fund (SWF), as other Gulf states have also done. Perhaps no issue in the political economy and international relations of the Gulf has been more controversial in the past few years than that of SWFs: state-held investment portfolio funds, often funded by foreign exchange earnings received by a state, that buy into domestic or international investments and that seek through these investments to earn a risk-based return on the investment, as capital growth or income (the latter often reinvested) or both.[76] They are somewhat akin to equity funds or pooled retirement funds in their aims and structure, only with the state being (usually) the sole owner and investor, although sometimes with a slightly different risk profile and investment strategy because of their very long-term approach. They are not new, even if much of the controversy surrounding them is very recent: the Saudi Arabian Monetary Agency's holdings of foreign currency and investments date to 1952; Kuwait's Investment Authority, which manages two large funds, was founded in 1953; and the Abu Dhabi Investment Authority (ADIA) was created in 1976 and Oman's State General Reserve Fund in 1980.[77] Despite this lengthy history, sovereign wealth funds became controversial around 2007 and 2008 when, fueled by the oil boom of 2003–2008, SWFs became worth much greater sums than in the past, more active and aggressive in their investments, and more prominent because of the fears surrounding the opacity of some funds and the lack at that time of any international regulatory framework for them.

Qatar's SWF, the Qatar Investment Authority (QIA), did not escape attention, although, valued at around US$115 billion at the end of 2012,[78] it lacks the size of some others, having been established only in 2005. Still, its rapid expansion in holdings, and the prospect of its becoming one of the world's largest funds in due course as Qatar accumulates enormous gas rents in the 2010s and beyond, have ensured that it nonetheless attracts some interest. While it does not publish much detail about its activities, it is structured around the QIA itself and wholly owned firms, and invests in a range of areas both within Qatar and abroad. Importantly, as a sign of its emphasis on diversification of the state's holdings away from oil and gas, it does not invest in the Qatari energy sector. It also owns and operates several firms through which it conducts much of its investment activity: Qatar Investment Company, which in turn owns Qatar Holdings; Delta Two, which holds some of QIA's assets offshore; and Qatari Diar, as mentioned earlier, which specializes in property development and management. It also established an agricultural investment firm, Hassad Food, to invest in food production assets and firms abroad. The QIA and its subsidiary firms hold a number of strategic-level stakes in international firms, including 27 percent of UK supermarket chain Sainsbury's (making the QIA the largest shareholder in that firm), 17 percent of Volkswagen, 15 percent of the London Stock Exchange, and smaller chunks of Barclay's Bank (6 percent) and the French media group Lagardere (6 percent).[79] It also owns the Harrods department store in London, which Qatar Holdings bought from Mohammed al-Fayed in May 2010 for £1.5 billion (US$2.23 billion).[80] The QIA also consolidated and expanded its investments during the global financial crisis of 2008–2009, through which Qatar traveled relatively unscathed,[81] in the process cleverly acting in a contrarian fashion in its investments and taking stakes in some key international firms. The purchase of Harrods was one example of this, but others include stakes in London property and businesses, international shares elsewhere, and increasing investments in sports and in other sectors in emerging markets.[82]

None of this is especially contentious. What has drawn attention to the QIA (and to most SWFs for that matter) are other issues of ownership, transparency, investment targeting, and independence. The first of these—what the fund buys—has been one of the key criticisms of state-owned firms and SWFs as their prominence has grown. The attempt by Dubai Ports World (DPW) to buy several key US ports from P&O Ports in 2006 is one of the more (in)famous cases of such an investment controversy involving a Gulf state-owned body, deriving from US ignorance about the UAE and its investment activities, and of course from a public fear in the United States about the security of its infrastructure after the 2001 terrorist attacks. Other investment controversies have been sparked by economic nationalism: as one example, there was uproar in 2008 when a firm held by Abu Dhabi's ADIA bought a majority stake in the Chrysler Center in New York City. The QIA has escaped this level of critical attention, and yet it still gained media attention after the May 8, 2010, announcement of its purchase of Harrods, less for the British icon being held in foreign hands and more simply because of the opacity surrounding the QIA compared to its seeming economic power. Later that year, there was debate surrounding the QIA's possible purchase of the Manchester United football team, with the QIA reportedly offering £1.5 billion (US$2.23 billion) to the Glazer family of the United States for the team in late 2010, and a higher sum still in 2011. The owning of the team was linked indirectly by many to the microstate "branding" issue, as it was seen as a fairly simple and effective way to build awareness and publicity for Qatar, in a positive way through an association with a sporting club that has a wide following in the United Kingdom and even more so globally.[83]

Not assisting the QIA's image was an article in 2010, published by the US-based Carnegie Endowment for International Peace, which ranked the

QIA as one of the world's least-transparent SWFs.[84] This echoed similar complaints made by political figures and others in target states that SWFs lack transparency and openness. The QIA has received criticism on three fronts in this respect. First, it does not publish many details about itself. Its website includes information on key figures, but not on its strategy or holdings, a practice that it claims is typical, noting rather obviously that "[t]he QIA does not publish its investment criteria but the criteria are based on the imperative of generating a strong financial return," and "as is usual with many global investment institutions which are not listed on the public markets, the QIA does not publish financial information."[85]

Another issue with the QIA is that of independent management. On the one hand, its website and official pronouncements suggest that it is run completely autonomously from the emir or others, and that investment decisions are made purely on their financial rationale. However, the composition of the QIA board makes this seem unlikely, as it is chaired by Crown Prince Tamim and includes as members the all-important Prime Minister Hamad bin Jassim bin Jabr and several other Al Thani family members. Granted, these figures possess financial or business skills and experience, but it is unthinkable that at least informally there is not some wider emiri or family influence on QIA board decisions. Moreover, the emir acknowledged his ability to influence the QIA during an interview with *The Financial Times* in October 2010: "If I have an idea, yes, I tell them I am thinking about this. But they are not obliged to do what I want."[86] It defies believability that, in such situations, the QIA would not interpret such a suggestion as a strong emiri wish.

A further issue is the question of the QIA's role and mission, and the specific issues of whether private money or breaches of confidentiality of the QIA's board deliberations take place. Remarkably, it remains unclear whether Al Thani family money is invested by the QIA or if the fund otherwise advises or assists the family, despite its being a national institution and supposedly autonomous from undue political or other influence. The QIA mission statement is telling, however; in Article 5 of the decree (Emiri Decision no. 22 of 2005) that established it, and detailed in its public pronouncements and online, its mission is stated as being to "develop, invest and manage the state reserve funds *and other property assigned to it*."[87] There is nothing in that wording that would preclude the QIA from acting for the family and its investments as well, which has occasionally been rumored, although counterclaims are made as well.[88]

Whatever the controversies, the QIA was created either primarily or partly as a deliberate strategy of the emir toward balancing out the fluctuations in energy rents and diversifying the economy.[89] While it may be naive to presume that this is purely a magnanimous action, it is not an unwise one in terms of economic management, given the financial stabilization benefits that can potentially be obtained from well-managed deposits and withdrawals from such funds.[90] It is also, of course, good politics, both at home and abroad. At home, apart from the stabilization benefits in ensuring macroeconomic steadiness, the fund sends a message that the regime is thinking of the longer-term and post-energy development of the country, and setting aside funds from a nonrenewable resource for future generations. It is in this way a sign of regime responsiveness to both actual and potential public opinion. It could also be construed as serving the regime's interests, since with a large enough fund and a small enough population, a well-managed set of state investments could sustain a rentier bargain into the very long term and certainly beyond the hydrocarbon era. Provided the population's standard of living were ensured, such a post-energy investment-based rentierism strategy would be plausible. Last, and somewhat separately, there is also an element of economic nationalism in such funds, as the QIA is seen as presenting a dynamic and competitive Qatari image to the rest of the world. This is crucial for an emir who is marking himself as reformist—transformationalist, indeed—and who has staked his legitimacy on, among other goals, an internationalization and globalization of Qatar's economy and greater linkage of it to the world economy.

Abroad, the benefits to the emir and the regime are greater still. There is some diversification benefit, not so much in terms of broadening the Qatari domestic economy, but more by diversifying the economic base of the regime, moving its revenue streams from an overwhelming reliance on oil and gas rents to one where increasing sums come from company profits and non-energy investments, and accrue from a wide range of foreign states and in a variety of currencies. This ought to expand the overall amount of revenue received over time, as rents are invested rather than spent and those investments bring returns. It is also useful in steadying the state's income and helping protect it against oil and gas rent fluctuations. At the international level, branding is also important. As argued in Chapter 6, the branding of Qatar as a liberal, reforming microstate, and the linkage of this to its trade and both inward and outward investments, are part of the regime's survival strategy and its strategy to flourish in the often-threatening and capricious security environment of the Gulf subregion. Finally, as with some other sovereign wealth funds in the Gulf, the QIA has begun branching into the area of food security, and Hassad Food was established under QIA ownership in 2008 for this reason. Qatar understandably is not food self-sufficient—it imports over 90 percent of its food—and would experience severe water strain were it not for desalination, which itself is the product of cheap energy. This prompted the government's national food security program,[91] to which initiatives such as the establishment of Hassad Food were related. Hassad was created to secure food supplies, especially of basic commodities, through investments in agricultural assets overseas; it invests less in land per se and more in agribusiness firms and technology that can assist with food production and reliability of supply, and in the process generate a profit.[92] Implicit in its mandate to supply food where it is most needed is that food products would be sent to Qatar, were that to be where they were deemed most required, and of course food security for Qatar is the first priority of the firm's strategic focus.[93] The national food security program aims for Qatar to be 60–70 percent self-sufficient by 2023, drawing both on domestic production and overseas production by firms such as Hassad.[94]

Given all of these dimensions to the QIA, its importance as a political economy actor is obvious. It exists ultimately for the political benefit of the political elite, and in particular for long-term regime survival and legitimacy, but this does not preclude its playing an advantageous role in society more widely as well. What it is *not* is an attempt to wield economic power overseas in the countries where it invests, a common claim made against SWFs but one that for the most part lacks any supporting evidence. It is overwhelmingly a domestic political actor because of its role in macroeconomic management, its appearance of regime concern for the future and for socioeconomic development, the potential benefits of the fund to national economic development and reform, and the fund's role in the diversification of state revenues into new and less variable streams. The QIA is a central actor in Qatar's entrepreneurial state capitalism, not only because it consists of rents reinvested for the long-term, even post-energy, future of the regime and the state, but also because it represents an attempt to develop a fund for state wealth that invests in emerging and explicitly non-energy areas, with an appetite for at least some risk. It reflects a new form of a well-established rentierism, being a new means of using rent income for regime maintenance and consolidation.

The Place of Energy

It is difficult to foresee any truly serious threats to the centrality of oil, and even more so of gas and gas-related industries, to Qatar's economy over the coming couple of decades. Even a major transformation of one of these sectors, while it may constitute an abrupt or unpleasant change for the firms or ventures most affected, would in all likelihood not translate into profound wider impacts on the political economy. It is only the most dramatic and global of crises or upheavals that would make certain of that. Otherwise, there are both gradual and unpredictable changes or events that might impact Qatar, including many related to energy, such as the risk of military conflict involving Iran, the emergence of alternative and renewable energies, and of course climate change both directly and indirectly. Qatar is aware of these problems, but they have had virtually no impact, probably not surprisingly, on its highest-level strategies for its energy sector, although there have been some modest attempts to bring environmental standards and renewable energy technologies to the economy.[95] If anything, an argument could be made that the Qatar Investment Authority represents an enduring importance for rents to the regime, even looking out to beyond the hydrocarbon age.

The mechanisms for rent accrual by the state are notable here, especially as those of oil, gas, and other aspects of the hydrocarbon sector all vary. It is in oil that Qatar is most traditionally rentier, with a powerful state-owned firm that controls both the oil assets still sitting underground or under the seabed, and the exploitation of oil and its sale. In contrast, gas is a much more internationalized affair. This is the case not just with Qatar, as many gas exporters need international partners to make expensive projects worth the risk of development and to ensure a long-term market for the gas that is eventually extracted. In Qatar's case, there has been a strong international relations element, with key gas firms deliberately brought into projects as a way for Doha to build links with regional and global powers as well, as mentioned here and discussed again in Chapter 7. As a final point on rent accruals, Qatar's state capitalism and in particular its attempts at diversifying and vertically integrating its hydrocarbon sector are important to note. In effect, the development of the petrochemical sector and the nature of the QIA point to a neo-rentier dynamic, in which rents are recirculated. They are reinvested to produce profits that then have a rentier-like impact in flowing to the state and in their effect when shared with society through state expenditure. There are many modalities to rentierism.

It could also be argued that, in many ways, Qatar has been very clever in its energy policies to date. It began development of the North Dome quite early—as early as international investor and buyer interest allowed. It developed a large and world-class downstream oil and gas sector, and was among the first of the Gulf states to recognize the need for such diversification and not simply to rely on rents from crude oil or natural gas sales. It also, as later chapters illustrate, has been very astute at leveraging energy wealth to develop other parts of the economy, including both those that feed into or support oil and gas and those that are much more separate.

However, it has not truly diversified its economy—that argument cannot be sustained when oil and gas exports alone remain at around half of GDP and over half of state revenue. Regardless, the fact that state revenue is now derived less from rents than previously, and increasingly from other sources such as state-owned firms' profits and investment returns, demonstrates that, despite a continued reliance on oil and gas, the state has developed revenue streams beyond very immediate and highly unpredictable hydrocarbon rents. This is a trend in the Gulf Cooperation Council that has already been noted in the case of other states,[96] and validates the argument that oil booms differ and that the impacts of a state's oil wealth on economies can vary. In other words—as suggested by the evolution of late rentierism as a new state-society dynamic—the state-society relationship is changing, but not the underlying rentier bargain that sits at its foundation.

Notes

1. QNB Capital, *Qatar Economic Review 2010,* p. 10; "The New Gas Giant," *Middle East Economic Digest,* May 18, 2007.

2. *BP Statistical Review of World Energy 2011,* p. 22, http://www.bp.com/assets/bp_internet/globalbp/globalbp_uk_english/reports_and_publications/statistical_energy_review_2011/STAGING/local_assets/pdf/statistical_review_of_world_energy_full_report_2011.pdf.

3. For more on these ideas, see Gray, "A Theory of 'Late Rentierism' in the Arab States of the Gulf"; especially on issues of definition and argument in the rentier-state theory literature, see pp. 2–18.

4. International Monetary Fund, "Qatar: 2010 Article IV Consultation," Country Report no. 11/64, p. 26 (tab. 2a); and International Monetary Fund, "Qatar: Statistical Appendix," Country Report no. 10/62, p. 10 (tab. 13).

5. Gray, "A Theory of 'Late Rentierism' in the Arab States of the Gulf."

6. As noted in the introduction, some examples of these works include Mahdavy, "The Patterns and Problems of Economic Development in Rentier States"; Beblawi, "The Rentier State in the Arab World"; and Luciani, "Allocation vs. Production States."

7. "Qatar Petroleum," *Middle East Economic Digest,* June 13, 2009. In some interviews, interlocutors claimed to me that Qatar Petroleum still has considerable redundant labor, something difficult to ascertain but at any rate not a significant-enough problem to be apparent from the firm's financials.

8. QNB Capital, *Qatar Economic Review 2010,* p. 15.

9. The point about Dukhan's life expectancy at current production levels is made in QNB Capital, *Qatar Economic Review 2010,* p. 15. The calculation at maximum production levels is mine.

10. "Qatar Petroleum Corporate Profile," 2010, http://www.qp.com.qa/Files/QP%20Profile/PROFILE%202010%20ENGLISH.pdf. Gravity is an inverse mea-

sure of the lightness of oil: gravity of over 10 means that the oil floats, and oil is "light crude" at 31.1 degrees or higher. The gravity for oil that attracts the best price is in the range of 40 to 45 degrees. A sulfur content of 1.2 percent is not high, but is not low enough to qualify as "sweet" crude oil (which indicates a sulfur content of ≤ 0.5 percent).

11. "Qatar Petroleum Corporate Profile."

12. Ibid.

13. Ibid.

14. "Qatar Enters Global Arena," *Middle East Economic Digest,* June 1, 2007.

15. QNB Capital, *Qatar Economic Review 2010,* p. 15.

16. What follows is from QNB Capital, *Qatar Economic Review 2010,* p. 15; "Al Shaheen Oil Field, Qatar," http://www.offshore-technology.com/projects/alshaheen; "*MEED* Special Report on Oil & Gas: Qatar," *Middle East Economic Digest,* January 13, 1997; and "Special Report on Oil & Gas: Qatar," *Middle East Economic Digest,* July 20, 2001.

17. Neil Ford, "Doha Looks Beyond North Field," *The Middle East,* February 2010, p. 46.

18. Energy Information Administration, "Country Analysis Brief: Qatar," p. 3.

19. "Qatar Special Report," *Middle East Economic Digest,* May 1, 1998.

20. Ibid.

21. "Qatar Special Report: Part 1," *Middle East Economic Digest,* August 28, 1998.

22. Most sources say over 200 years, presumably because they are including in their calculations other gas such as the reserves of associated gas fields.

23. "Cover Story: Qatar LNG Arrives," *Middle East Economic Digest,* November 8, 1999.

24. Gina Coleman, "Qatar Survey," *The Middle East,* August 1998, p. 24.

25. Tom Owen, "Qatar Gas: Returns Vindicate Energy Policy," *The Middle East,* July–August 2001, p. 32.

26. The details that follow, unless otherwise cited, are from QNB Capital, *Qatar Economic Review 2005,* p. 15; QNB Capital, *Qatar Economic Review 2010,* pp. 19–20; and company fact sheets published online at http://www.qatargas.com/Media.aspx?id=96.

27. QNB Capital, *Qatar Economic Review 2010,* p. 19; and QNB Capital, *Qatar Economic Review 2005,* p. 15. The downstream project was a massive undertaking, involving some US$2 billion of investment at the time, plus about 65 million person-hours, at times with up to 10,000 personnel on site, to complete the project: "*MEED* Special Report on Qatar: Qatargas—Breaking Into the Global Gas Market," *Middle East Economic Digest,* August 26, 1996.

28. These details on Qatargas 2, 3, and 4 are from QNB Capital, *Qatar Economic Review 2010,* p. 20.

29. "Qatar: A Beacon of Stability in Troubled Times," *The Middle East,* June 2010, p. 37.

30. Ibid.

31. QNB Capital, *Qatar Economic Review 2010,* p. 19.

32. Ibid.

33. The details that follow, unless otherwise cited, are from QNB Capital, *Qatar Economic Review 2005,* p. 15; QNB Capital, *Qatar Economic Review 2010,* pp. 19–20; and company information published online at http://www.rasgas.com/l_3.cfm?L3_id=11&L2_id=5.

34. Coleman, "Qatar Survey," p. 24.

35. QNB Capital, *Qatar Economic Review 2010,* p. 20.

36. QNB Capital, *Qatar Economic Review 2005,* p. 16 (tab. 3.8); and QNB Capital, *Qatar Economic Review 2010,* p. 21 (tab. 3.9).

37. QNB Capital, *Qatar Economic Review 2007,* p. 19 (tabs. 3.6, 3.7).

38. Again the details that follow, unless otherwise cited, are from QNB Capital, *Qatar Economic Review 2005,* pp. 17–18; QNB Capital, *Qatar Economic Review 2010,* pp. 21–22; and company information published online at http://www.rasgas.com/l_3.cfm?L3_id=11&L2_id=5.

39. Specifically, the Japanese firm Chiyoda Corporation, the Italian firm Snamprogetti, and the Qatari Almana Group.

40. "Qatar: A Beacon of Stability in Troubled Times," p. 37.

41. Dargin, "The Dolphin Project," p. 1.

42. Ibid., pp. 28–32; Gina Coleman, "Qatar Encourages Foreign Investment and Joint Ventures," *The Middle East,* January 2000, pp. 32–34; and Tom Owen, "Qatar's Dolphin Project Takes Off," *The Middle East,* May 2001, pp. 22–23.

43. QNB Capital, *Qatar Economic Review 2010,* p. 23.

44. Dargin, "The Dolphin Project," pp. 2–3, 50.

45. Author interview, Doha, January 2011. The point is also made in Ulrichsen, *Insecure Gulf: The End of Certainty and the Transition to the Post-Oil Era,* p. 102.

46. QNB Capital, *Qatar Economic Review 2010,* p. 24.

47. GTL takes natural gas as feedstock and produces and reforms the hydrocarbon chains into high-grade products such as paraffin, naphtha, and lubricants. Pearl and Oryx GTL both mostly manufacture naphtha for high-grade and very clean diesel fuel, but produce other products in smaller amounts.

48. Dargin, "The Dolphin Project," p. 2.

49. Quoted in "Special Report: Qatar—Interview: Abdullah bin Hamad al-Attiya," *Middle East Economic Digest,* October 17, 2003.

50. Ibid.

51. This point has been made by others, although using other specific examples. See, for example, Dargin, "Qatar's Natural Gas."

52. Not only do they share the North Dome/South Pars field, and cooperate as members of the Organization of Petroleum Exporting Countries (OPEC) and other multilateral bodies, but the two have multiple other bilateral agreements and linkages.

53. "Turning Up the Gas," *The Economist,* July 18, 2009.

54. "Boom Puts Contractors Under Pressure," *Middle East Economic Digest,* November 6, 2009.

55. Author interview, Doha, January 2011.

56. "Boom Puts Contractors Under Pressure."

57. "Qatar's Peaking Energy Market," *Middle East Economic Digest,* February 12, 2010.

58. "Moving Beyond the North Field," *Middle East Economic Digest,* January 9, 2009.

59. The main producing parts of the North Dome are at about 3,000 meters below the seabed—not unusually deep for a gas field—with the ocean depth at a quite shallow average of about 60–65 meters.

60. "An Unconventional Glut," *The Economist,* March 13, 2010.

61. Jean-François Seznec, quoted in Kern et al., "Symposium: Gulf Oil and Gas," p. 12. The point is also made in "Qatar's Peaking Energy Market."

62. "An Unconventional Glut."

63. QNB Capital, *Qatar Economic Review 2010,* p. 25.

64. Ibid.

65. According to the QAFCO website; see the "About QAFCO" page at http://www.qafco.com/about-us.html.

66. QNB Capital, *Qatar Economic Review 2010,* p. 25.

67. Coleman, "Qatar Survey," p. 24.

68. QNB Capital, *Qatar Economic Review 2010,* p. 26.

69. Coleman, "Qatar Survey," pp. 24–25.

70. "Qatar Special Report," *Middle East Economic Digest,* August 28, 1998.

71. "*MEED* Special Report on Qatar: Projects—Small Place That Likes to Think Big," *Middle East Economic Digest,* August 26, 1996.

72. MTBE is a chemical compound used to raise the octane level of fuels and as a solvent.

73. Olefins are synthetic fibers made out of polymers. They are used in a wide range of products, including clothing, furniture, carpets, and ropes. Aromatics—the best-known is perhaps benzene—are used in fuels and as solvents, among other things. Synthesis gas is a mixture of carbon monoxide and hydrogen, used in the process of making synthetic natural gas (from where its name is derived) or for making ammonia (used as a fertilizer among other things) or methanol (used for fuel or as a solvent or antifreeze).

74. "Boom Puts Contractors Under Pressure."

75. For a list beyond the examples here, see QNB Capital, *Qatar Economic Review 2010,* pp. 14–29.

76. This definition is my own, but see also the similar definitions in Drezner, "Sovereign Wealth Funds and the (In)Security of Global Finance," pp. 116–117; and Xu, "The Political Economy of Sovereign Wealth Funds," pp. 1–5.

77. Information on the various funds from around the world, including their value and establishment date, is available online from the Sovereign Wealth Fund Institute website, http://www.swfinstitute.org.

78. Sovereign Wealth Fund Institute website, http://www.swfinstitute.org/fund-rankings.

79. These figures are from the "Qatar Investment Authority" page of the Sovereign Wealth Fund Institute website, at http://www.swfinstitute.org/swfs/qatar-investment-authority and the "Qatar Investment Authority" page of the Sovereign Wealth Fund News website, at http://www.sovereignwealthfundsnews.com

/qatarinvestmentauthority.php. More specific information on the QIA is scarce, and the QIA does not publish more sensitive information such as details on its investment strategy.

80. "Doha's Diversification of Revenue," *Middle East Economic Digest,* June 4, 2010.

81. On Qatar and the global financial crisis, see, for example, "Qatar: A Beacon of Stability in Troubled Times," *The Middle East,* June 2010, pp. 35–39.

82. "Qatar, the Tiny Gulf State That Bought the World," *The Independent* (London), May 11, 2010; "Fuelling a Knowledge Economy," *Middle East Economic Digest,* June 4, 2010; and "Qatar's Global Spree Shows No Signs of Slowing," *The Independent* (London), October 31, 2010.

83. Author interview, Doha, January 2011.

84. "Time to Take Call on Transparency," *Middle East Economic Digest,* June 4, 2010. The Carnegie Endowment for International Peace article referred to by the *Middle East Economic Digest* was Behrendt, "Sovereign Wealth Funds."

85. See the "FAQs" page of the QIA website, at http://www.qia.qa/faq.html.

86. "Interview Transcript: Qatar's Sheikh Hamad," October 24, 2010, http://www.ft.com/cms/s/0/9163abca-df97-11df-bed9-00144feabdc0.html#axzz1UWReOddR.

87. Emphasis added. See the "Governance" part of the "About Us" page of the QIA website, at http://www.qia.qa/about.html#Governance.

88. Author interviews, Doha, October 2011. The counterclaims of independence, of course, are made by the QIA, in its marketing material and on its website.

89. Author interviews, Doha, October 2011.

90. This point is made in multiple sources on sovereign wealth funds, but see, for example, Askari et al., "An Economic Manifesto for the Oil Exporting Countries of the Persian Gulf"; but on the economic and stabilization benefits, see especially pp. 365–368.

91. Details of the program are available at http://www.qnfsp.gov.qa/home.

92. On Hassad, see the website of Qatar's national food security program, at http://www.qnfsp.gov.qa/about-us/qnfsp-task-force/hassad-food; and the website of Hassad Food, at http://www.hassad.com.

93. As stated on the "Strategic Focus" page of the "About Us" section of the Hassad Food website, at http://www.hassad.com/Aboutus/strategicfocus/tabid/67/Default.aspx.

94. "Qatar to Secure 60% to 70% of Its Food by 2023," *Qatar News Agency,* February 19, 2011, http://www.qnaol.net/QNAEn/Local_News/Economics/Pages/QatarToSecure60To70ofItsFoodby2023.aspx.

95. Ulrichsen, *Insecure Gulf,* p. 136.

96. For example, in an excellent piece, Steffen Hertog has examined changes in rentier impacts in Saudi Arabia by comparing the oil booms of the 1970s and 1980s with the oil boom of 2003–2008, and argues that rentier states are not static and instead evolve as rents are recycled and as the state accumulates both rent wealth and other forms of wealth purchased with rents. See Hertog, "The Evolution of Rent Recycling During Two Booms in the Gulf Arab States: Business Dynamism and Societal Stagnation."

5

Energy-Driven Economic Diversification

Qatar not only grew its economy and gross domestic product after the year 2000 as new gas production came online, but also made significant strides in economic diversification and in developing some of the non-energy sectors of the economy, often backed by government initiatives and funding. Such was the extent of the changes in its economy that by 2009—while many states in the Atlantic were in recession and many in other parts of the world were also struggling against the global financial crisis—Qatar was being lauded as an economic success story.[1] That year, at the height of the financial crisis, Qatar was the second-highest recipient of inward foreign direct investment (FDI) in the Arab world after Saudi Arabia, with over US$8.7 billion invested, a sum that extraordinarily, in light of the international economic environment at the time, represented a 112 percent increase over 2008.[2] By 2009 it had the lowest sovereign risk rating of any of the Gulf Cooperation Council (GCC) states (long-term ratings of AA from Standard and Poor's and Aa2 from Moody's).[3] In 2010, the World Economic Forum's *Arab World Competitiveness Review* placed Qatar at the top of its rankings for the Arab world and at the top of its "efficiency-driven economies" ranking.[4] Qatar's rankings in the World Economic Forum's *Global Competitiveness Report* are similarly strong: in the 2010–2011 report Qatar ranked seventeenth, the highest in the Arab world and ahead of economies such as Austria, Belgium, and Israel.[5] Further, it had significantly improved its ranking in that period.[6] The 2010–2011 report's assessment of Qatar was similar to that of many such reports on its economy and business environment: "Its strong competitiveness rests on solid foundations made up of a high-quality institutional framework, ranked 10th overall, a stable macroeconomic environment (8th), and an efficient goods market (12th). Low levels of corruption and undue influence on government decisions, high government efficiency, and excellent security are the cornerstones of the country's solid institutional framework."[7]

But what are the sources of this reform, and of the economic diversification that has been its goal? Is it as substantial as these reports suggest? In fact, while the Qatari development strategy has been impressive in some ways, in others it has been less successful, and aspects of the economy remain weak. For example, at the same time that Qatar was earning these competitiveness rankings, the World Economic Forum was also noting that business confidence remained much less impressive (Qatar ranked sixty-second on that), and there were problems in particular with ingraining innovation in the economy. The economy's vulnerability to energy price shocks remains an issue as well, and is a barrier not only to generating employment but also to improving investor confidence beyond current levels. A further problem is the limited involvement of Qatari citizens in the private sector, supposedly the economy's long-term, post-hydrocarbon source of growth and development. Remarkably, according to a 2006 World Bank report, out of a Qatari (citizen) labor force of 50,000 people, only 2,200 workers were employed by the private sector.[8] This excluded the self-employed and a sizable number of public sector employees with private sector interests or investments, of course, but regardless, the fact that only 4.4 percent of Qatari citizens who were participating in the labor market were employed by the private sector was extraordinary and alarming. Moreover, this 4.4 percent figure was a marked decline from the figure of 10 percent in 1986.[9] It suggests that the challenges faced in developing the economy, and the long-term prospects for it, are probably more complex than simple macroeconomic indicators, reform policies, or performance on many competitiveness measures might indicate.

This chapter considers some of the aspects of economic development and diversification beyond and outside of those already considered in the energy sector, and brings into the discussion some case studies of specific sectors such as higher education, aviation, tourism, and banking and finance. Three things are ultimately addressed and argued. First, while there has been impressive progress in some aspects of economic reform and diversification, and while the transformation and globalization of the country and its economy since the mid-1990s have been handled in a measured, considered fashion, there are still problems remaining in the structure of the economy and in progress toward making it truly global, diverse, competitive, and innovative. Second, even though some sectors seem to be very separate from oil and gas, in fact these sectors often have discreet links to energy, and as a result the economy still remains energy driven. Some of these sectors are derived from the oil, gas, and petrochemical industries or rely on them for a critical mass of core business. In other cases these sectors and key businesses in them have been supported or underwritten by the state, meaning that in effect they are at least partly underwritten by rents. Diversification, after all, has been state driven, and the state's concerns not only are about development per se but also include alleviating employment pressures, bringing technology and innovation to the economy, and avoiding problems such as economic bimodalism and price shocks. Third, this chapter reiterates an overall theme of the book: even though there has been some true reform and diversification of the economy, little *economic power* has shifted from the state to the private sector. The political economy ultimately is still late rentier because of the centrality of energy rents and their allocation by the state; it is still entrepreneurially state capitalist given the state's role as owner or regulator in the various sectors about to be studied; and the political economy, despite the reforms since the mid-1990s, remains driven by a small group of elites who seek to control the nature and pace of development for national benefit, certainly, but very much for their own advantage as well. Arguably, attaining this advantage is ultimately, whether directly or not, their highest purpose.

The chapter begins by briefly outlining the *Qatar National Vision 2030*—the central development-policy document of the state, in other words what the state *says* it is aiming to do—and then considers how much and what types of broad economic liberalization have occurred and what other reforms have been undertaken as well, such as those amending business regulation or administrative procedure. It then looks at the case studies mentioned, placing them in the contexts of economic reform and diversification.

The *Qatar National Vision 2030* and Its Objectives

The *Qatar National Vision 2030* (QNV) is the Qatari government's central strategic document on socioeconomic development and other development-related national initiatives. It is, therefore, the first point of reference in terms of what the government says its development goals are and serves as a foundation for many of the policies and reforms that are undertaken. The QNV was developed over the period from 2003 to 2008, deriving partly out of the impetus for reform created by the development and endorsement of the permanent constitution in the first few years of the 2000s—hence the specific statements that it "embodies the principles of the Permanent Constitution" and "protects public and personal freedoms."[10] In practice it stems even more from the need for greater cohesion and consistency in economic policies and actions by public sector institutions, which became apparent during the dramatic economic boom of the 2000s and given the emir's ambitious reform agenda.

The QNV is based around four development pillars: human, social, economic, and environmental.[11] All of these have bearings on the political economy, and all feed into the focus here on economic development and diversification. The first, human development, includes an emphasis on education, health, and in effect the policy of "Qatarization"—that is, of getting a greater number of Qatari nationals into the work force to take over roles currently performed by expatriate workers. In mentioning a global economy that is increasingly "knowledge-based,"[12] the implication is that Qatar is seeking to consolidate its status as a late-late developer—that is, as a state that rapidly gains the capacity for a sophisticated, competitive services sector, largely bypassing the industrialization and manufacturing stages typical of the development paths of most states. The second pillar, social development, in focusing on goals such as social care, the preservation of culture and tradition, and international relations, is essentially seeking a moderately paced, measured development, something that distinguishes Qatar strategically from Dubai and the so-called Dubai model.[13] The third pillar, economic development, has driven the sectors that are the focus here. It is core to the strategy of economic diversification, but also the strategy of deriving as much value as possible from the hydrocarbon sector (coincidentally, another way in which Qatar's development approach has varied from Dubai's). It also emphasizes the importance of the economy being competitive, an area where particular focus is needed, as will be discussed shortly. Finally, environment development is prominent in the QNV, partly because of the limited water resources in Qatar, but also because of the longer-term impacts and limitations of carbon-based energy use.

The QNV includes some interesting elements that distinguish it from the approaches of Qatar's neighbors to development and from Dubai's in particular. One is the importance of deliberately and meticulously preserving the Qatari identity and culture. For most Gulf states this is a dilemma, introduced in part because of globalization and rapid social change, but also because of the risk to identity that comes from the enormous expatriate populations in these states. In Qatar's case, around 85 percent of residents are expatriates, many of them Muslim but, even so, all of them bringing different cultural and social perspectives and values into the host society. There is also some interaction between Qataris and expatriates, and the two groups work together and socially interact more than in some other Gulf states, though still not extensively. Thus far Qatar has been very careful to preserve its culture and construct as harmonious a cohabitation as possible between Qatari and global identities and values, something that has long been a concern in the country but that has come into sharper relief as the changes under Hamad have occurred. The identities that are being reasserted are constructed, of course, but the point remains that the QNV is a tool for the state to articulate and communicate these identities. Second, the QNV is very clear about the exactitude and appropriateness of Qatar's economic development and diversification. It is not promoting an unbridled economic growth, endorsing instead "reasonable and sustained" growth rates, financial and economic "stability," and "responsible" and "optimum" exploitation of energy resources.[14] To belabor a point, this is a clear, and obviously deliberate, differentiation of Qatar's development approach from that of Dubai. At the same time, the QNV is not promoting a "Qatar model" either, beyond laying a policy foundation for Qatar's own development. The idea of a "model" implies a very static formula of development policies, which the QNV is not.

Beyond the literal aspects of the QNV, and what it says are the goals of development, what aims and dynamics underlie it? In a way, it is a politically honest document because the state and regime are not making any claims that are contradictory to the underlying rentier emphasis and mechanisms of the political economy. The QNV accepts that the energy sector and its rents will dominate the economy and contribute a large amount of state revenue for the foreseeable future. It also accepts that diversification will need to be driven in part by rents, and also by what is possible in light of the importance of them to the economy. It does not promote the type of diversification whereby the state simply uses rents to cross-subsidize other sectors of the economy, as was very ineffectively attempted by Saudi Arabia, among others, in the 1970s and 1980s. Nonetheless, an element of that exists in the cheap energy, low rental prices for land, and very low taxation levels that the state has created for indigenous and international business.

Lurking beneath the QNV is an acknowledgment of some of the political motivations for it. The political implications for the state and its leadership are implied in the QNV's warning about the need to pace development carefully: "Once inflation becomes ingrained, or hurried development projects are implemented, or public services can no longer cope with bourgeoning demands, there will be risks to sustaining prosperity and to social cohesion. Skillful and farsighted economic management and effective and agile institutions will be needed to attenuate these risks."[15] In effect, this is an acknowledgment that any real or perceived failure of the government in the economic realm will have social, and by implication political, consequences. Indeed, a characteristic of late rentier states is the determination to spend (at least some) rental income widely and responsively to public preferences, and to be seen to be doing so by the population. This is a key reason for oil money being more easily accounted for and more responsibly spent in the 2003–2008 oil boom than in earlier such booms, including a larger proportion of it being spent on public infrastructural and socioeconomic development rather than being lost in royal family finances, spent on defense, or wasted.[16]

Second, the political risks of a societal backlash against globalization and rapid social change are acknowledged in the QNV in an economic sense when it says that "future economic success will increasingly depend on the ability of the Qatari people to deal with a new international order that is knowledge-based and extremely competitive."[17] To meet this, it prescribes high-quality public services, especially healthcare, and above all an emphasis on education. Tellingly in terms of the cultural awareness lying beneath Qatari development strategies, mention of education includes stress on a system that promotes "Qatari moral and ethical values, traditions and cultural heritage" and a "strong sense of belonging and citizenship."[18]

Finally, the focus of the QNV on economic diversification is perhaps its most important element. Certainly the success of many aspects of its four pillars depends on successful diversification. Such success would create employment, including meaningful and productive jobs, and would create a favorable impression of the state among those in society who benefit from such policies—ideally the overwhelming majority, of course. This would enhance regime and state legitimacy and support, and reduce the risk of popular political dissatisfaction. The logic behind the implementation of the policy is to use hydrocarbon resources to begin a diversification process, which would then become self-sustaining once there a critical mass of activity in the non-energy sector is achieved:

> Converting these natural assets into financial wealth provides a means to invest in world-class infrastructure; build efficient delivery mechanisms for public services; create a highly skilled and productive labour force; and support the development of entrepreneurship and innovation capabilities. If attained, these achievements would in turn provide a broader platform for the diversification of Qatar's economy and its positioning as a regional hub for knowledge and for high value industrial and service activities.[19]

What has been done to date, and just how successful this is likely to be, are at the core of this discussion.

Economic Liberalization and Business Reform

One of the most contentious policy issues in the Middle East over the past generation has been that of economic liberalization—economic reforms that increase the role of the market and the power of market forces in determining the generation and allocation of resources, and that at least in theory also involve a retreat of the state from the economy vis-à-vis the private sector. However, both the simplistic nature of common definitions such as this, and the often-antagonistic and ideological nature of the debate about the desirability or otherwise of it, mean that economic liberalization has dominated debate about reform.[20] While Qatar has had a certain amount of economic liberalization, it has not shifted dramatically toward economic neoliberalism as did Egypt during the early and mid-2000s, nor has it sluggishly adopted haphazard, politically despoiled, and often only partial reforms as have Syria, Iran, and others. Reform is wider than neoliberal economic marketization (most of which is macroeconomic), and Qatar—although it has indeed undertaken certain such market reforms and baulked at others—has also embarked on other reforms that enhance the business context or improve business processes, as well as making other socioeconomic policy changes with implications for the business environment and the role of the market.

There are specific reasons for the nature and extent of the reforms that Qatar has made since the mid-1990s, and for the mixture of economic liberalization, business process reforms, and other socioeconomic policy changes. Ultimately, the pattern of reform reflects the political imperative of the regime, the desire to maintain both the overarching rentier bargain between state and society—which would almost certainly be upset by a genuine neoliberal transformation—and the new state capitalist character of the state. The certainty of very long-term rental income—some two centuries' worth in the case of natural gas, if the assessments of the North Dome are correct—means that there is little financial pressure for dramatic economic liberalization to develop and expand a private sector that will supply taxation revenue and provide large measures of employment. A large proportion of the state's revenue needs for multiple generations is ensured from rents, meaning that society too is very sure of a certain level of income or public services via the state. There is little desire on the part of the state, or for that matter among most of society, to upset this arrangement.

Yet some reforms have been necessary. At one level, reform suits the firms that are at the core of the entrepreneurial state capitalist system. An easing of restrictions or regulations on state-owned firms improves their profitability and prospects of expansion. Greater room to operate in a market environment gives them potential new customers, and increasingly the possibility to operate and invest abroad, as some leading state-owned firms such as Qatar Petroleum (QP) have begun to do. At a more sophisticated level, some economic liberalization and other reform is necessary for Emir Hamad and others to be able to argue convincingly that they are globalizing and innovating the political economy. Just as senior Qatari figures, the state, and bodies such as the Qatar Investment Authority (QIA) seek to invest abroad, they are actively seeking foreign investment into Qatar, not only for the funds it brings—which, bluntly, Qatar's balance of payments has not needed since the late 1990s—but also for technology, innovation, and other intangible benefits; as one official from the Ministry of Economy and Commerce remarked: "We don't need FDI for the money, although capital is always welcome. We want the transfer of systematic know-how. Local companies can bring in individuals, but [international] companies bring institutional knowledge, and that is the biggest plus."[21]

Normally in non rentier states, the cost of economic liberalization is a change in the business-government relationship and, more precisely, the surrender of some power by the state to the private sector in exchange for the economic and political benefits bestowed by the reforms. However, Qatar is different, as are many rentiers with small populations or weak commercial classes. The Al Thani family, the commercial institutions of the state, and the key commercial families linked to the royal family are so strong that the business-government relationship is far less about a zero-sum power relationship between the two, but instead and in typical rentier fashion, more one of allocative opportunities from one (the state) to the other (business). In this way the state has much greater room to decide how much reform it will implement, and indeed the power to undertake much less of it and to cherry-pick what it will do, than in a non-rentier, extractive economy.

That noted, Qatar has undertaken some reforms of both the more economywide economic liberalization variety and, to a greater extent, more administrative but still important commercial and legal reforms. The former have not transformed Qatar into a neoliberal economy—nor sought to—but rather have specific aims behind them. The bulk of the reforms took place in the middle to late 2000s, as the economy was booming and as the emir's goals, later mostly enshrined in the QNV, were implemented. Notable in the 1990s, however, as already mentioned, were Hamad's rapid liberalization of the media and creation of the stock market, and later an expansion of Qatar Airways and some reforms in the tourism and hospitality sector.[22] In 1997 the laws on foreign investment were amended slightly as well, by emiri decree, to allow for the formation of a specific type of firm that could have foreign nationals as an equity partner.[23] This set of reforms sent a message of continuity and stability, and yet also the prospect of longer-term reform, to both the indigenous and foreign business community in Qatar, and was partly the emir signaling a more liberal social policy. In other respects, however, the economy remained centered on oil and gas, and the environment in which wider agriculture, industry, and service sectors operated did not profoundly change in Hamad's first few years in power, even if the state began paying them closer attention and talking increasingly of diversification. The late 1990s was a period of low oil prices, and also one in which the gas sector was still consuming enormous investment resources but was yet to return the dividends of a decade later. For this reason, the first few state budgets under Hamad were quite cautious and austere, and his first to balance, after a decade of deficits, was not until 1999–2000.[24]

Since then there have been many reforms, numerous of which proved significant. An early step, in the early 2000s, came when the laws governing foreign ownership in the economy were significantly liberalized. From 1963 to 2000, non-Qataris could not own real estate, apart from those already holding title over a piece of land or building, except with special approval from the emir.[25] The first reform was in 2000, when Law no. 13 established the legal framework for foreign investment, but the major change came in 2004, when amendments to the 2000 law allowed for new investment terms. For the first time, foreigners were permitted to invest in banking and insurance and were allowed to own up to 25 percent of the listed shares of a firm listed on the Doha Securities Market, as it was then called. Furthermore, Law no. 17 of 2004[26] allowed foreigners to acquire freehold property in a few of the big real estate projects (West Bay Lagoon, The Pearl-Qatar, and Barwa al-Khour) and to possess long-term leases over property in defined other areas of the country that could be renewed or sold forward to other non-Qataris. Related to this was a clarification of the residency rights of foreign nationals who owned property, under Law no. 2 of 2006, which allowed for residency permits to be given to non-Qataris by the minister of the interior in cases where the person had investments under the 2000 and 2004 investment laws and their amendments.

This was quite a remarkable reform. It was a rare instance in the Gulf that foreigners could be given residency without a sponsor and on the basis of their economic interest in the country alone, and was among the most liberal property laws applying to non-GCC nationals in the Gulf. It is important to recall, however, that these reforms were predominantly in the real estate sector, or affected foreigners owning particular pieces of the capital of a joint venture project. In terms of the ownership of a company established in Qatar by foreigners, generally the 49-to-51 rule applied, with the foreign individual or firm limited to 49 percent ownership of the capital of the firm. The investment law did reform this slightly, however: under Article 2(2) a foreigner could own up to 100 percent of the capital if the investment was in certain sectors either where the state was trying to attract investment and technology—agriculture, health, education, tourism, and some industry and mining areas—or where the investment was specifically made under one of Qatar's development plans.[27]

Changes to the property law were predominantly guided by the need to attract foreign investment and ensure that investor confidence in their legal position was strong. Other legal amendments around the same time were important too, in targeting investment or in enhancing business confidence more widely. In 2004, the 1971 civil code was partly amended by a new law, the Civil Law no. 22. As the civil code is a fundamental law of the country, this amendment was a more significant change to the legal system than many assumed, but it also was important specifically for some of its commercial impacts. The most important of these was a reform of lender-borrower rights and powers. For the first time, for example, it allowed a lender to take a security interest over movable assets and fixed plant equipment;[28] previously, in the absence of such rights, borrowers had great difficulty raising loans for such capital and had needed to obtain finance for such things from abroad or put up additional land or other such security. The new law also changed the interest the creditors may have, allowing for a mortgage, lien, or contractual pledge, and was also important in clarifying and updating laws related to large projects such as those involving creditor and debtor rights with respect to assets located on land owned by a third party and suchlike.[29]

Also in 2004, the new labor law was promulgated (Law no. 14). It established equal pay for men and women, although somewhat controversially it still barred women from some jobs that involved arduous physical labor or that were deemed hazardous (to be determined by the minister of civil service affairs and housing, under Section 94). Qatari law also allows workers to form committees (though not trade unions as such) where there are over a hundred employees and, uniquely for the GCC, to strike in certain circumstances—although few have been able to do this without being evicted from the country, despite Qatar's history of strikes and industrial quarrels, especially in the 1950s. Still, it was notable that the labor law articulated such rights.

Another of Qatar's steps in reforming its economy has been to promote greater commercial competition. One example of this is in the telecommunications sector, where legal reforms in 2006 ended Qtel's monopoly on telephone and Internet service provision and encouraged greater and more liberal use of the Internet.[30] The changes also made the Supreme Council of Information and Communication Technology (ictQATAR), which had been established in 2004 as a broad telecommunications and e-commerce adviser and agent for the state, the sole independent regulator of the telecommunications sector for the government. However, the subsequent outcomes of the reform have been controversial and contested.[31] Vodafone Qatar, a consortium of firms that included Vodafone UK as a minority shareholder,[32] won the country's second mobile phone license in December 2007 and entered the market in early 2009. Due in part to name recognition, Vodafone Qatar quickly gained a sizable minority market share among expatriates. Qtel, unsure what to do in the face of competition—with which it had little experience, at least in its home base of Qatar—entered into a partnership with the United Kingdom's Virgin Group and began marketing Virgin Mobile in Qatar. However, it did this solely with Virgin's branding, not jointly, which prompted Vodafone Qatar to lodge a complaint with ictQatar that Qtel was trying to pass off Virgin as a separate, third mobile provider. In July 2010, ictQatar ruled in favor of Vodafone, essentially agreeing that Qtel had acted in a misleading manner and forcing Qtel to correct the public impression created by the issue. It was a lesson for both the established, state-owned provider and the new entrant into the market of the difficulties and risks of a new competition environment, and indeed ought to have demonstrated to the government the difficulties in establishing genuine competition in a small, previously monopolistic market.

Finally, in 2009 and 2010 the government introduced substantial reforms in taxation.[33] Previously, under Income Tax Law no. 11 of 1993, non-Qatari-owned firms with a permanent presence in Qatar had paid tax on a sliding scale, ranging from 10 to 35 percent, except in the oil and gas sectors, where foreign joint venture partners were taxed according to the agreements underlying their contracts, at a minimum rate of 35 percent. Qatari-owned firms were not subject to tax. In 2009, Income Tax Law no. 21 replaced the 1993 law and amended the company tax rate to a flat 10 percent as of 2010. While the company tax rate fell, the 2009 law also broadened the tax base by imposing company tax on foreign-owned resident firms and taxing some offshore activity conducted under contract with Qatari-owned firms, and placed responsibility for a withholding tax for other payments to nonresidents onto Qataris and non-Qatari residents. Qatari and GCC national-owned firms remained untaxed. The reforms of the 2009 law are an example of the dubious advantage of many reforms. Law no. 21 was widely seen as a positive reform and a reduction in taxation—which it was for most firms that were already paying tax, and this was probably the expectation of the government; however, in creating new categories of taxpayers, including some Qataris, and broadening the tax base, it probably did not reduce the state's tax take and in fact may have increased it.[34]

As significant as some of these reforms have been, there are a range of economic liberalization measures that have not been conducted. The currency has remained pegged to the US dollar at the same rate since 2001, despite the inflationary impact of this during the boom of the middle to late 2000s. This is likely to remain the case in the 2010s, given the low levels of inflation since 2009 and the high foreign debt, much of it denominated in US dollars. More widely, the environment in which business operated, especially foreign business, remained constrained throughout the 2000s as well, and despite the legal reforms made, further structural adjustment was not forthcoming. The labor laws were and are highly favorable to Qatari employees, and contractual law also tends in practice to favor the Qatari party if a dispute ends in court action.

Perhaps most telling, there has been virtually no privatization in the sense of sales of state-owned firms, even if joint ventures have brought foreign private sector actors increasingly into some new areas of the economy. These dynamics all result from the fact that reforming them would provide little gain for the Qatari state, yet would probably bring problems for the Al Thani family's legitimacy given that the Al Thani, and a handful of other families close to them, would be the main financial beneficiaries of a broad privatization. This reinforces the argument that Qatar has not undertaken reforms out of ideological commitment to neoliberalism or market efficiency, nor because of a desire by the state to step back from its role in the economy. Rather, those reforms that strengthen, or at the very least do not threaten, the economic base of the regime, its political legitimacy, or its international reputation have been pursued or permitted, while wider-ranging reforms that might upset the political order or appear unfair or crony remain disregarded.

This is similar to what has occurred with other reforms, such as those affecting the regulation, administration, and mechanics of conducting business. Such changes are different in their scope and nature compared to economic liberalization, but often have a positive impact on business confidence and operations. A second but important set of reforms since about 2004 has been in this area, with changes to ease the establishment, operation, management, and closure of a business. Some of the reforms stemmed from the wider legal changes already mentioned, and others arose out of reforms that aimed to streamline or simplify the procedures for firms in certain sectors. The amendments to the foreign investment laws provide examples of both types of reforms. Accompanying their implementation were specific initiatives to attract foreign investment. In 2004 the Qatar Science and Technology Park was established both to attract foreign investment in the science and technology fields and to encourage and support Qatari entrepreneurs in establishing firms in these sectors.[35] The park was also co-located with Education City in an attempt to bring together scientific and technological investment, research, operations, and education. Legal changes in 2005 made the park in effect a free zone, meaning that on top of tax and customs incentives, foreign firms could own up to 100 percent of the capital in a registered firm. Similarly, in 2005 the Qatar Financial Centre (QFC) was opened to develop the financial sector and link it more closely with international financial firms.[36] Importantly in the context of an energy-driven economy, the QFC also sought to attract finance for the energy sector, including for downstream projects, by bringing in both financial and technical expertise from overseas. In this way, even an apparent diversification into the finance sector is the result in substantial part of the economy's centeredness on hydrocarbons.

These types of reforms helped Qatar receive high ratings, for the most part, on indexes and measures such as the *Global Competitiveness Index,* cited earlier, and the World Bank's *Doing Business* reports.[37] Such reports typically make note of administrative reforms that assist businesses, and not just the macroeconomic climate. A comment in the 2011 *Doing Business in the Arab World* report is typical: "Today, 6 out of 20 economies in the Arab world have some kind of one-stop shop for business registration [including Qatar]. This type of reform does not necessarily require legal changes, just administrative ones. Furthermore, entrepreneurs and governments alike often see immediate benefits."[38] Similarly: "Economies with well-designed tax systems are able to encourage the growth of businesses and, ultimately, investment and employment. . . . Yet there is great variation within the Arab world: the Republic of Yemen requires 44 payments a year while Qatar requires just 3 . . . [and the] total tax rate in these types of economies ranges from just 11% in Qatar to 72% in Algeria."[39]

Such reforms have political as well as commercial importance. They raise Qatar's attractiveness for investment and, equally, improve the impressions held by the indigenous business community toward the state and regime. This is especially true in Qatar, where its state capitalism reduces many opportunities available to the private sector or relegates them to partnerships with state-owned firms, and given remaining problems in the transparency of the business environment due to state controls and the opaque, highly informal influence of key business figures. This is also less politically charged and less administratively complex to introduce, as *Doing Business* noted when arguing that many reforms to the processes of business can be achieved with simple administrative changes or by emiri or ministerial decree rather than more substantial legal reforms. Whether intentionally or not, therefore, the undertaking of these particular types of reforms sends a specific message about how much and what kind of private sector power the emir and the state will allow, and the limited depth of liberalization has meant that the state has remained firmly at the center of economic management (and indeed ownership). Wittingly or not, Qatar has sent a message to foreign firms that investment is welcome, but on the state's terms. Above all, the state is not seeking, through such changes, to make any reforms that would seriously impact or jeopardize its own political position. Thus the reforms since the late 1990s do not mark a retreat of the state from the economy; rather they symbolize a reassertion and rearrangement of that role through partial liberalization and attempts at a measured, appropriate diversification of the economy. The examples of particular sectors where reforms and diversification policies have been attempted demonstrate this dynamic.

Direct Beneficiaries of Rents: Construction and Infrastructure

At the simplest level, there are a few sectors that are not part of the Qatari energy sector but nonetheless directly and obviously benefit from it. Among these are construction, infrastructure, and to some extent the small agriculture and agribusiness sector. Such sectors are direct beneficiaries of hydrocarbons for a few reasons. The most obvious is the flow of state spending to these sectors—sizable proportions of energy rents are directed into major public works projects that directly sustain the construction sector. The drive by the state to develop Qatar's infrastructure, including the need for state funds in major initiatives such as the Qatar Financial Centre, Education City, and the like, are important drivers of construction activity. The state is at least partly motivated by its role in leading economic development, but the outward signs of development that major construction and infrastructure projects exude are politically useful for the state as well and reinforce its role and the emir's vision to modernize the economy and society. Moreover, as rents circulate through the economy, a portion of them ends up being injected by individuals and firms into such sectors as private investment. Very often, Qataris' first thoughts of investment are directed toward property and real estate, adding new demand and income to the construction industry.

It is for these reasons that the fortunes of the construction sector have largely followed the growth of rents. As of about 2003, as oil prices began to rise and as gas increasingly came online, the construction and property sectors gained international attention. The Ministry of Municipal Affairs and Agriculture unveiled a massive infrastructure program in 2002 worth some US$3 billion, the result partly of a drive to improve infrastructure and begin major projects as rents increased, as they were expected to, and also partly the result of a spending boom resulting from Qatar being chosen to host the 2006 Asian Games. On top of this, major public projects and the beginnings of a real estate boom were under way.[40] From about 2004 to 2009, a major set of construction projects were undertaken, including as examples The Pearl, a US$2.5 billion artificial island off the West Bay, and the ongoing Lusail project, a US$5 billion city that will ultimately house some 200,000 residents.[41] There were also a range of different infrastructure projects implemented in the same period, such as in road construction and expansion, water supply, and new government facilities,[42] not to mention the construction associated with initiatives such as Education City. Similarly, transport facilities were further developed, including the development of a US$5.5 billion port near Mesaieed, and the new Doha airport, due for completion in phases over 2011–2015 and costing some US$11 billion.[43] Many of these projects have been driven by government departments and funded through the state budget, and others have been investments by state-owned firms or joint ventures involving them, again sometimes using public funds but often raising their own capital. In any event, the link to rents had been either direct or indirect, but has usually been present in the large infrastructure and construction projects. With very high rental income virtually guaranteed into the foreseeable future, further projects will be prominent through the 2010s, including the construction of a road and rail bridge to Bahrain, the development of a rail system in Qatar, and of course construction of buildings and infrastructure for the 2022 World Cup.[44]

Such was the expansion of property and infrastructure that by the time the global economy went into crisis in 2008, there was an oversupply of office space in Doha and yet complaints among some Qataris of a paucity of low-cost housing.[45] In fact, the risk of property price fluctuations reached the point that the state controversially stepped into the sector in 2009 and 2010. A year earlier Qatar had been supplying cheap land to developers and capping rental prices, but as the global financial crisis unfolded the state began leasing additional office space for its departments and institutions and encouraging firms based in residential offices to move to commercial facilities; in some cases businesses reported being coerced, under pressure of not having their commercial registration renewed, if they failed to move into commercial premises.[46] Despite these steps, in 2010 there was a 15–20 percent occupancy rate in commercial property, with new supply still due to come onto the market.[47]

This boom in the construction sector is evident from Table 5.1. The sheer number of people employed in the sector is telling—from around 56,000 in 1997 to some 559,000 in 2009, or a tenfold increase in a dozen or so years—but the number of employees as a percentage of the work force—20 percent in 1997 versus 44 percent in 2009—represents a dramatic increase as well. This is by far the largest growth, both percentage-wise and by sheer numbers, of any sector in the period, although it is worth noting the rise in numbers involved in other sectors as well, in areas like manufacturing, wholesale and retail, health, and real estate, which look less impressive only because of the enormous overall population growth in the period. Coincidentally, the population growth itself is indicative of the energy boom in Qatar over 2003–2008, and indeed of the rentier characteristic of the political economy: recall that the *indigenous* natural population growth rate in the period was about 2.5 percent per annum (an exact figure is difficult to ascertain), meaning that the number of economically active people should have increased, at this rate, from 280,000 in 1997 to no more than 400,000 in 2009. The difference between this and the much larger actual figure of 1,262,000 is nearly completely accounted for by the influx of expatriate workers and their families. The energy dominance of the Qatari economy is partly demonstrated by this increase in the number of foreign residents, and also by the increase in the number of people employed in the energy sector (upstream mostly captured in the "mining and quarrying" category, midstream and downstream in "manufacturing"), compared to the very small overall numbers of people employed in the capital-intensive industries. The energy dominance of the Qatari economy is also evident in the expansion of sectors that support an energy economy, such as construction of course, but also areas such as retail, hospitality, finance, real estate, and to some extent domestic services.

Higher Education

One of the starkest examples of diversification, leading on from the major projects just mentioned, is the higher education strategy—since this is, itself, a major infrastructural undertaking, but also one that supports the goals of human, social, and economic development, especially in the creation and development of Education City. Qatar is not alone in its emphasis on higher education, as other Gulf states, most of all Dubai and Abu Dhabi, have actively sought to develop the sector and have sought to establish a presence in foreign universities. However, Qatar's method of developing higher education and the nature of Education City are unique.

Table 5.1 Qatari Employment by Sector, 1997–2009

	1997 Census		2004 Census		2009 Survey	
	Number of Employees	Number of Employees as Percentage of Total Work Force	Number of Employees	Number of Employees as Percentage of Total Work Force	Number of Employees	Number of Employees as Percentage of Total Work Force
Agriculture, hunting, forestry	9,044	3.23	10,200	2.33	16,955	1.34
Fishing	1,303	0.47	1,825	0.42	2,822	0.22
Mining and quarrying	9,364	3.34	17,997	4.11	62,774	4.97
Manufacturing	24,143	8.62	40,039	9.15	108,786	8.62
Electricity and gas	3,206	1.14	4,364	1.00	6,158	0.49
Construction	56,106	20.03	117,049	26.75	559,066	44.29
Wholesale and retail trade	30,622	10.93	54,438	12.44	138,358	10.96
Hotels and restaurants	6,068	2.17	10,280	2.35	24,940	1.98
Transport, communications, etc.	9,614	3.43	15,218	3.48	55,900	4.43
Financial intermediation	3,094	1.10	4,766	1.08	15,422	1.22
Real estate, renting, etc.	4,644	1.66	11,859	2.71	46,326	3.67
Public administration	49,873	17.80	53,438	12.21	64,808	5.13
Education	13,954	4.98	19,877	4.54	31,105	2.46
Health and social work	5,434	1.94	11,554	2.64	30,090	2.38
Other social services	7,663	2.74	10,130	2.32	16,387	1.30
Domestic services	45,100	16.10	53,356	12.19	80,342	6.36
Extraterritorial bodies	595	0.22	1,171	0.27	2,024	0.16
Other	295	0.10	—	—	—	—
Total	280,122	100.00	437,561	100.00	1,262,263	100.00

Source: Author calculations from statistics provided in QNB Capital, *Qatar Economic Review 2010*, p. 8, and *Qatar Economic Review 2007*, p. 8.
Note: Percentage numbers may not sum to 100.00 because of rounding.

There are several challenges facing Qatar that link to education policy. One is the relatively low level of employment creation for Qatari citizens during the 2003–2008 boom,[48] which disproportionately resulted in the creation of many jobs, both skilled and unskilled, for expatriates, but comparatively few that were suitable or desirable for Qataris. Importantly, too, the state has been relatively open to the employment of foreigners, and although there is a Qatarization policy in place, the state has not pursued the nationalization of the work force as vigorously as have other Gulf states.[49] Third is the fact that rents only go so far in terms of buying support. Even where a state can afford to provide make-work positions for its citizenry, some of the political benefit for the state in employing the citizenry, if people see their roles as lacking value or importance, is lost. By this logic the state thus needs to not just help create any work, but work that has some meaning and prestige attached to it. Finally, Qatar arguably suffers from what several scholars have identified in the Gulf as a "manager (*mudir*) syndrome," whereby, as the term implies, people seek out positions that have particular status or respect attached to them, particularly professional careers, management, brokerage roles, and the like.[50] While some Qataris are to be found in unskilled roles, most are not.

For all of these reasons, the Qatari government has been keen to develop the education and high-end training sector, to enhance the employability and prospects for Qataris in particular in more skilled and prestigious roles. Education reform has occurred across the schooling and higher education systems, but three reforms are worth noting: the primary and secondary school reforms; Qatar University (QU) reforms and amendments to the higher education strategy and curriculum; and the creation of Education City. Primary and secondary school reforms are linked to the more extensive higher education reforms, because of the need to better prepare students for tertiary study and to help them develop the skills and interests that will match their later academic pursuits to what the economy is seen as most needing, particularly science, technology, and commercial expertise.

The education system in Qatar, as noted in Chapter 2, evolved in line with the development of oil. Prior to the 1950s, there were virtually no schools at all except for the *kuttab,* an informal schooling for children at mosques or homes conducted by literate adults. The formalization of modern public education did not begin until 1948 with the opening of a boys' school, which gained government support in 1951, followed by the opening of the first girls' school in 1956.[51] The system developed from there. The Ministry of Education was formed in the mid-1950s and followed an Egyptian education model for the first decade or so. By the 1970s, male and female curricula were unified, and the public system was more centralized, although private schools also began appearing around this time. By the 1990s, Qatar had a modern, centralized education system, albeit one that was ready for reform; however, it is worth recalling that barely half of Qatari males born around 1950 had any schooling at all.[52]

An attempt at rapid modernization and improvement of education began after Hamad's ascension to power and especially after the late 1990s. In 2001, the government, bringing in the RAND Corporation to advise and assist it, began a reform of the primary and secondary schooling system. The reform led to the 2002 "Education for a New Era" policy.[53] The specific initiatives within this included the development of curricula around specific educational outcomes and focused on the core subjects of Arabic, English, mathematics, and science, as well as better facilities and higher teacher salaries.[54] Crucially, the policy centered on independent schools funded by the state, with qualified people, even those from outside the teaching profession, able to apply to establish and operate a new school under contract with the state.[55] The aim was to create students who were better equipped in general, but especially well prepared for higher education, with the independent schools focusing on such skills as critical thinking, problem solving, and teamwork.[56] As clever and seemingly appropriate as the reforms were—especially compared to the prior old-fashioned rote-learning approach to education—their success remains uncertain in the long term, since such schooling requires significant resources; as of 2009, students still were not meeting the government's new standards for the core subjects.[57]

At the higher education level, the reforms have been even more far-reaching, feeding qualitative improvements and better matching of education to the labor market. An initial study of the sector in 1997 drew some sobering conclusions about the poor educational and technical competencies of many public sector employees and the propensity of students to choose courses in social or religious studies rather than in the technical and scientific areas most needed by the economy.[58] Moreover, this came on top of the economic imperatives caused by rapid population growth and the strategy of using energy resources to transition away from a reliance on the energy sector and rents. Qatar produced only a relatively small number of graduates until the 1990s. Qatar University was not established until 1973 and remained a relatively small university. By the late 1990s it was producing considerably more female than male graduates, which was a problem since many women graduates either did not enter the work force or, if they did, usually ceased employment once they began a family. Some Qataris studied abroad under government scholarships, but the number who did so was relatively small. A greater number of males studied abroad, but not in large enough numbers to offset the much greater number of female students at Qatar University. Table 5.2 illustrates some of these trends.

The state's approaches to reforming higher education have been manifold, driven by these dynamics and some of the existing problems with the labor force and graduates. The creation of the Qatar Foundation in 1995 was arguably the first key step toward educational reform, given the importance of the foundation itself and the role of the emir's wife, Shaikha Muza, within it. One of the flagship developments of the Qatar Foundation is Education City, a campus in the suburbs of Doha that aims to bring together local campuses of globally renowned international universities. Inaugurated in October 2003, by 2010 Education City had established campuses of nine universities on its 14–square kilometer grounds, including Texas A&M University, teaching various engineering degrees; Carnegie Mellon University, focused on business and computer sciences; Georgetown University School of Foreign Service, teaching international relations, diplomacy, and related fields; Northwestern University, teaching journalism and communication; Weill Cornell Medical College, teaching pre-medicine and medicine; Virginia Commonwealth University, teaching fine arts, interior design, and fashion; HEC Paris, delivering management education, especially executive development programs; University College London, offering archaeology and conservation-related instruction; and Qatar Faculty of Islamic Studies, offering graduate education in Islamic studies.[59] To maintain quality, at least in theory, these campuses are required to offer programs as they would on their home campuses, with the same methodologies, curriculum standards, and delivery.[60]

To a lesser extent, Education City also aims to link and align more tightly the government's and business's interests in education, and to bring technology and methodologies in teaching and education into the economy. The fact that the foreign university campuses are highly specialized in their research and teaching is important, too. The research remit is a direct element of the state's focus with Education City, and in light of the subjects being offered is a sign of both the ongoing importance of energy resources and the desire of the state to diversify the economy into new areas. It is noteworthy that, beyond specialized secondary educational facilities and supporting infrastructure, Education City also includes a hospital, which is the teaching hospital for Weill Cornell program,[61] and that Qatar Science and Technology Park is co-located with Education City. Because of this, Education City is a somewhat different education hub compared to those in Dubai and Abu Dhabi, in particular given the strate-

Table 5.2 Higher Education Dynamics in Qatar, 1995–2000

	1995–1996		1996–1997		1997–1998		1998–1999		1999–2000	
	Male	Female	Male	Female	Male	Female	Male	Female	Male	Female
Qatar University students										
Pre-specialization	515	1,580	493	1,576	401	1,197	430	905	158	62
Education	257	1,995	261	1,982	264	2,173	245	2,070	222	2,434
Humanities	238	866	221	914	211	880	200	893	225	1,193
Islamic law/studies	72	393	72	392	68	348	130	338	146	426
Science	289	516	290	606	304	746	276	867	301	951
Engineering	362	—	426	—	447	—	419	—	399	—
Administration/economics	412	316	399	416	358	553	475	664	367	782
Technology	159	301	118	309	152	322	199	365	274	395
Parallel teaching	—	—	—	—	—	—	—	—	384	174
Total	2,304	5,967	2,280	6,195	2,205	6,219	2,374	6,102	2,476	6,417
Qatari students abroad										
Training	55	6	52	—	88	13	—	—	—	—
Specific courses	2	4	3	2	2	2	1	1	1	1
Undergraduate	472	182	464	227	399	261	346	262	446	263
Postgraduate	239	129	250	129	226	143	214	140	272	182
Total	768	321	769	358	715	419	561	403	719	446

Source: Qatar Statistics Authority, *Annual Statistical Abstract 2000*, tabs. 94 and 98.

gic and careful selection of the institutions to be represented there, which are less liberalized compared to those in Dubai. Education City's focus on research is unique as well.[62]

A skeptic might argue that such an initiative is not difficult to implement given the resources of the state. This indeed does highlight one of the criticisms with Education City, namely, that the quality of its education is very good—although this is occasionally questioned too—but that the expense involved per student is especially substantial. The other issue is that Education City remains nascent. It promises the same education as provided on US campuses, but students do not usually study across both campuses. Coordination across the various campuses is weak, too, making it questionable as to whether Education City is a cohesive educational vehicle, or more of a collection of small, specialized college outposts. Finally, Education City is a reminder of the underlying rents and rentierism of the Qatari political economy: a state without the energy income and resources available to Doha would not have been able to create Education City without substantial reductions in spending elsewhere, and it is arguably a product of rentierism because, in light of the cost, there is an aspect of co-optation through the gift of education, and a state-driven attempt at diversification as well.

Finally, policy reform and institutional changes at Qatar University have also been important. Again with the involvement of RAND, the government has sought to amend higher education policy and practices, beyond just introducing initiatives such as Education City. One initiative was the creation and operation of the Qatar National Research Fund (QNRF), which was established in 2006, along lines similar to those of state research-funding bodies in Western economies, to promote and fund scholarly and other original research of national benefit.[63] Another development was the restructuring and reform of Qatar University. While in theory the university at the turn of the 2000s was akin to a Western university in terms of power and autonomy, in reality it was subject to considerable political oversight and influence, and was not as efficient as it could have been. The reforms that RAND recommended and that to a large extent were implemented as of 2003 included enhancements to the university's autonomy, greater administrative decentralization, closer integration of teaching and research, improvements to pedagogy, better management and administration, and improved academic standards and quality assurance.[64] As suggested by Table 5.3, these reforms did not expand enrollments but rather aimed at enhancing the efficiency of the university.

Beyond these changes, there has even been discussion from time to time about reforming the expectations and career mechanisms of graduates, to improve competition among them and their overall performance,

Table 5.3 Higher Education Dynamics in Qatar, 2008–2011

	2008–2009		2009–2010		2010–2011	
	Male	Female	Male	Female	Male	Female
Qatar University students by faculty						
Foundation program	714	2,296	813	2,275	733	2,324
Education	84	388	65	277	24	161
Arts and science	248	2,096	220	1,950	205	1,955
Islamic studies	112	330	86	289	121	482
Engineering	473	538	470	603	518	627
Administration and economics	276	694	322	869	344	944
Law	61	137	55	157	80	228
Pharmacy	0	60	0	110	0	165
Community college	—	—	—	—	237	437
Parallel teaching	0	0	0	0	0	0
Nonspecialized	0	0	0	0	0	0
Specific courses	5	19	0	10	0	3
Postgraduate	72	84	58	76	77	128
Total	2,045	6,642	2,089	6,616	2,339	7,454
Private university students in Qatar						
Bridge program	65	170	68	130	116	159
Carnegie Mellon	10	7	9	15	5	18
College of Islamic Studies	2	4	8	10	2	2
College of the North Atlantic	6	12	14	24	18	44
Georgetown	2	8	3	6	3	8
Northwestern	1	11	0	0	0	0
Qatar Aeronautical	0	0	0	16	1	10
Texas A&M	8	19	11	21	14	26
Calgary	0	1	0	5	0	5
Virginia Commonwealth	2	19	2	28	2	31
Weill Cornell	4	13	7	5	5	9
Total	100	264	122	260	166	312
Qatari students abroad on scholarship						
Doctoral	4	3	3	0	4	4
Master	8	6	17	8	16	18
Bachelor	57	14	87	32	98	40
Associate	—	—	0	0	0	0
Diploma	—	—	0	0	0	0
Other	4	—	6	2	10	1
Total	73	23	113	42	128	63

Source: Qatar Statistics Authority, *Annual Statistical Abstract,* various years and tables.

remove some of their presumption of entitlement, and ensure that they are motivated to attend the best possible institution and to earn to best possible grades. Typical was the statement by the *Middle East Economic Digest* in 2005, endorsing such changes and suggesting they may be forthcoming: "One of the recommendations now being evaluated is to encourage the country's top employers—public and private sector—to hire students on the basis of their degree, the level they have attained and the institute they attended. One suggestion that has also been mooted for the long term is to cut traditional government subsidies to nationals to ensure students take their education seriously."[65] Such dramatic changes to the state's employment bargain with young people would seem unlikely in the foreseeable future, however. This would bring with it too great a sense of relative deprivation or intergenerational unfairness, as many young Qataris have come to expect the same opportunities, income, and prestige experienced by their parents. Moreover, for as long as Qataris struggle to perform to the same level as foreign students in standardized examinations, they will find it difficult to compete for positions against expatriates.

In light of this, it is difficult to easily characterize Qatar's higher education reforms as a success or failure, and equally difficult to determine to what extent they represent genuine and efficacious diversification. To a proponent of the reforms, they represent a significant state investment to kick-start a set of reforms that will improve the performance of the higher education sector, better link teaching and research, and much more closely align the graduates produced by universities with the most important sectors of the economy. By these arguments, Education City and other such initiatives are expensive, but only as a first step in a reform process that will become increasingly autonomous from the state and ultimately, as the profile of graduates and the outputs and standards of universities increase, self-financing. To a critic, this is subsidized diversification, not dissimilar to what was tried in the Gulf a generation ago, just more sophisticated and in theory better linked to the economy's comparative advantages. Without cultural changes such as greater prestige in private sector employment, more incentives among students to maximize their qualifications and match them to what the market needs, and a willingness for new graduates to be globally competitive, a critic would argue that such reforms will continue to have limited prospects.

Banking and Islamic Finance

The other sector, along with education, where reform has been especially noticeable is in banking, finance, and related areas, including sharia-compliant (i.e., Islamic) finance. Since the late 1990s the Qatari government has actively sought to expand and develop the sector and to turn Qatar into a financial center of the Gulf. Arguably it has been more successful in the former of these than in the last, although Qatar is becoming increasingly competitive as a hub or regional center for banks and other financial institutions and as a place for firms to raise capital locally.

The diversification of the banking sector actually predates the economic diversification strategy of Hamad and began with the creation of the Qatar National Bank (QNB) as the country's first Qatari-owned financial institution. Previously, the banking sector had consisted entirely of foreign-owned banks, both Arab and Western, operating branches in Qatar. The QNB was established in 1964, half owned by the state and half by businesspeople. It retains this balance to this day, being now 50 percent owned by the QIA and 50 percent by the public.[66] It has become the country's leading financial institution: in May 2011 (see Table 3.1), it was the largest company on the Qatar Exchange by market capitalization—almost twice the size of Qatar Industries, the next-largest firm, and over two and a half times the size of the next largest bank, Masraf al-Rayan. It holds about a 40 percent market share by banking sector assets.[67] It is also the leading bank in terms of influence in the political economy, since due to its history and ownership structure it is favored by government departments and state-owned firms, and is preferred by many large foreign firms in Qatar as well. Also important in its political reach is the fact that several prominent Al Thani family members are on its board, alongside some figures from key shaikhly and merchant families as well.

The QNB is not without competition, and as of 2010 there were sixteen other banks authorized to operate in Qatar. In its early years it had to compete to gain market share from the foreign banks operating in the country, and many international financial institutions maintain a presence in the market: those with a license to operate in Qatar as of 2012 included Arab Bank, Bank Saderat Iran, BNP Paribas, HSBC, Mashreq Bank, Standard Chartered, and United Bank.[68] Furthermore, six locally owned banks operate in the market; apart from QNB, these are Ahli Bank, Al-Khaliji, Commercial Bank, Doha Bank, and the International Bank of Qatar.[69] Finally, there are four Islamic, or sharia-compliant, banks: Barwa Bank, International Islamic, Masraf al-Rayan, and Qatar Islamic Bank.[70] Somewhat separate from these institutions but still a financial institution is the Qatar Development Bank. It is a nonprofit state-owned institution set up by the government, under an emiri decree in 1997, to assist the economic diversification policy by lending and providing general banking and financial services to small and medium-sized firms in key sectors such as tourism, education, healthcare, industry, agriculture, and other primary and secondary economic sectors.[71] Table 5.4 provides an outline of the size and value of the main Qatari banks, both conventional and sharia-compliant.

Other parts of the financial sector have been developed through state reforms and initiatives since the late 1990s. One initiative was the creation of a stock market, launched in 1997. In some ways this was not a dramatic change, as in many cases shares in firms were already being traded over the counter, and the stock market simply formalized this trade.[72] However the creation of the Doha Securities Market, now the Qatar Exchange, actu-

Table 5.4 The Qatari Banking Sector: Comparative Financial Standing and Statistics, 2011 (QR millions)

	Total Assets	Loans	Deposits	Net Profit[a]	Capitalization[b]
Conventional banks					
Qatar National Bank	301,955	193,943	200,123	7,509	91,874
Commercial Bank	71,540	41,614	37,989	1,884	16,925
Doha Bank	52,420	30,704	31,699	1,241	11,162
International Bank of Qatar	27,129	16,729	19,426	572	n/a
Ahli Bank	17,734	12,155	12,690	442	6,335
Al-Khaliji	27,003	11,314	12,130	487	5,944
Sharia-compliant banks[c]					
Qatar Islamic Bank	58,286	29,596	27,657	1,365	17,958
Masraf al-Rayan	55,271	34,766	46,264	1,408	20,213
International Islamic Bank	23,400	10,589	18,091	653	7,341
Other Qatari banks					
Qatar Development Bank	3,647	1,125	n/a	50	n/a
International banks					
HSBC	17,542	6,439	10,106	360	n/a
Arab Bank	4,549	2,101	2,904	120	n/a
BNP Paribas	2,278	628	1,616	69	n/a
Standard Chartered	3,217	898	2,189	23	n/a
Mashreq Bank	3,196	1,565	1,919	23	n/a
United Bank	716	351	542	20	n/a
Bank Saderat Iran	744	302	362	37	n/a

Source: QNB Capital, *Banking Sector Review 2012*.
Notes: a. For foreign banks, profit is after tax.
b. As at June 20, 2012.
c. Figures are not available for Barwa Bank.
n/a = not applicable.

ally proved important, as it sent a message of pro-business reform by the then-new emir. It sent a message to business that reform and modernization were expected of them and not to be undertaken solely by the state. It also sent a message of globalization and liberalization to Qataris and international investors when foreign nationals were given permission to own a minority of shares in listed firms, under the 2004 amendments to the investment law as previously discussed.

The late 1990s was a transitional period during which Qatar's economy was rapidly changing. This included the banking sector having to transition from simpler processes, mostly as a recipient of capital for key projects, into a more sophisticated sector able to generate its own capital and supply a variety of firms and sectors.[73] With low oil prices in the late 1990s, high capital demands from the development of gas production, and then unstable markets in the West after the correction to technology stocks that began in March 2000 and again after the terrorist attacks of September 11, 2001, this was not a tranquil transition. It was at this time that the bond market was first created, and that the first leveraged buyouts in Qatari firms were attempted with local banks; both were tortuous because of the inexperience of the sector and the environment at the time. The first state bond issue, in 1998, was delayed,[74] but ultimately was successfully concluded later, and within a few years state-owned firms quickly began to issue bonds and other debt instruments to raise money. By 2005, a range of methods were being used to finance projects.[75] The state has even issued bonds, such as a US$7 billion issue in 2009, not out of necessity—rent surpluses are sufficient, not to mention the QIA holdings—but in order to set an example for the financial sector so as to encourage corporate and bank issuance of debt.[76]

Finally, the other, nonbanking, financial area that is important and that has an established history is insurance. Qatari insurance companies, not surprisingly, trace their origins to the development of the oil industry and the need for insurance products by the energy sector. As with banks, some foreign insurance companies were present in the market in the 1950s and serviced international firms entering the market, but reforms in the 1960s initiated the Qatarization of the sector. The Qatar Insurance Company (QIC) was established by emiri decree on March 11, 1964, and then the sector as a whole was brought under a regulatory framework by reforms in 1966.[77] In supplying paid-up capital at the start of the firm's operations, the government took a 12 percent shareholding in the QIC, which it still maintains.[78] The insurance sector then essentially followed the growth of the oil sector, expanding in the 1970s and again in the 1990s as foreign companies entered the market at these times, and given in particular the influx of oil income in the 1970s and the growing sophistication and reform of the economy in the 1990s. Additional Qatari firms established at these times were Qatar General Insurance and the Al-Khaleej Insurance and Reinsurance Company, both in 1978, and the Qatar Islamic Insurance Company in 1993 and Doha Insurance in 1999.[79] These were in addition to four foreign firms[80] that entered the market in the 1960s prior to a 1971 decree banning new foreign entrants into the insurance sector. The sector developed further as a result of the economic boom of 2003–2008, although it was impacted as well by the fluctuations in premiums in the global insurance sector over the same period, and arguably was somewhat hobbled by the relatively small size of the economy at the time.[81] Perhaps partly for this reason, one of the focuses of the Qatar Financial Centre is on developing insurance, reinsurance, and captive insurance as part of its strategy of making the financial sector larger and more sophisticated.[82]

All the Qatari insurance firms remain major actors, and all are listed on the Qatar Exchange, although the QIC is by far the largest: measured by gross premiums it constitutes about half the market, and by equity it accounts for a similar share of the market's total value.[83] It is also the largest insurance company in the Gulf when measured by market capitalization. Its position stems not just from its history, however, as it is also the best-connected insurer to the political elite. Its board is heavily represented by the Al Thani family and others among Qatar's commercial and political elite. Apart from its chairman and managing director, Khalid bin Muhammad bin Ali Al Thani, there is Hamad bin Faysal bin Thani Al Thani, who is chairman of the Al-Khaliji bank, a former minister of economy and commerce, a former vice chairman of the QNB, and a former director of customs. He is both politically and commercially influential. So too is Jassim bin Hamad bin Jassim bin Jabr Al Thani, a son of the exceptionally powerful prime minister and chairman of Qatar Islamic Bank. There is another Al Thani on the QIC board as well, plus several other members of prominent financial and merchant families, the most notable of whom is the deputy chairman, Abdallah bin Khalifa al-Attiyya, who serves as chairman of Commercial Bank and also serves on the boards of other key firms.

Once the hurdles of low oil prices and a small, fairly isolated economy had been overcome, the finance sector became the target of significant reform. Obviously the sector benefited from the wider economic liberalization of the early 2000s, especially the 2000 investment law and its 2004 amendments, and from the construction boom noted earlier, which had a profound impact on the sector by creating demand for massive amounts of capital and for new methods of capital-raising. Several other reforms are also worth emphasizing.

Perhaps the most important—certainly the one to gain the greatest attention in the financial media—was the creation of the Qatar Financial Centre. Created by Law no. 7 of 2005 and effective from May that year, it sought to encourage foreign investment in banking and the associated financial sector, especially to supply the capital expected to be demanded because of the major infrastructure and project work planned for the late 2000s and early 2010s.[84] It targeted above all investment banking, corporate finance, and private banking firms that had already built up some involvement in the market but were not invested with a permanent presence there, but also sought out foreign and Qatari startups and more specialized firms.[85] Supporting legal structures were put in place quickly,[86] as was a permanent board, appointed in 2006 and consisting of specialists in the finance sector.[87] The benefits of the QFC to investors in the finance sector were numerous: a three-year taxation holiday, freedom to move funds in and out of the country, permission for 100 percent foreign ownership of a registered firm, and, initially, the ability to operate under specific laws of the QFC's regulatory authority, separate from those of the Ministry of Economy and Commerce, which usually dictate business operations.[88]

Other reforms were important too. In 2007 the finance sector was harmonized by a unification of the regulations covering it. This was a major step that put banking, insurance, securities, asset management, and other financial services under the same laws and regulator, with better transparency and efficiency.[89] Finally, as the global financial crisis unfolded in 2009, the Qatari government stepped in to shore up confidence in the banking sector by buying small stakes in the Qatari banks—reportedly spending over several stages around QR21.5 billion (US$5.9 billion)—and taking over or guaranteeing some project finance arrangements.[90] This happened before other measures such as the purchase and leasing of real estate to avoid a price collapse, and also reportedly involved the state pressuring the QIA to buy into the banks as well.[91]

A final reform worth reiterating is the expansion of sharia-compliant finance, which has been prominent in Qatar's finance sector and in which Qatar has been prominent internationally. There are the four sharia-compliant banks already noted—Barwa Bank, International Islamic, Masraf al-Rayan, and Qatar Islamic Bank—but beyond this, a number of conventional banks operated separate sharia-compliant services as well,[92] until a controversial central bank directive in February 2011 ordered them to cease doing so by the end of that year.[93] Technically this reform will enhance transparency and improve regulation of the sector, as new regulations are brought into the sharia-compliant subsector, but it was also an abrupt directive with a negative impact on conventional banks' assets and bottom line. Despite this, however, the state has actually been quite active in supporting sharia-compliant banking, bringing some of its business to the four main sharia-compliant banks and also to the sharia-compliant windows at the large commercial banks.[94] Qatar has also encouraged the development of sharia-compliant bonds (*sukuk*) in line with its development of more sophisticated capital-raising methods and products for the private sector and for state-owned firms.

The result of these policy changes and reforms has been in many ways quite impressive, albeit more in the case of the former impacts than the latter. A commonly cited measure of the competitiveness and relative strength of financial centers is the Global Financial Centres Index, which measures the various aspects that support a financial center, such as human capital, the regulatory context, market access, infrastructure, sectoral competitiveness, productivity, living costs, and the like, and uses both quantitative and qualitative methodologies—a score for the opinions of practitioners from the international finance sector is weighted strongly as well.[95] Under it, Qatar has done extremely well. It began by placing forty-seventh in the first index, in March 2007, with Dubai at twenty-fourth,[96] but by the ninth index, in March 2011, it was ranked thirtieth—second in the Middle East after Dubai, which it was now only two places behind. It is also well ahead of its next closest Middle East competitor, Bahrain—once a contender for the role of financial hub of the Middle East—in forty-ninth place.[97] This rating captures the improving environment for and the growing confidence in the Qatari finance sector, but also reflects the financial troubles in Dubai—in 2009 Qatar overtook Dubai for the first time as a stock market investment destination[98]—as well as political uncertainty in some other states, and is probably not therefore a perfect measure of QFC performance and reform impact in finance sector development.

However, a not dissimilar conclusion is derived from other measures and reports, which suggest that both sectoral reforms and the QFC have assisted in the development and expansion of the Qatari finance sector. An International Monetary Fund (IMF) report on Qatar's economy was positive about its financial sector, citing an appropriate regulatory presence, successful results from stress-testing of the banking sector, and a good culture of risk management.[99] Qatar also performs well on the IMF's vulnerability indicators.[100] On other financial sector indicators it performs well too, as indicated by Table 5.5, which suggests that the sector has grown strongly in both deposits and lending, and has become increasingly linked to international finance as well.

The only significant questions around the finance sector involve three issues, none of them dramatically negative. One is whether credit has

Table 5.5 The Qatari Finance Sector: Performance Indicators, 2006–2011

	2006	2007	2008	2009	2010	2011
Qatar Central Bank						
Reserve money (M0)[a] (QR millions)	10,154	30,652	23,623	45,903	91,809	31,186
Net foreign assets (QR millions)	19,694	34,747	35,790	67,118	112,170	59,698
Deposits rate (%)	5.15	4.00	2.00	2.00	1.50	0.75
Lending rate (%)	5.50	5.50	5.50	5.50	5.50	4.50
Commercial banks						
Total deposits	119,304	162,841	198,050	224,840	277,107	343,777
Private deposits	76,407	102,602	122,215	156,663	205,036	217,902
Total domestic credit	94,773	146,329	220,807	251,916	293,920	376,695
Private sector credit	73,236	110,427	160,218	177,459	190,862	227,525
Net foreign assets	41,557	26,696	13,079	–19,965	–48,185	–42,093

Source: Derived from statistics in Qatar Central Bank, *Quarterly Statistical Bulletin,* various editions.

Note: a. M0 is a term used by economists to refer to all physical notes and coins in circulation or reserve, but not other monies such as saving accounts, travelers' checks, commercial paper, etc.

expanded too rapidly, and debt levels are starting to become excessive. This debate is explored in Chapter 8, but the short answer is that much of the debt on Qatar's books is project debt, underwritten by long-term gas income in particular and therefore not as concerning as the property debt that threatened Dubai's economy so seriously in 2008 and 2009. The second question is whether the expansion of credit in the late 2000s actually contributed to the sharp rises in gross domestic product. Invariably it did, which suggests that easier credit as much as state policy was responsible for the (nonetheless still rather modest) economic diversification that took place in the same period. This credit, backed by state investments into the banks, also helped Qatar sail so smoothly through the global financial crisis of 2008–2009. Finally, there remains the question of whether the finance sector is yet as efficient and world-class as it needs to be for Qatar to emerge as a true international financial center—that is, not of the size and status of London or New York, but along the lines of second-tier but global centers such as Singapore, Geneva, Frankfurt, and the like. The economic base and diversity of the underlying economies is smaller and much narrower in Qatar than in most of these centers, and arguably Qatar has experienced problems with developing greater innovation and productivity.

That said, Qatar's enormous projected rents—likely to keep the country one of the wealthiest in the world per capita perhaps for the rest of the century or longer—are crucial here. They provide for a stability of government revenue, and thus for a predictable and strong amount of capital and social expenditure, into the foreseeable future. Here again is a reminder, if one was needed, that despite some modest successes in economic diversification, rents dominate the Qatari economy, and are likely to continue to do so for the duration of the hydrocarbon age.

Aviation: Qatar Airways

A final sector that is worth considering in the context of Qatari diversification and development is aviation, and dominating the sector is Qatar Airways. The national carrier is a dynamic, state-driven, and hybridly owned firm that is interesting in itself but also symbolic of a couple of key features of the Qatari political economy.

Qatar Airways was founded in 1993 and began operations in 1994.[101] It was a small, quite basic airline in its early years, operating leased aircraft and privately owned by members of the Al Thani family. In its first year, it expanded to serve multiple destinations in the Arab world, plus London and some South Asian cities. Its claimed aim was to provide Qatar with better international air links, which is probably true but masks the fact that Qataris by this time were becoming increasingly frustrated with Gulf Air, in which they had a 25 percent stake and which was not as aggressive or as helpful to shareholder states such as Abu Dhabi and Qatar as these shareholders wanted.[102] Qatar Airways then transformed itself in 1997 when it was relaunched under the same name but with a completely new management, with new branding, better services, a higher-quality feel and approach to capture Gulf and business travelers, and an aggressive market development and growth strategy.[103] It remained a privately owned airline at this stage, but was receiving state loans.[104] The state formally bought into the carrier in 1999, and now has a 50 percent stake in it.[105]

Thereafter the airline expanded still further and faster. The impact of the September 11, 2001, terrorist attacks in the United States was limited, and did not stop the airline's expansion plans or the upgrade of the terminal at Doha airport.[106] In fact, the airline's passenger numbers rose by 40 percent from 2001 to 2002—consistent with an average 35 percent increase in passengers per annum over 1998 to 2003[107]—and by this stage it was flying to some thirty-three destinations, although it still was not profitable.[108] Importantly, Qatar withdrew from Gulf Air in the same year. Gulf Air's management had asked for further capital, which in light of the development and likely success of Qatar Airways the government was not willing to provide. The remaining partners in Gulf Air—Abu Dhabi, Oman, and of course Bahrain—provided some of the requested capital and in so doing took over Qatar's 25 percent stake in Gulf Air.[109]

By 2010 and 2011 the airline was a regional and global carrier of some repute.[110] In 2011 it was named "Airline of the Year" by Skytrax, was serving a hundred destinations, had ninety-four aircraft in its fleet, and was continuing its expansion, all at a time when many other airlines were struggling for profitability due to continued sluggish economic growth in the United States and Europe. The airline ran multiple subsidiaries related to aviation, including a catering company, duty-free, and an aviation services firm. Crucially, in 2010–2011 it planned to record a profit for the first time; the lack of urgency to enter profitability had long been one of the criticisms leveled at it as it expanded rapidly. There have been rumors of a public float of at least part of the airline for some years, and of it launching a low-cost carrier to compete on the regional market, but both of these remain unlikely as long as the airline remains unprofitable. Such rumors may return to prominence in the early and middle 2010s if the airline can reach and sustain profitability.

Given this impressive rise and expansion, is Qatar Airways an example of successful non-oil diversification and the development of a globally competitive international firm by Qatar? The question is complicated by the profitability issue, which plagued the airline for some dozen years after its 1997 relaunch. The apparent indifference of its executive to profitability suggested both that it has some type of underlying guarantee from the government and its other shareholders, and that it viewed its mission as much in nonfinancial terms as in commercial ones. This latter explanation is potentially strong, since as with many such carriers, the airline has had a strong role in branding Qatar and acting as a national symbol. In this it has followed the example of Dubai's Emirates Airline, arguably also a flagship for its home city and country. Both airlines have had aggressive expansion goals, avoided airline alliances that might dilute the brand or any other uniqueness, and emphasized quality across all classes. In particular, they have shared some strategies too, especially in serving not just major centers but also secondary cities where there is no local carrier and high demand for international services to third ports. This is why several major airlines have been able to emerge in the Gulf—Emirates Airline, Qatar Airways, and Etihad—despite the region's relatively small market size: the major carriers, while not ignoring inbound and outbound travelers, have focused heavily on transit passengers, often traveling between secondary international points, thus allowing the carriers to serve a larger number of passengers than they could if they were focused only on their home base, and to build high passenger loads on very regular flights. It also means, crucially, that these airlines are only mildly competing with each other; they are competing much more with carriers based in other transit cities such as those in Southeast Asia, and with major carriers in Europe and Asia that focus on serving mostly large global cities.[111]

Even with Qatar Airways there is some link to the energy sector as well, although this is as much a feature of its ownership as it is of being in the aviation sector. The ports that the airline serves include major energy and financial centers, but also some less global (and less expected) ones, especially energy-centered cities such as Houston, Algiers, and Baku. This is partly linked to the strategy of serving secondary cities but is related to Qatar's energy-centeredness as well. Even more clearly, the state and royal family ownership is important in encouraging the airline to act as a national symbol, and to undertake initiatives that promote national interests. One example is a flight that the airline undertook from London to Doha on October 12, 2009, which used as fuel a mixture of kerosene and synthetic gas-to-liquid (GTL) fuel. The flight's aim was to demonstrate the viability of a fuel not refined from crude oil, to show what was possible with sophisticated natural gas processing. It served the government's aims of promoting that sector and, in so doing, linked it to the aviation sector. The airline's press release after the flight in effect said this, in quoting the then–deputy prime minister: "Qatar's position as the GTL capital of the world has been further enhanced with today's achievement [the Qatar Airways flight]. GTL technology enables us to produce liquid fuels and other products from natural gas. Commercial aviation is one of the exciting new markets that this opens up, helping us maximise the value from our natural resources."[112]

The airline does, however, also support diversification. In particular, Qatar has begun developing a more ambitious tourism strategy, which the airline will be integral in supporting. Previously, tourism was mostly centered on business travelers, conventions and other such work-related visits, education arrivals, and attracting visitors for major sporting and cultural events. These remain important, and Qatar is unlikely to give up its emphasis on higher-end tourism, but a US$20 billion tourism and culture strategy was unveiled in mid-2010 that nonetheless aimed to dramatically develop and expand the sector.[113] Part of this strategy was to expand the areas of current focus, as much of the funds were for new or upgraded cultural, exhibition, and supporting facilities. Some of this will flow through to other forms of tourism, including international leisure tourism, since the strategy also encourages high-end visitors, including a target of 5 percent of airline transit passengers staying for two days more than the usual layover.[114] These visitors are addressed through the development of cultural facilities such as galleries and museums, on top of business plans for new resorts and other such facilities. Qatar is also targeting new areas of inbound tourism growth, especially Asian tourists. In both its strategic approach and the type of visitors it is seeking, Qatar is different enough from regional competitors such as Dubai, Abu Dhabi, and Bahrain that the strategy of doubling the number of short-term visitors to Qatar may indeed work. Regardless, the expansion and strategy of Qatar Airways is vital to the pursuit of Qatar's tourism goals.

The State and Economic Diversification

Qatar has undertaken some substantial reform, but in a measured way, and only undertaking certain reform policies. It is very different in this regard than Dubai, despite the comparisons that are often made, including the claim that Qatar is "copying" Dubai; it is copying at best only some specific policies that seem suitable for transposition from one state to the other. Qatar perhaps looks somewhat similar to Dubai in terms of economic diversification and the development of sectors such as construction, transport, tourism, and finance. Indeed, Qatar's diversification strategy has been somewhat successful, more so than Dubai's, but its ultimate success is uncertain because the economy remains so energy centered. Very important in any comparison is to note that Qatar's diversification has been underwritten much more directly by rents than has Dubai's, and while debt levels in Qatar are not modest, overall the debt is of a far more desirable type than that which threatened Dubai's economy in 2008 and 2009.

Returning to the wider themes of the book, where Qatar is similar to Dubai is in the rentierism that underlies the state-society relationship—but a "late" rentierism with greater sophistication than the simple allocative bargains of the Gulf in the 1970s and 1980s—and in its state capitalism, but again a newer form in which the state is entrepreneurial and friendly toward business that is involved in areas of the economy that do not threaten the state's interests and indeed that the state is seeking to develop.

Despite the enormous growth of the economy since 2000, despite the successes of economic diversification, and despite the sophistication of the political economy and of society that has evolved, the fact remains that Qatar's political economy is still dominated and overwhelmingly controlled by a small elite of royals, well-connected merchants, and a few other key families. This elite has deliberately paced reform and selectively chosen what reforms will and will not be undertaken, because the ultimate aim is to preserve the current political and economic arrangements, even if the scope is also present to develop new opportunities for other actors and to expand the size of this elite somewhat. The overarching rentierism and state capitalism are unlikely to change, however, for this reason. Related to this also is the dynamic of national branding and image—and the promotion of these for economic as well as political ends—to which this book turns next.

Notes

1. As noted in Moin Siddiqi, "Qatar Stands Firm in the Face of Global Financial Storm," *The Middle East,* July 2009, p. 47, citing several reports on Qatar in 2009 by international investment banks.

2. Moin Siddiqi, "Investing in the Growth Revival," *The Middle East,* December 2010, p. 29.

3. QNB Capital, *Qatar Economic Review 2010,* p. 5.

4. Hanouz and Khatib, *The Arab World Competitiveness Review, 2010,* pp. 9, 46–47.

5. Schwab, *The Global Competitiveness Report, 2010–2011,* p. 16.

6. Ibid., pp. 15, 282; Hanouz and Khatib, *The Arab World Competitiveness Review, 2010,* pp. 9, 46. Also noted in Hvidt, "Economic Diversification in the Gulf Arab States," p. 49.

7. Schwab, *The Global Competitiveness Report, 2010–2011,* p. 37.

8. "Rebalancing the Labour Load," *Middle East Economic Digest,* April 21, 2006.

9. Ibid.

10. Qatar General Secretariat for Development Planning, *Qatar National Vision 2030,* p. 5.

11. Ibid., p. 6.

12. Ibid.

13. Martin Hvidt has published widely on the idea of a "Dubai model." See, for example, "The Dubai Model" and "Economic and Institutional Reforms in the Arab Gulf Countries."

14. Qatar General Secretariat for Development Planning, *Qatar National Vision 2030,* p. 15.

15. Ibid., pp. 13–14.

16. Maloney, "The Gulf's Renewed Oil Wealth."

17. Qatar General Secretariat for Development Planning, *Qatar National Vision 2030,* p. 6.

18. Ibid., p. 8.

19. Ibid., p. 13.

20. The economic liberalization debate in itself is background to the issues being considered here and therefore beyond the scope of this book. However, for

details see, among many works on the topic, Henry and Springborg, *Globalization and the Politics of Development in the Middle East;* Heydemann, *Networks of Privilege in the Middle East;* the older but still useful Harik and Sullivan, *Privatization and Liberalization in the Middle East;* and Richards and Waterbury, *A Political Economy of the Middle East,* especially chaps. 8–9 (pp. 205–250).

21. Khaled Alderbesti, a senior official at the Ministry of Economy and Commerce, quoted in Siddiqi, "Qatar Stands Firm in the Face of Global Financial Storm," p. 48.

22. Gina Coleman, "Qatar Survey," *The Middle East,* August 1998, pp. 23–30; "Qatar: Sheikh Hamad Bin Khalifa Al Thani," *Middle East Economic Digest,* September 22, 2003.

23. "Qatar: Sheikh Hamad Bin Khalifa Al Thani."

24. "Special Report: Qatar," *Middle East Economic Digest,* March 10, 2000.

25. This was under Law no. 5 of 1963. Much of the discussion here on foreign ownership law reform is from Glenn O'Brien and Alexis Waller, "Changes in Qatar Property Ownership Law," October 2007, http://www.clydeco.com/knowledge/articles/changes-in-qatar-property-ownership-law.cfm.

26. Its full name was Law no. 17 of 2004 Regulating Ownership and Usufruct of Real Estate and Residential Units by Non-Qataris, and was also known as the Foreign Ownership of Real Estate Law.

27. Latham and Watkins, *Doing Business in Qatar,* December 2009, online at http://www.lw.com/upload/pubContent/_pdf/pub2782_1.pdf.

28. "Investor Security in Qatar," *Middle East Economic Digest,* December 3, 2004.

29. Ibid.

30. Specifically in 2006, promulgation of Telecommunications Law no. 34.

31. Much of what follows is taken from "Competitor Shakes Up Market," *Middle East Economic Digest,* September 17, 2010.

32. The precise ownership of Vodafone Qatar is 40 percent public, based on its listing on the Qatar Exchange; 15 percent by Qatari institutional investors (the Qatar Foundation, the Military Pension Fund, and others); with the remaining 45 percent owned 51-to-49 by the Qatar Foundation and Vodafone Group. See the "Shareholder Structure" page on the Vodafone Qatar website, at http://www.vodafone.com.qa/go/en/investorrelations/shareinformation/shareholderstructure.

33. Much of the following detail is from Deloitte Qatar, "International Tax and Business Guide: Qatar—Highlights," January 2011, http://www.deloitte.com/assets/Dcom-Global/Local%20Assets/Documents/Tax/Intl%20Tax%20and%20Business%20Guides/2011/dtt_tax_highlight_2011_Qatar.pdf; and Leigh Hall, Julian Pope, and Martin Brown, "The Qatar Update: Supplement—Tax Law no. (21) of 2009: Key Provisions," April 23, 2010, http://www.mondaq.com/x/95778/Corporate+Tax/The+Qatar+Update+Supplement+Tax+Law+No+21+of+2009+Key+Provisions.

34. Hall, Pope, and Brown, "The Qatar Update."

35. QNB Capital, *Qatar Economic Review 2010,* p. 52; Moin Siddiqi, "Qatar: A Beacon of Stability in Troubled Times," *The Middle East,* June 2010, p. 38;

Siddiqi, "Qatar Stands Firm in the Face of Global Financial Storm," p. 48; Latham and Watkins, *Doing Business in Qatar,* pp. 4–6.

36. Siddiqi, "Qatar: A Beacon of Stability," p. 38.

37. World Bank, *Doing Business in the Arab World, 2011*.

38. Ibid., p. 17.

39. Ibid., p. 35.

40. "Qatar: Managing the Spending Spree," *Middle East Economic Digest,* February 7, 2003.

41. "Qatar Poised for Take-Off," *The Middle East,* August–September 2006, p. 42.

42. Ibid.

43. QNB Capital, *Qatar Economic Review 2010,* p. 28.

44. Shadi Hamid, "The Qatar Model: A New Way Forward in the Middle East?" *The Atlantic,* December 13, 2010, http://www.theatlantic.com/international/archive/2010/12/the-qatar-model-a-new-way-forward-for-the-middle-east/67908; and "Qatar's 2022 Rail Challenge," *Middle East Economic Digest,* February 18, 2011.

45. "State Supports Property Sector," *Middle East Economic Digest,* November 19, 2010.

46. Ibid.

47. Ibid.

48. Donn and al-Manthri, *Globalisation and Higher Education in the Arab Gulf States,* p. 49.

49. Ibid.

50. Champion, *The Paradoxical Kingdom,* pp. 200–202. Daryl Champion was writing on the case of Saudi Arabia, although other writers, both scholars and journalists, have argued a similar thing without using the term "*mudir* syndrome." Another source that cites Champion makes the point that employment is part of an individual's identity, and so it is natural for people to seek out certain roles. This source also is focused on Saudi Arabia, but the point could be made of Qatar (or almost anywhere) too; see Bensahel and Byman, *The Future Security Environment in the Middle East,* pp. 113–114. This issue was also raised by some Western managers and employers in Doha during my interviews with them in October 2011.

51. Brewer et al., *Education for a New Era,* p. 20.

52. See the Qatar General Secretariat for Development Planning, Department of Social Affairs, "Social and Human Development Profile no. 2: Features of Education in Qatar—Trends and Patterns," p. 3.

53. Donn and al-Manthri, *Globalisation and Higher Education,* p. 50.

54. See Wendy Wallace, "Qatar Invests in a Vision," *The Middle East,* July 2005, pp. 58–59; and Brewer et al., *Education for a New Era,* throughout but especially pp. 57–89. On progress in the policy, see RAND-Qatar Policy Institute, "Qatar's K–12 Education Reform Has Achieved Success in Its Early Years," research brief, 2009, http://www.rand.org/content/dam/rand/pubs/research_briefs/2009/RAND_RB9455.pdf.

55. Wallace, "Qatar Invests in a Vision," p. 58.

56. Ibid.

57. RAND-Qatar Policy Institute, "Qatar's K–12 Education Reform Has Achieved Success."

58. Donn and al-Manthri, *Globalisation and Higher Education,* p. 50.

59. For more, see the education section of the Qatar Foundation website, at http://www.qf.org.qa/education.

60. "Developing a Meritocracy," *Middle East Economic Digest,* March 18, 2005; "Special Report: Qatar—Education City," *Middle East Economic Digest,* October 17, 2003.

61. "Qatar: New Hospital and Research Centre for Education City," *Middle East Economic Digest,* June 25, 2004.

62. "Special Report: Qatar—Education City."

63. For details on the QNRF, see Greenfield et al., *Design of the Qatar National Research Fund.*

64. For details on the reforms, see Moini et al., *The Reform of Qatar University,* throughout but especially pp. 33–69.

65. "Developing a Meritocracy."

66. From the "About QNB" page of the QNB website, at http://www.qnb.com.qa/csportal/qnb/innerPage.jsp?currentPage=QNBHistory&LangPref=en.

67. Ibid.

68. Omar M. el-Quqa et al., *Qatar Banking Sector,* p. 6; and QNB Capital, *The Qatari Banking Sector 2009,* available online at http://www.qnb.sy/csportal/BlobServer?blobcol=urlenglishdoc&blobtable=QNBNewDocs&blobkey=id&blobwhere=1246522745172&blobheader=application%2Fpdf.

69. QNB Capital, *The Qatari Banking Sector 2009.*

70. Ibid.

71. For details, see the Qatar Development Bank website, http://www.qdb.com.qa.

72. "*MEED* Stock Markets Special Report: Qatar," *Middle East Economic Digest,* February 9, 1998.

73. "Special Report: Qatar—Banking," *Middle East Economic Digest,* March 9, 2001.

74. "Qatar: Debut Bond Issue Delayed," *Middle East Economic Digest,* July 6, 1998.

75. "Special Report: Qatar—Project Finance: Taking Credit from All Sides," *Middle East Economic Digest,* March 12, 2004; "Bonding for the Future," *Middle East Economic Digest,* June 9, 2006.

76. Pamela Ann Smith, "Interview with Shashank Srivastava, Acting CEO, Qatar Financial Centre," *The Middle East,* October 2010, p. 47.

77. From the "History of QIC" page of the QIC website, at http://www.qatarinsurance.com/site/topics/static.asp?cu_no=1&lng=0&template_id=499&temp_type=42&parent_id=498.

78. Ibid.

79. David Anthony, Neil Gosrani, and Jan Willem Plantagie, "The Qatari Insurance Sector in 2009: Short-Term Weaknesses Offset by Long-Term Strengths," *Standard & Poor's RatingsDirect,* January 26, 2009, p. 3.

80. These were American Insurance (established in 1963), Arabian Insurance (1966), Lebanon-Suisse Insurance (1966), and the National Insurance Company of Egypt (1969).

81. "Qatar: Time to End the Roller-Coaster Ride," *Middle East Economic Digest,* June 6, 2003.

82. Smith, "Interview with Shashank Srivastava," p. 49.

83. Anthony et al., "The Qatari Insurance Sector in 2009," p. 3.

84. "May Day Moment for Qatar's New Financial Centre," *Middle East Economic Digest,* April 29, 2005; "Legal Briefing: Qatar Financial Centre—QFC Seeks to Benefit from Good Foundations," *Middle East Economic Digest,* October 14, 2005.

85. "May Day Moment for Qatar's New Financial Centre."

86. Ibid.; "Legal Briefing."

87. "Board Appointed to Run Qatar Financial Centre," *Middle East Economic Digest,* April 28, 2006.

88. "Qatar Financial Centre: One of a Kind," *Middle East Economic Digest,* October 14, 2005; "Legal Briefing." See also the QFC regulatory authority's 2011 brochure "A Guide to the Qatar Financial Centre Authority," available online at http://www.qfc.com.qa/Files/Brochures%202011/Final%20General%20Brochure%20(low%20resolution).pdf.

89. "Rewriting the Rules," *Middle East Economic Digest,* July 20, 2007.

90. Pamela Ann Smith, "Qatar's Banks: Navigating the Storm," *The Middle East,* August–September 2009, p. 42.

91. Ibid.

92. For example, QNB's sharia-compliant window accounted for about 20 percent of the market and about 15 percent of QNB's profits, assets, and deposits. Robin Wigglesworth, "Islamic Directive Shocks Qatari Banks," February 14, 2011, http://www.ft.com/intl/cms/s/0/0ab164e0-3858-11e0-8257-00144feabdc0.html#axzz1VNNBfVBS.

93. Wigglesworth, "Islamic Directive Shocks Qatari Banks."

94. Author interviews, Doha, October 2011.

95. Chatham House, *The Gulf as a Global Financial Centre,* p. 34.

96. Ibid.

97. Mark Yeandle et al., "The Global Financial Centres Index 9," March 2011, p. 20, http://www.zyen.com/GFCI/GFCI%209.pdf.

98. "Qatar Overtakes Dubai for Investment," *Middle East Economic Digest,* February 6, 2009.

99. See International Monetary Fund, "Qatar: 2010 Article IV Consultation," Country Report no. 11/64, pp. 19–20.

100. Ibid., p. 30.

101. What follows on the period 1993–1997 is from "*MEED* Special Report on Aviation: Qatar Airways—New National Carrier Heads for the Sky," *Middle East Economic Digest,* August 29, 1994.

102. This was a quiet complaint in the United Arab Emirates at the time, too, and accounted in part for the earlier creation of Emirates Airline in Dubai in the 1980s, when Gulf Air refused to expand, and actually cut, services to Dubai.

103. Angus Hindley, "Special: Aviation—Qatar Airways: New Team Revamp and Relaunch," *Middle East Economic Digest,* June 2, 1997.

104. Ibid.

105. Angus Hindley, "Special: Aviation—Qatar Airways: Upmarket Move Is Starting to Pay Back," *Middle East Economic Digest,* May 31, 1999; and the Qatar Airways briefing "The Qatar Airways Story," July 2011, available online at http://www.qatarairways.com/global/en/newsroom/presskits/qr-story-jul11.pdf.

106. "Special Report: Aerospace—Qatar Airways," *Middle East Economic Digest,* November 9, 2001.

107. "Special Report: Qatar—Qatar Airways: In for the Long Haul," *Middle East Economic Digest,* October 17, 2003.

108. "Qatar Airways Takes Off," *Middle East Economic Digest,* May 24, 2002.

109. "Qatar Exits Gulf Air," *Middle East Economic Digest,* May 31, 2002.

110. What follows is from "Qatar Airways Declares Profit Breakthrough, Roll on IPO," December 22, 2010, http://www.centreforaviation.com/news/2010/12/22/a-profit-breakthrough-for-qatar-airways-roll-on-ipo/page1; the Qatar Airways briefing "The Qatar Airways Story"; and other company information available on the Qatar Airways website at http://www.qatarairways.com/uk/en/ceo-message.html.

111. "Briefing: Aviation in the Gulf," *The Economist,* June 5, 2010.

112. "World's First Commercial Passenger Flight Powered by Fuel Made from Natural Gas Lands in Qatar," Qatar Airways press release, October 12, 2009, available online at http://www.qatarairways.com/global/en/newsroom/archive/press-release-12Oct09-2.html.

113. Pamela Ann Smith, "Qatar Pledges $20 billion for Tourism and Culture," *The Middle East,* July 2010.

114. See the "Vision & Strategy" page on the Qatar Tourism Authority website, at http://www.qatartourism.gov.qa/about/index/1.

6

The Strategy of National Branding

Qatar is a small state, and by most measures definable as a microstate in both geographic and demographic terms. This, to a certain extent, accounts for the attempts by the Qatari government to "brand" the country with a particular global image: an image of an economically successful, globalizing, pro-business, and independent state. It is also the reason why it has followed an independent foreign policy, which mixes a close strategic relationship with the United States with close economic and other ties with other regional actors, including Iran.

Most states and governments seek to undertake some form of national "branding." It is usually the purpose behind major national facilities such as museums, art galleries, and the like, and often a consideration in the architecture of public buildings, too, such as government offices, bridges, universities, and other such visible national socioeconomic assets. What is important about the branding of Qatar is not that it occurs, but that it occurs to such an extent and in such a strategic way as it does. Important also is the centrality of economic and commercial concerns to this branding. The branding is not done solely, or even primarily, out of state- or nation-building concerns, even if they are also a (rather minor) aspect of it, but instead is an attempt to communicate with the Qatari population and the international community. Branding links to the emir's reformist agenda and the image that the regime attaches to that. Stemming from this, the branding also seeks to increase the commercial and diplomatic attention that Qatar receives, thus attracting investment, trade, and cultural linkages that will sustain and consolidate the Al Thani power base and underwrite the security required by the country as a microstate to survive and develop—and for the Al Thani dynasty to thrive too, of course.

What follows is a discussion of these themes, and various case studies either where a political economy actor is used for branding and national image efforts or where issues of branding impact the political economy or create a dynamic of it. There is a discussion of some sectors that so far have not been given much attention in their own right, such as the mass media, specifically Al-Jazeera; the sports sector, including Qatar's successful bid for the 2022 World Cup and its attempts to host a Summer Olympic Games; and public spaces such as the redevelopment of the old Souq Waqif markets and initiatives such as the development of the Museum of Islamic Art. The aim, however, is to consider them particularly in light of their central roles in branding Qatar. They all play key roles in the attempt to show Qatar to the world as a developing, open society that has managed to retain its culture and values, and in so doing, to enhance both the security and the prospects of the country and its political elite.

Why and How Qatar Is Branded

At its simplest, the discussion here about Qatar as a "brand" or as a state that is "branding" itself refers to the attempts by the state and regime to create unique and distinctive characteristics or features that will make Qatar more recognizable and, in effect, more favorably viewed and valuable than otherwise.[1] It is similar to the way in which firms create and brand products or services, or brand the firm itself. However, this branding, in being done around a nation-state, is typically more vague in its imagery and more general in approach; that is, things such as color or appearance that are important in branding a physical product in the case of a nation-state are supplanted by factors (and goals) such as name recognition, positive mass media discussion, foreign visits to the country, and uses by foreigners of products from the country (as examples, in the case of Qatar, passenger numbers on Qatar Airways, television viewers of Al-Jazeera or of major sporting events being hosted by Qatar, and suchlike). As with physical products, branding a state includes not only creating factual knowledge about it but also creating a positive or pleasant feeling around it, which in turns increases both the uniqueness and the desirability of the state "brand."[2] Thus, many of the efforts to brand Qatar involve functional decisions not only about what will seem a positive attribute or action by the state but also about how the country will be remembered by those who engage with it at some level, and about how intangible aspects of its image and brand will be interpreted across cultures and time. Being seen in a positive light is important, but so too is being *remembered* in such a light and associated with other positive images or experiences.[3]

There is an attempt, therefore, to construct a specific and unique image of Qatar in the mind of influential foreigners, such as businesspeople, diplomats, senior public officials, academics, journalists, and others, and to reiterate this image repeatedly until it becomes in effect a consolidated "brand"—a particular and cohesive image and feel attached to the idea of the country. This brand is distinct from that of other Gulf states—even if many people, especially Westerners, still assume that Qatar and Dubai are similar or even near identical—and from that of other microstates. Qatar's status as a microstate is important because, as with most other micro- and small states, there is a perceived need by such states to build international linkages, ensure strategic or other protective alliances, and create economic niches that fit with regional or global economic needs so as to guarantee the economic success and, in some cases, even the continued political viability of the state and its ruling regime. Such states are variously defined but usually have a limited geographic and demographic size and a small number of economic specializations that set them apart from larger, more diverse economies.[4] Most scholarly focus has been given to the microstates of the Pacific and the Caribbean, typically with populations of under 250,000 or so, and of tiny geographic size. Yet the research on other states beyond the Gulf suggests that there are in fact benefits to be gained from states that are small in size but that possess clear economic strategies or that link in well with regional blocs or the regional economy.[5]

Each brand created by a microstate, however, has to be unique, and Qatar since the mid-1990s has realized this and sought to build a unique brand based on real or constructed images of political and media freedom, active diplomatic engagement in the Middle East, economic openness and a willingness to host investment in most sectors, and a desire to globalize and socially adapt to technological and social change, albeit on the country's own cultural terms.

The construction of Qatar's national image and brand, and the nature of that image, derive from both a nationbuilding goal and economic imperatives, in turn linked to the international security environment that is faced by the ruling elite. At its most basic and fundamental level, it serves to ensure the political survival of the Al Thani dynasty, especially more recently Hamad's wing of the family, now entrenched in the constitution as the emiri line. National image supports the regime and its legitimacy more generally by assisting in the development and diversification of the economy, creating a larger segment of the domestic population and a larger pool of international actors who have a stake in the long-term survival and stability of the country.

While most states seek to project a positive image internationally and domestically, Qatar's national branding has been especially strong and prominent, and is an international public relations strategy by a reformist emir and his elite. By promoting the image of a comparatively very free and liberal mass media and through hosting international sporting, cultural, and other events, the political elite send a powerful message of reformism and openness both to the Qatari population and to the wider world. This is not unimportant—the emir and the political elite, like Qataris in general, genuinely care about their personal and family image and reputation and, at a national level, about the country's international image[6]—but it is not the sole reason for the emphasis that has been placed on branding under Hamad. Image and branding also link the emir, in the minds of the population, to major events and to Qatar assuming a global economic, diplomatic, and cultural role; again, this is important in itself at a base political level.

At a simple but important level, there is a direct element of branding in the ways in which the national colors—maroon and white—are used by ministries and state-sponsored bodies in their promotional activities. These colors come from the current and previous national flag and ensign.[7] They are used quite consistently by key government ministries, national carrier Qatar Airways, the Qatar Investment Authority, and state-supported bodies such as the Qatar Olympic Committee, the Qatar Financial Center Authority, and others. Even the Qatar Football Association uses these colors.[8] While many states do this type of thing, Qatar's small size and even smaller political elite make the coherent use of such colors and other symbols especially easy to achieve.

There are in fact more specific tactics behind the way in which Qatar has been branded as it has, and the extent to which this has been done. These ultimately have economic and commercial aims, even if the extent to which economics, versus factors such as security and nationalism and nationbuilding, drives them varies. At one level, of course, if Qatar is to be considered in part a large family business—an economy that is disproportionately owned by and revolves around the emir and the Al Thani family—then branding is, in effect, a business development tactic. Foreign investors are encouraged into certain sectors (and of course not some others), and to attract them and send a message that Qatar is a secure and stable investment destination, branding becomes important. Thus some of the messages from key figures inviting links with the outside world are, in their "marketing" message, partly an attempt at branding or very close to one. A statement by the emir is one such example: "In addition to the increased attention we are paying to the various aspects of human development, the strategy [the *Qatar National Vision 2030*] reflects our keenness to improve economic infrastructure and diversification, expand the production cycle, secure sound management of our financial resources and protect the environment."[9] It is not surprising that he should say something like this, but at regular opportunities he stresses the range of initiatives that Qatar is undertaking under his stewardship, and often links initiatives that elsewhere might be considered separate, for example trade promotion, diplomacy, and environmental protectionism. In a similar vein, others with a role in promoting the country do likewise, for example the acting chief executive officer of the Qatar Financial Centre (QFC) in late 2010:

> Qatar is opening itself up to the world across many fields. These include culture, education and sport—for example, our bid [since successful] to host the World Cup in 2022. We are also striving to become an attractive destination for international investment, one of the world's leading locations for international business and finance and a pre-eminent financial services marketplace. Our goals may seem at first to be somewhat ambitious, but we have no doubt that we will achieve them.[10]

In seeking more specifically to attract international investment and business, Qatar's minister of economy and commerce said explicitly in 2005: "The story of Qatar is selling the QFC: people realize that Qatar has a good story to tell. That is a blessing in the marketing."[11] There is, in other words, a marketing narrative for the country as a whole, which gives it a unique brand that can be applied to specific initiatives.

Another interesting example is from a 2009 interview by the German newspaper *Der Spiegel* with Emir Hamad, in which the emir talks about wanting to see low oil prices during the global financial crisis in order to support the world economic recovery. The language in the interview and the seeming magnanimity of the emir were, again, very close to branding in terms of the intended impact of the message on how the country is seen abroad, and were also delivered adroitly:

> *Spiegel:* How do you believe oil prices will develop now?
>
> *Hamad:* I think the oil price should continue (to stay) in the $40 range for at least one or two more years.
>
> *Spiegel:* Why so modest?
>
> *Hamad:* Because this way we can help the world out of this crisis. If the world economy recovers, it will be good for us, too. Automati-

> cally, the price of oil will go up again. I don't see why OPEC countries should continue to cut production just to keep the price of oil high. This will not affect the industrial countries alone, it will also hit poor countries in Africa, Asia and Latin America. Who will look after them?
>
> *Spiegel:* That's not the kind of argument you often hear when talking to oil producers.
>
> *Hamad:* Yes, but I believe this battle is a battle for the whole world. Everybody should be helping each other for the next two years.[12]

This was a stroke of marketing genius and good for the Qatari brand. In his sentiments in the interview, the emir was, in effect, expressing solidarity with those economies that were suffering from the global financial crisis and were fearful, at that time, of a return to the high oil prices of the previous year. Given the political sensitivities of petroleum retail prices in most Western markets, and the perception among some that the Gulf was profiteering, this claim that Qatar not only was sympathetic to consumers in these markets but also shared the same view about the ideal price level for crude oil was very cleverly made. Similarly, the comment also targeted developing states. It demonstrates the importance of international ties and image to Qatar and its emir, for branding and ultimately for foreign relations as well, which link into its search for international physical and economic security, which in turn will underwrite the regime's domestic legitimacy and stability.

In fact, this international focus of branding links to specific economic initiatives too, such as the diversification goal discussed in Chapter 5 and the attempts at greater "Qatarization" (i.e., indigenization) of the work force. In terms of diversification, put crudely, more foreign investment and business activity in more diverse economic areas feeds into the regime's survival: it creates employment in new areas of the economy, including at senior and professional levels for Qataris; it consolidates and flattens out the financial base and rental income of the regime, allowing for a continuity and greater predictability in the funding of major initiatives—most with a branding element to them—as well as protecting the rentier bargain with society; and as a link to Qatar's national security, a better international brand that increases trade and investment will thus lead to a larger pool of international investors and businesspeople with a stake in the stability of Qatar and its regime.

Cultural initiatives and international cultural links, and major events that receive transnational news coverage or broadcasting, all also serve to create an image of Qatar as a defined, specific state, and in turn serve to offer both economic opportunities and regime consolidation. At their crudest, cultural initiatives such as the development of the Museum of Islamic Art—now one of the best such collections anywhere in the world—are about branding and international image, as most museums, galleries, and other cultural production with a link to nationalism or national identity typically are. They take on a special importance for a state such as Qatar, however, which is relatively new and still underdeveloped in its popular sense of national identity. To some, especially in the West, Qatar is still often confused culturally with neighboring states, or simply seen as a place that was, prior to oil, mostly undeveloped and nomadic and that thus possesses little unique history. Much of the effort that has gone into the museums and public spaces such as the Souq Waqif has been designed to address and, where possible, counter this impression. These efforts are discussed in depth shortly.

Qatar's bids to host major sporting events such as the 2022 World Cup, and its continuing attempts to host a Summer Olympic Games, are similarly efforts at branding through major events and the publicity and attention that such events receive. Its hosting of the fifteenth Asian Games in 2006 was the first time that it deliberately used a major event to showcase the country and its achievements and raise awareness of it abroad.[13] More specifically, it sends a message to Qataris and foreigners alike that the country and its political leadership are not simply accepting globalization and economic change on Western terms but also responding to globalization actively and creatively, and reconfiguring Qatar socially (and by implication, politically and economically) to benefit from change.[14] The benefits of this internationally are obvious, as are the effects of it on the domestic political legitimacy and support enjoyed by the emir, who attaches himself to these events very prominently. Likewise, the art and culture initiatives, on which the emir has spent a massive sum, have been designed at least in part for the publicity message attached to them, namely that Doha is "a cosmopolitan city where artists and patrons from both East and West mingle."[15] Thus such initiatives are, coincidentally or not, useful politically as well. One report on Qatar after the 2011 Arab Spring demonstrated this in effect when the reporter noted that "the few young Qataris I met showed far more interest in the country's sudden emergence as a 'country that matters,' as one young woman put it, than in its becoming more democratic. The Arab Youth Survey . . . found that 88 percent of young Qataris thought their country was 'going in the right direction.'"[16] Of course, such cultural activities furthermore link into commercial goals and are impacted by commercial considerations, which in turn broaden the economy and strengthen the rule of the emir; they form part of the emir's attempts at economic diversification of course,[17] while a higher profile is generally useful not only in cultural terms but in commercial ones as well, whether from flying visitors into the country, building the business links to support the events, or simply making potential investors aware of the country.[18]

Finally, branding links into the national security and foreign relations imperatives and goals that are the focus of the next chapter. These stem from Qatar's microstatism too, since the state does not have the means to defend itself adequately against major external actors, and indeed is worried about the nonmilitary but politically important threat of undue Saudi influence over its policies and activities. A creative and active foreign policy, and strong defense ties to a major power, are therefore essential. At the most basic level, the regime is also seeking to avoid domestic threats, too, concerned as it is about foreign intervention through domestic opponents such as some distant parts of the Al Thani family and some politically marginalized tribes and families. As noted in Chapter 4, joint ventures in the gas sector in particular can be seen as possessing a strategic element, given that partnerships have been formed with most major international energy firms. This is also a political goal—if not the main one—behind economic diversification, since the regime is seeking to globalize the economy and expand inward investment so that firms based in major economic and military powers have a long-term interest in Qatar.[19] Finally, Qatar has chosen its foreign relations, especially its diplomatic and strategic engagement, carefully. It has links to the US military for, primarily, the favor and military security that come from hosting a global superpower, but it also maintains quite close commercial relations with Iran, and increasingly with emerging powers, especially China, in the diplomatic and above all economic realms.

Al-Jazeera: The Political Economy of Branding by Media

When looking at the question of branding, the first example that is cited when Qatar is discussed in contemporary media and academic circles is usually Al-Jazeera. It is, in fact, probably the thing for which Qatar is still best-known in the West, and in the Middle East for that matter. It is not the aim here to discuss in much detail, except where relevant, the role of Al-Jazeera as a media group or the international relations impacts of its operations, since these have been investigated in depth elsewhere.[20] Rather, the aim is to look at how Al-Jazeera is used as a tool to brand Qatar internationally, and for that matter to enhance the regime's impression at home among the population, and to consider how this branding impacts the political economy dynamics of Qatar and supports its existing political structures.

The creation of Al-Jazeera was one of Hamad's first major acts after seizing power. The media firm was established and commenced operations in 1996, modeled in terms of its appearance, editorial style, and willingness to entertain multiple viewpoints and controversy on major Western news and current affairs broadcasters such as CNN. It is fully state owned, controlled by Qatar Media Corporation, which owns most of Qatar's domestic media as well. Al-Jazeera began operations as an Arabic satellite television broadcaster, focused on news and current affairs, and not coincidentally it was established at around the same time that the Ministry of Information was abolished and press freedoms were enhanced. In effect, it represented a first stage of what many saw as Qatar's political liberalization—a liberalization that was at some levels quite genuine and important, even if the much deeper political reforms that many expected would follow thus far have not so been.

Al-Jazeera has become something of a trendsetter for Arab media since its establishment. It expanded its operations to twenty-four-hour daily broadcasting quite quickly, as well as sharply increasing its reach to subscribers across the Arab world and beyond. It became almost a household name across the Middle East and in the West after the terrorist events of September 11, 2001, when it reported from Kabul and CNN was given use of this reportage. It also gained notoriety after its offices in Kabul were hit by US bombs on November 13, 2011, and especially after a similar US air strike on its Baghdad office on April 1, 2003, killed Tareq Ayyoub, one of its journalists. Since its early years it has transformed into a much broader media firm, developing its online offerings and starting additional news and other channels in other languages. It began publishing online in English in 2003, and launched an English-language television news channel in 2006. It also has multiple sports channels, a children's channel, a documentary channel, and others. By 2010 it was a truly international media firm, with several main broadcasting offices around the world, some 3,000 staff at its headquarters and at sixty-five bureaus worldwide, and reaching into some 220 million households in over a hundred countries, and it had in place plans for yet further expansion of its offerings.[21]

However, despite its success at these levels, it is difficult to see Al-Jazeera as exclusively or even primarily a commercial creation of the Qatari state. It loses money, and has done so throughout its existence, occasionally needing to have its coffers topped up by the Qatari government. There is some validity to the argument that this is a feature of media in the wealthier Arab states, where paid subscriptions to media are for the most part unpopular and outlets therefore often require state support.[22] Al-Jazeera certainly is not alone in receiving state financial support. However, there are other explanations for Al-Jazeera, and the political goals that lie behind it, all of which either contain an element of, or contribute to, the goal of national branding and the redevelopment of the state's and emir's image domestically and abroad.

In considering the political goals behind Al-Jazeera, most commentators begin with the timing and manner of its creation. Indeed, it was clearly intended by the emir that Al-Jazeera would send a political message both to the Qatari people and to key international actors, including presumably the United States and major Western governments, but probably to international business actors as well.[23] It was part of the emir's image-construction to expand and liberalize the media, while at the same time to dismantle the Ministry of Information. Hamad's first decade or so in power was a time of political liberalization in general, and Al-Jazeera was both a sign of this liberalization and an actor through which the emir's reform ideas and agenda were transmitted, and through which the emir's name could be attached to them.

At the same time, it is important not to overstate these reforms. In terms of political change, the introduction of a popularly elected parliament did not occur in the early 2000s as long promised and expected. In the media sector specifically, all publishers and broadcasters, including Al-Jazeera, have remained subject to the strict print and publication law of 1979 throughout Hamad's rule to date, despite promises to enact new, more up-to-date legislation. Above all, the reformist nature of Al-Jazeera has never been absolute. Domestic political issues, especially controversies involving the royal family, such as Hamad's legal battles with the deposed father or issues of corruption, remain unaddressed by the channel.[24] Moreover, there remains some censorship and bullying of the media,[25] albeit on a fairly modest scale compared with much else of the region. To some this is a sign that Al-Jazeera is still operating within an (albeit soft) authoritarian environment and with less profound change occurring than many proponents of such media will claim,[26] while for others it more innocuously shows the international focus of the channel and the lack of interest in Qatar's politics, a topic that to most viewers outside the country is, to put it bluntly, very boring.[27]

Other factors were behind the creation of Al-Jazeera. The channel was also a method through which the emir could expand Qatar's international role; in effect, Al-Jazeera is an international relations actor. First and most, of course, it was an international publicity vehicle just as it was a domestic one, sending a message of media freedom and political change and dynamism to the Arab world and, later, beyond. It was also a tool through which Qatar could compete regionally; famously, it has often challenged Saudi Arabia's strategic and political dominance over the smaller shaikhdoms on the Arab side of the Gulf. In so doing, Al-Jazeera has managed to offend the Al Saud family more than once, especially in its early years when Abdallah, then crown prince of Saudi Arabia and now king, objected to it directly to Emir Hamad.[28] It has offended a range of other states, several of which have expelled its reporters or closed its offices in their countries.[29] While upsetting other states may seem contradictory to the goal of using Al-Jazeera as a foreign policy tool and to promote Qatar's external image, in fact it was still very useful in this regard. It sent a message that Qatar and its emir were planning to act independently, and with a stronger commitment to political freedoms than to diplomatic sensitivities. That it was popular in the Arab world also gave Qatar's image an enormous boon in the region, in effect making Al-Jazeera, as a tool for national branding, a public diplomacy actor. Finally, important as the relationship with the United States is for the emir and ruling elite, the United States could hardly complain about the freedom of speech that the channel promoted, even if the messages conveyed by that freedom at times have angered US leaders.

It is also likely that the emir intended Al-Jazeera to be an economic actor within Qatar, although this was probably a much more minor consideration in its establishment compared to its publicity potential. Still, it offered some benefits for the Qatari political economy beyond image. Perhaps most important, prior to 1996 the Qatari state had very conventional state capacity vis-à-vis society. It had a basic repressive capability, in particular, but a relatively modest one even compared to that of most other Arab Gulf states. At the same time, its co-optive mechanisms were impressive and (normally) very large in terms of economic largesse, although the economic strains of the late 1990s have in fact been proposed as a source for the emir's emphasis on political reforms at that time.[30] However, despite this capacity, the ability to influence opinion through state discourse and narrative, and to influence societal impressions of those in power, was both very conventional and very limited. The old state apparatus of a Ministry of Information had become less and less effective, and by the 1990s was virtually useless in promoting state legitimacy, while conventional media lacked dynamism and more traditional state-society networks (whether tribes and families, or institutions such as civil society bodies) were comparatively weak. In this sense the creation of Al-Jazeera can be viewed as an outcome of Qatar's late rentier structure. Oil and gas rents provided the state with the repressive capability and financial co-optation capacity that have always characterized rentier states, but the pressures of rent fluctuations and a desire to respond proactively (or be seen to be so doing) to regional and global change encouraged Qatar's late rentier leader to redefine the role of the media and in so doing to create and strengthen newer areas of state capacity.

Other initiatives beyond Al-Jazeera have served a similar political purpose for the emir and the regime. Perhaps best known outside of media are the "Doha Debates." These debates, which began in 2004, are a public forum in which controversial issues of the day are discussed by key figures and motions are developed and passed with audience participation. The debates are sponsored and financed by the Qatar Foundation, but otherwise are not influenced by the Qatari regime, as evidenced by the controversy of some of the topics and motions passed. Despite the apparent risk of having such debates, and broadcasting them globally, they still well serve the emir and his elite. They are, like Al-Jazeera, an image-making initiative, sending a message of Qatari leadership reformism and openness to the international community. Given that they are broadcast through the BBC and other channels in key states such as the United States, Canada, and Pakistan, the debates potentially reach an audience of 350 million people or more. They are also a domestic political outlet: normally a majority of the audience is comprised of university students of different nationalities, including a sizable number of Qataris, and the freedom to speak openly, take controversial positions, and vote on motions provides an outlet for popular political grievances and wishes that is at the same time comparatively politically nonthreatening to the Qatari regime. The Qatar Foundation's funding and the attachment of Qatar's name to the debates provide enough link to the emir and regime to serve a political purpose both at home and abroad, without the debates appearing stage-managed or crudely influenced by the government.

This is little different to the case of Al-Jazeera, for which state funding guarantees its operations and discreetly constrains its coverage of a handful of topics, but which otherwise operates fairly freely while at the same time promoting the Qatari name and the regime's image of openness and liberalism. Qatar's leadership in the Arab trend toward new satellite news and new media is a case of soft power at work abroad to brand the country and promote its image, in the process branding and legitimizing the regime at home as well. Not only were these foundational goals of Al-Jazeera, but they have also continued to account for how and why the channel has been able to—indeed, encouraged to—operate in the way that it has.

Sports, Major Events, and National Branding

Al-Jazeera has probably been the single largest contributor to Qatar's international image and reputation since 1996, but not far behind has been its role as host of major sporting, cultural, and other global events. Important have been some diplomatic events such as Doha's holding of the Organization of the Islamic Conference (OIC) summit in November 2000 and especially its hosting of the ministerial-level talks in 2001 that commenced what subsequently became known as the Doha Development Round of trade liberalization negotiations. Such events have raised Qatar's international profile, and promoted an activist diplomatic image of it as a state that punches above its weight. Even more notable in terms of image and branding, however, have been sporting and cultural events, in particular Qatar's hosting of the 2006 Asian Games, its successful bid for the 2022 Soccer World Cup, and its attempts to host a Summer Olympic Games. These are in marked contrast to the situation in the 1980s, when Qatar began implementing a proper sports and sporting infrastructure policy, and began construction of six main modern sports clubs, formed a tennis federation for the country, and built its first international-standard stadium.[31] For much of the decade that followed, facilities expanded and improved in line with population growth, but it was not until the twenty-first century that sports events became a core development and international branding strategy for the Qatari government.[32]

Qataris and longer-term expatriates alike often point to the 2006 Asian Games as the turning point in Qatar becoming known internationally and in its strategy of competing for the chance to host global events.[33] The Games tied in well with sports and leisure policy in Qatar, and especially with the emir's desire not only to develop higher-level sporting prowess among young Qataris but also to promote sports and other physically active leisure activity.[34] The Games came on top of attempts to maintain traditional sports as well, such as camel-racing and falconry, with the view being that these fostered national identity and nationalism.[35] It was certainly, as has been argued elsewhere, also a case of "modernization through sport,"[36] and linked into attempts to develop other sectors of the economy. Branding and publicity are not the sole reasons behind this effort, and in the course of preparing to host the FIFA World Cup, Qatar will spend some US$60 billion on sports and related infrastructure over 2011–2022, including building over 50,000 new hotel rooms in the same period.[37] It is also using the Cup as further justification for other major projects, such as the US$40 billion worth of rail transport projects it has planned for the years leading up to 2022.[38] As the chairman of the 2022 World Cup bid, Shaikh Muhammad bin Hamad bin Khalifa Al Thani, put it: "We can see huge progress between [the bids for] each event based on [i.e., flowing onto] areas such as technology, travel, accessibility, hotels, and so on."[39] As the Asian Games represented the first such major spectacle that Doha held, in the view of many it encouraged the emir and the country to seek out other such prestigious, image-enhancing international events and to begin pursuing such events as branding and publicity opportunities beyond the sports-specific benefits they might offer.

Certainly the Asian Games did much for Qatar. Perhaps above all, they provided Qatar with the experience and confidence to pursue other such events and contributed to some extent in its winning in late 2010 the right to host the 2022 World Cup. At the simplest level, the Games delivered a boost to Qatar's image and helped with the recognition of its name abroad, and especially its image in the Arab world and in East and Southeast Asia. The Games prompted the creation of the Aspire Dome and Aspire Academy,[40] which opened in 2005 and subsequent to the Games became a key actor in the promotion of Qatar's national image abroad through the academy's scholarships and other support to aspiring sportspeople in the developing world. The Games also, of course, had wider economic implications, helping to create and sustain the economic boom that characterized most of the 2000–2010 decade; the boom over the first half of that decade in construction, in particular, but also in hospitality, tourism, and other sectors, was due in some significant part to Qatar's winning bid to host the Asian Games in 2006. At the same time, however, there were some problems and controversies with the Games, including a drenching rainstorm immediately after the opening ceremony that the Games organizers were underprepared to handle, the death of a Korean equestrian rider during a distance tournament in wet weather, and questions being raised, despite the overall success of the Games, about whether Doha was yet fully capable of hosting larger events such as the Summer Olympics. These may all have been reasons why Qatar lost its bid to host the 2016 Summer Olympics, although the extreme heat during the usual summer Olympic time window was the main reason.[41]

The bid for the 2022 World Cup was a natural extension and outcome of the Asian Games. It had similar aims, if arguably on an even larger scale given the enormity of the World Cup as an event and the global popularity of soccer as a sport—arguably the Summer Olympics and perhaps the Winter Olympics are the only sporting events that are larger and more complex than the World Cup, and even then, the duration of the World Cup is considerably longer than that of the Olympics. It is a crucial event, though, because of the popularity of soccer in both the West (especially Europe) and the developing world, and it is difficult to conceive of any other single sport that has such a wide and deep global following, nor another event that would have as much positive impact on Qatar's image among the global public.

In December 2010, Qatar was declared the winner of the bidding process to host the 2022 World Cup, following a unique and creative bid.

Qatar addressed some of the problems anticipated with its bid for the 2016 Summer Olympics, for example, by including in its bid for the World Cup a promise to use a novel—some would add untested—solar-powered, carbon-neutral air conditioning system to cool stadium air to around 25°C/77°F, in contrast to outside temperatures likely to be 45°C/113°F or higher. The bid also included an undertaking to dismantle parts of some stadiums and donate them to developing countries that lack sporting and major event infrastructure—a creative way in which to promote the bid, while also presenting Qatar as a bidder that had taken a holistic, including an international and economic-developmental, view of and approach to the bid and to the responsibility of hosting of the Cup.

The problem with the bid subsequently, however, has been that considerable controversy followed it, especially allegations in May 2011 that corrupt payments may have been made by Qatar, via an intermediary, to secure the bid. The allegation, which emerged in the United Kingdom, was that an informer involved with the Qatari bid, and subsequently the *Sunday Times* newspaper, claimed to possess evidence that four FIFA executive committee members had sought favors in exchange for supporting the Qatari bid. Moreover, the Qatari Muhammad bin Hammam was forced around the same time to withdraw his bid to become president of FIFA and was banned for life from all FIFA activities, because of a ruling against him by a FIFA ethics committee, after claims that he had attempted to use bribery to secure the presidency. He had been a key figure in the Qatari World Cup bid, leading some media commentary to question what role he might have played in any alleged corruption related to the World Cup bid. Regardless of the ultimate outcome of these claims for Qatar's plans to host the Cup—Qatar has very vigorously denied the claims, of course[42]—they are a problem because they undermine the publicity goals of the event, which are a key driver in the bid to host it, and harm Qatar's relatively clean image in terms of corruption and other undue influence in processes that are meant to be impartial.

The accusations of corruption do not affect the fact that there has been an underlying strategy of branding to Qatar's bids to host such spectacles. The realm of sports is, ultimately, a tool of public relations and public diplomacy: in effect, as one article put it: "[As] sports economist Frederic Bolotny rightly notes: 'Global sports is for sale.'"[43] Accusations of corruption aside, international sports have become increasingly commercialized and thus are increasingly exposed to the interests and practices of business and economic actors, including issues of branding through sports. Part of this "purchasing" of sports arguably involves using economic power to obtain major events, since they bring both diplomatic prestige and international public name recognition to a country that otherwise is too small to receive much attention. This need not be through corruption; indeed, more common than criticisms of Qatar or claims of corruption among observers have been observations that the country has become one of the wealthiest in the world in terms of gross domestic product. The rentierism and new state capitalism of its political economy have manifested in an increased desire, and capability, to host major sporting events and to raise awareness of the country through its involvement in various sports and other such events.

Almost as important in terms of branding have been Qatar's purchase and sponsorship of sporting teams and events overseas. This is a situation where Qatar's energy wealth, sovereign wealth fund, external security goals, and domestic political imperatives all overlap in the sporting realm. The dynamic is summed up well by a report on the issue:

> Sports diplomacy reaches European countries in the form of the purchase or sponsorship of top soccer teams. Sheikh Mansour, a member of the Abu Dhabi royal family, spent hundreds of millions of euros for his soccer team, Manchester City. Emirates Airline is a sponsor for English Premier League team Arsenal, the French Team Paris-Saint-Germain (PSG), and others. Qatar Sports Investment (QSI), founded by Heir Prince of Qatar Sheikh Tamim bin Hamad Al-Thani, just bought 70% of PSG. The Qatar Foundation will spend 30 million euros a year from 2011 to 2016 to be featured on the FC Barcelona jersey. And Qatar Airways announced last Friday that it is to become the official airline of the Tour de France.[44]

While there is arguably a strong financial aspect to such investments, they are important too as branding and publicity vehicles for Qatar, giving it reach to sports fans in numerous countries. Similar in strategy to this is the further initiative by Qatar to use the Aspire Zone and its facilities as a tool of foreign branding and publicity. One of Aspire's roles is to seek out young Qataris with a talent for sports, whether soccer or otherwise, and to sponsor intensive training for them, with the ultimate aim of developing world-class athletes. However, as part of this role, Aspire also offers training and development opportunities to young students from other countries and at various times has offered training, scholarships, or other help to young people from most parts of the developing world. Beginning in 2006, Aspire began offering scholarships to talented eleven-to-fifteen-year-old students from a range of countries in West Africa, South America, and elsewhere, including both top-quality sports training and a full concomitant academic education. Aspire's "Football Dreams" project subsequently tested over a million students in its first four years of operation.[45] This is part of Qatar's international development aid activities, flowing originally from the creation of Aspire in the lead-up to the Asian Games, and it has become a high-profile, popular, and well-respected route for talented young athletes in poor countries to gain the training and support they need to build a career in sports. In this, Aspire has become a very useful and successful method of national branding. It has created a very broad, positive image of the country across large parts of the developing world.

All of this symbolizes the centrality of sports as both a social policy and a diplomatic and political-economic strategy for the emir and his inner elite. Not dissimilar—if even more difficult to win a bid to host—is the Olympic Games. Qatar has made a concerted effort since 2007 to win the chance to host a Summer Olympics. When Qatar launched its bid for the 2016 Games in 2007, it possessed at best marginal chances of winning, even before its chances disappeared the following year when key members of the International Olympic Committee became concerned about the weather. Its bids for 2020 and 2024, while the first was dropped, reflect a genuine seriousness about hosting a Summer Olympics, as well as its need to appear serious in this respect. Many observers presume that the 2020 bid was driven by a strategy of awareness-raising, and that the most serious bid was always the 2024 one. By then, the argument goes, Qatar will have hosted the 2022 World Cup and will have both the infrastructure in place and the experience necessary to host an event as large, diverse, and operationally complex as an Olympic Games.[46]

The reasons why it would want to host the Olympics are the same as for the World Cup or the Asian Games. Doing so would be a boost to national pride and a boon for the emir's legitimacy and support at home; it would cement Qatar's growing position as a diplomatic and economic actor in the Gulf region, the Arab world, and globally; and it would create a more positive mood among the global public toward Qatar, which in all likelihood would flow through to greater investment interest, a more positive attitude toward Qatari investment abroad, and new commercial opportunities more widely. All this is good for the emir politically and as head of the (in effect family-owned) economy.

Arts, Culture, and Tourism: Discovering and Reinventing Qatar

A final group of sectors that are integral to Qatar's attempts at international branding, and indeed to how Qataris view the state and its role in economic and social development, are arts and culture, and tourism. The state has very ambitious but very precise strategies to develop these sectors, aiming in so doing to enhance the ongoing nationbuilding effort and the state-society relationship, and to create a very positive image abroad of Qatar as a society that can happily combine traditions and Islamic values with modernity, globalization, and economic success. As with media and sports, while there is certainly significance placed on the arts and culture and tourism sectors for their financial and economic diversification potential—the total contribution of the tourism sector to the economy in 2011 was estimated at about QR20.5 billion (US$5.6 billion)[47]—their value to the state also comes from their capacity to brand the country and, in contributing to other sectors and to how the country is viewed, how they enhance the state's position both vis-à-vis society and as an international actor.

The role of arts and cultural facilities in national branding and nation-building are fairly obvious: most states construct and finance galleries, museums, national monuments, and other facilities as a way of both engendering and supporting national pride and reinforcing nationalism by educating or reminding people about their shared history and cultural values. In many cases this extends to international branding, too, as tourists and other visitors from abroad are shown such facilities and monuments as a way of promoting the country and its values and thus projecting national values, historical memories, and mythologies internationally. In Qatar's case it is certainly doing this, through the Qatar National Museum. This opened in 1975, in an old palace that belonged to Emir Abdallah, but with a newer and larger site being developed and due to open in late 2014. Qatar also promotes an image of itself as protecting and promoting Arab and Muslim culture and values more generally, through facilities such as the Museum of Islamic Art and the Museum of Modern Art (Mathaf). The former is a world-famous museum that opened in December 2008 and is home to perhaps the best collection of Islamic manuscripts, textiles, and pottery in the world, acquired from the 1980s onward. The building that houses the museum was designed by I. M. Pei[48] to project traditional architectural principles on the most modern of building facilities. Mathaf, on the other hand, houses a very different collection, yet one equally impressive in its size and scope. It is the largest collection of Arab modern art in the world.[49]

The strategy of cultural marketing and branding, and the cultural production that goes with it, are also reflected in sites such as the Souq Waqif, which has become one of Doha's main tourist attractions. This is a redeveloped and expanded area where the traditional marketplace at Doha was originally established around a century ago. The modern iteration of it includes extensive traditional markets selling clothes, foods, spices, and famously even an array of birds, while the main street that runs diagonally through the Souq is structured to cater to tourists and visitors, and has a range of international restaurants and coffee shops as well as sites such as the Souq Waqif Art Gallery. As with most such deliberately structured sites, therefore, the Souq Waqif is a combination of a genuine original site and a deliberate piece of cultural production; the camels that are housed near the Souq's carpark and released through the market's streets each day are an example of an artificial feature that has been added to the site to match visitors' expectations of authenticity, rather than actually being an authentic feature of the place.

Katara Cultural Village is similar in its aims. It is a designated area, constructed in the years leading up to its soft launch in 2010, designed as both a residential area and a location for events and productions and to promote Arab and Qatari culture. Cultural societies were beginning to establish themselves at Katara in 2011 as the village began public operations, and the longer-term plan is for it to become a cultural center for Doha. The Doha Film Institute, which hosts the Doha Tribeca Film Festival, is based there.[50] Even the large residential projects possess similar aims. The Pearl, for example, is not just a residential project, but also includes an extensive shopping district, marina, and other facilities that attract international visitors and send a message of globalized development and cultural harmony. Lusail City, still under development as of early 2013, will be similar, with a marina, shops, and other facilities designed to make the city an independent and self-supporting residential area (of some 200,000 people, ultimately), but with explicit links to Qatar's tourism strategy and national branding goals.[51]

Like the museums, sites such as the Souq Waqif, Katara, and the large residential projects reflect a deliberate attempt by the Qatari government to brand the country in a particular way, and specifically in a way that is consistent with the country's traditions and values, even if not necessarily an accurate reflection of the past and its traditions. It is cultural production of a sort and on a scale that meets visitors' expectations of what they will find—a feature of much modern, commoditized tourism infrastructure anywhere in the world, it should be stressed—while being consistent with how the state would like Qatar and its society and culture, and by extension the state, to appear to foreign visitors. These sites not only provide a tourism "experience" for visitors but also are designed to consistently and clearly reinforce the message of how the state wishes Qatar to appear and be interpreted by visitors, and this in turn translates into greater international influence and a consistent international image for the state and the country.

So too is it with tourism more widely. Non-oil economies, of course, are attracted to tourism for financial reasons, in particular for its ability to generate foreign exchange earnings and, as a labor-intensive sector, to create large numbers of jobs. The circulation of tourism income within the economy flows on widely to a range of other sectors, too, making the benefits felt across the economy. For energy-driven economies like Qatar, however, these considerations carry little weight: the state does not need the foreign currency generated by tourism, and most jobs created by it are held by foreign workers, not Qataris, who will only work in the most skilled and prestigious niche roles related to tourism. Qatar is also keen to avoid the negative social consequences of tourism, especially the hedonism and cultural conflict that many associate not just with major tourism exporters in the region such as Egypt and Turkey, but also closer to home, even with neighboring Dubai.[52] Thus, while the state has a very ambitious tourism policy, it is also a very careful one, driven primarily not by economic considerations—although tourism does link to Qatar's economic diversification strategy—but rather to the goals of supporting major events and thereby raising awareness and positive impressions of the country. Tourism in Qatar is important and booming, as Table 6.1 shows, but in a more unique and niche way than in most other Arab states.

Qatar has long sought to develop tourism. The first significant wave of tourism reform came in the late 1990s, when the laws covering the availability of alcohol were liberalized and the state supported the modernization and expansion of hotel capacity through the state-owned Qatar

Table 6.1 Hotel and Tourism Expansion in Qatar, 2000–2011

	Number of Tourist Nights	Number of Hotel Occupants
2000	434,901	377,979
2001	506,505	375,954
2002	697,616	586,645
2003	848,395	556,965
2004	982,619	732,454
2005	1,023,698	912,997
2006	1,146,922	945,970
2007	1,245,191	963,573
2008	1,992,636	1,404,850
2009	1,535,145	1,658,569
2010	1,722,944	1,866,471
2011	2,684,346	2,905,300

Source: Qatar Statistics Authority, *Annual Statistical Abstract,* various years.

Notes: "Number of Tourist Nights" refers to the total number of nights that tourists rented hotel rooms. "Number of Hotel Occupants" refers to how many total people stayed in hotel rooms that year.

National Hotels Company (QNHC).[53] The financial austerity of the late 1990s impacted these developments to some extent, as did the dominance of Dubai as the main emerging Gulf destination at the time, but still the plans for tourism were already quite ambitious at that stage. Further reforms followed, including the creation of the Qatar Tourism Authority in 2000 as a specific tourism promotion body for the state[54]—the QNHC had, in effect, filled the role previously[55]—and the early 2000s also saw new initiatives in tourism such as the development of further top-quality hotels and the creation of plans for new attractions such as the redevelopment of the Souq Waqif and some of the major real estate projects mentioned. Importantly, some of the large projects such as the City Center shopping mall, the plans for which were developed in the early 2000s, presumed and required an expansion of tourism or the expatiate population in order for them to ultimately succeed.[56] By this time, of course, planning and development for the 2006 Asian Games was under way.

The reforms and liberalization that have occurred, which either targeted or strongly impacted the tourism sector, have been not insignificant and have begun to demonstrate an impact on the size of the tourism sector. Remarkably, the number of hotel rooms in the country more than tripled between 2008 and 2010 alone, from some 2,700 rooms to 8,500, with almost the same number of rooms again under construction in 2010.[57] The goal set in 2010 for tourism overall was for a doubling in the number of visitors by 2015, to some 2.5 million, and the construction of facilities and development of services that would support such a number.[58] The strong state investment role in infrastructure and services related to tourism was important in the late 2000s, as the global financial crisis caused other developed economies, and even other Gulf tourism destinations such as Dubai, to cancel or scale back such investment, while Qatar's financial position remained strong.

It is important to understand, however, that Qatar's tourism development is not unbridled or unconditional. It is focused on certain subsectors of tourism, some already discussed, including especially major events, business and convention travel, stopover traffic on Qatar Airways, and higher-end and niche tourism. Some of these types of tourism—major events and stopover visitors in particular—point to the centrality of branding as a goal behind Qatar's tourism policy, since there is a clear publicity element to major events, and a limit on the financial value of stopover visitors. This also reinforces that Qatar is not blindly following a "Dubai model" of development. In comparison with Dubai, Qatar is deliberately seeking to avoid an unbridled expansion of tourism and a complete liberalization of the sector, and instead has taken a more precise approach to tourism policy. It is focused on ensuring that tourism remains consistent with its social values and is sustainable. Shaikha Mayassa bint Hamad bin Khalifa Al Thani, chair of the Qatar Museum Authority, perhaps acknowledging that Qatar cannot compete with Dubai but can still carve its own tourism niche, noted in an interview that "there is no point replicating what is taking place next door, as people have different tastes and preferences. . . . People like to discover different things."[59] Importantly, she also pointed to the domestic goals of culture and the arts in the same interview, saying that "Qatar is working to ensure that the young generation does not forget where it came from and that our culture and heritage is preserved and continued."[60]

Development Strategies Beyond Economics

While branding and image do not dominate Qatar's political economy, they are a very important element of it, and have traditionally been ignored or underemphasized by observers. Sectors such as media, sports, tourism, and culture are all aspects of the political economy, but they also help link the political and the economic. They are in some cases economic activities that take on political meaning, or contribute to how power is organized or elite structures are maintained. In other cases, they contribute both economically and in other ways to wider political dynamics, especially at the domestic level to how society views the state, and internationally to how foreign governments and publics view the Qatari emir, state, and people.

These sectors are a reminder that political economy is not just a matter of economic performance and the political impacts thereof, nor of how political and commercial elites and forces interact with and influence each other. Rather, elements of political economy are manufactured as economic activities with political dynamics and benefits. Other sectors remain more integral to development and to political stability, and Qatar is an energy-driven economy above all else. However, energy has footed the bill for the state-driven expansion of sectors like media and tourism, and for the enormous infrastructure and other investments that have been needed for events like the Asian Games and that will be even greater still for the World Cup. The dynamics illuminated in this chapter show the importance of rentierism, but in a new light, and given that Qatar is a microstate with very specific domestic and regional security imperatives, the sectors discussed also shed light on the patterns and goals of Qatar's new state capitalism. The next chapter continues with the themes of new state capitalism conduct and microstatism, in the case this time of how Qatar's foreign and defense policies link to and interrelate with its political economy.

Notes

1. This definition is similar to that in Peterson, "Qatar and the World," p. 743.

2. Peterson, "Qatar and the World," pp. 743–746.

3. Author interview, Doha, October 2011. A strategy consultant stressed to me that the goal behind Qatar's branding was to have a regular reiteration of the country's brand and image in the mind of foreigners, across several key sectors such as news and current affairs media, sporting and cultural events, and, through the flag carrier Qatar Airways, international business travel.

4. The definition of a microstate is so arbitrary and contested that any technical or quantitative criteria are nearly pointless. By various measures and definitions—population, physical size, economic size, and the like—Qatar either is a microstate or, slightly exceeding the population or physical size of some definitions, might instead be considered a small state. Still, it is worth noting that despite a size of 11,437 square kilometers, Qatar is in effect a microstate since about half of its population reside in the capital, Doha, and a majority of the remainder in a few other urban centers (mostly oil and gas towns and cities); the population figure is deceptively large too, since out of 1.6–1.7 million people residing in Qatar, only about 280,000–300,000 hold citizenship.

5. See, for example, Mehmet and Tahiroglu, "Growth and Equity in Microstates"; and Wilkinson, "Strategies for Tourism in Island Microstates." There is also, of course, the now-famous article by *The Economist* arguing for the advantages of small states: "Small but Perfectly Formed," January 3, 1998, available online at http://www.economist.com/node/109387.

6. Author interviews, Doha, October 2011. This point was raised repeatedly, but not exclusively, when the question of image and branding was put to interlocutors.

7. The maroon is said to symbolize the Qatari blood that was shed in national wars, particularly those of the latter half of the nineteenth century, and the white is a symbol of peace, as it is in most of the world.

8. Some of course do not; such branding is not universal. The Qatar Foundation, for example, has very different marketing colors and mood in its publications and online; however, this is perhaps deliberate, as an attempt to stress the autonomy of the foundation from the Qatari government. The ministries and bodies that are most visible to foreigners—the Ministry of Foreign Affairs, the airline, the major state agencies, and the like—do, however, usually carry this color branding.

9. Sheikh Hamad bin Khalifa Al Thani, "A Solid Core," in Oxford Business Group, *The Report: Qatar 2011*,, p. 24.

10. Pamela Ann Smith, "Interview: Shashank Srivastava, Acting CEO, Qatar Financial Center," *The Middle East,* October 2010, p. 49.

11. "Getting Qatar Going," *Middle East Economic Digest,* October 14, 2005.

12. "SPIEGEL Interview with the Emir of Qatar: 'We Are Coming to Invest,'" *Der Spiegel,* March 29, 2009, http://www.spiegel.de/international/world/0,1518,616130,00.html.

13. "Bright Horizons," *Middle East Economic Digest,* October 14, 2005.

14. Amara, "2006 Qatar Asian Games," especially pp. 501–505.

15. "Increased Momentum," in Oxford Business Group, *The Report: Qatar 2011,* p. 229.

16. Hugh Eakin, "The Strange Power of Qatar," *New York Review of Books,* October 5, 2011, http://www.nybooks.com/articles/archives/2011/oct/27/strange-power-qatar/?page=1.

17. Amara, "2006 Qatar Asian Games," p. 498.

18. These points are made in numerous sources, including, for example, throughout two pieces in Oxford Business Group, *The Report: Qatar 2011:* "Increased Momentum," pp. 226–230; and "Ready, Set, Go," p. 234.

19. Author interview, Doha, January 2011. This point is also made in Ulrichsen, *Insecure Gulf,* p. 102.

20. As noted in Chapter 1, there are numerous book-length works on Al-Jazeera, including, for example, Miles, *Al-Jazeera;* al-Nawawy and Iskandar, *Al-Jazeera: The Story of the Network;* and Zayani, *The Al Jazeera Phenomenon: Critical Perspectives on New Arab Media.* There are of course a variety of scholarly and popular articles and similar such shorter works on Al-Jazeera as well.

21. These figures are from the "About Us: Facts and Figures" page of the Al-Jazeera website, at http://english.aljazeera.net/aboutus/2010/11/20101110131438787482.html.

22. "Global Force," in Oxford Business Group, *The Report: Qatar 2011,* p. 237.

23. The exact reasons for Al-Jazeera's establishment and the target audiences for it in a political sense remain unclear and highly contested, but domestic and international image were invariably major goals behind Al-Jazeera's creation. Bahry, "The New Arab Media Phenomenon," pp. 89–90.

24. al-Nawawy and Iskandar, *Al-Jazeera: The Story of the Network,* p. 83.

25. Ibid., p. 76; and author interviews, Doha, October 2011.

26. Mitchell, "Political and Socioeconomic Transformation in the GCC," pp. 281–282.

27. Author interviews, Doha, October 2011.

28. Foley, *The Arab Gulf States,* p. 118. This is especially notable given the image of Abdallah as a moderate within the Saudi royal family.

29. Foley, *The Arab Gulf States,* p. 118; Bahry, "The New Arab Media Phenomenon," p. 94; al-Nawawy and Iskandar, *Al-Jazeera: The Story of the Network,* p. 83; Tom Owen, "Qatar Leads the Way," *The Middle East,* September 2000, pp. 4–5; and Shankar Vedantam, "Qatar Advances Plans to Privatize Al-Jazeera," *Washington Post,* January 31, 2005, p. A16. Among those states that have been offended by the channel are Kuwait, Jordan, Bahrain, Algeria, Libya, and, farther afield, the United States, where in 2001 then–US secretary of defense Donald Rumsfeld criticized Al-Jazeera for repeatedly playing Taliban propaganda. The George W. Bush administration more widely complained about bias by Al-Jazeera and expressed concern that it was providing a mouthpiece for Islamic extremists.

30. Lambert, "Political Reform in Qatar," p. 95.

31. "*MEED* Has Reported on the Sports and Leisure Scene in Qatar," *Middle East Economic Digest,* June 15, 1985.

32. "Qatar Aims to Produce Best Performers," *The Times* (London), May 31, 2010.

33. Author interviews, Doha, October 2011.

34. Amara, "2006 Qatar Asian Games," pp. 500, 503–504.

35. Ibid., p. 500.

36. Ibid., p. 504.

37. "Doha's World Cup Challenge," *Middle East Economic Digest,* January 28, 2011.

38. "Race to the Finish," in Oxford Business Group, *The Report: Qatar 2011,* pp. 119–124. On the rail project, see Ed Blanche, "Gulf Rail Network: The Dream Becomes Reality," *The Middle East,* February 2011, pp. 12–16.

39. Quoted in "Qatar Aims to Produce Best Performers."

40. The academy is part of the Aspire Zone set of facilities, which also house Aspire Dome, an indoor sports center, and the 15,000-seat Khalifa Stadium. The full name of the academy is the Aspire Academy for Sports Excellence.

41. See, for example, "Six Cities Bid to Host 2020 Olympic Games," *BBC News,* September 2, 2011, http://news.bbc.co.uk/sport2/hi/olympics/14687584.stm; Ossian Shine, "Qatar Ponders Bid as Games Chiefs Rule on Dates," *Reuters,* August 26, 2011, http://uk.reuters.com/article/2011/08/26/uk-olympics-qatar-idUKTRE77P0YV20110826.

42. Regan E. Doherty, "Qataris Brush Off Allegations of Buying World Cup Rights," *Reuters,* May 30, 2011, http://www.reuters.com/article/2011/05/30/us-soccer-fifa-qatar-idUSTRE74T4J420110530.

43. Moustapha Kessous, "Sports as Diplomacy: How Small Gulf Countries Use Big Sports to Gain Global Influence," *Time/Worldcrunch,* June 27, 2011, http://www.time.com/time/world/article/0,8599,2080062,00.html (translation of an article originally published as "Pays du Golfe: Les Nouveaux Rois du Sport," *Le Monde,* June 24, 2011).

44. Ibid.

45. See the "Aspire Football Dreams" page on the Aspire website, at http://www.aspire.qa/inthecommunity/aspirefootballdreams.aspx.

46. Author interviews, Doha, October 2011.

47. "Increased Momentum," p. 229.

48. I. M. Pei is a Chinese American architect, among the most famous modern architects in the world. He is perhaps most famous for designing the glass-and-steel pyramid at the Louvre, which was completed in 1989. Born in 1917, Pei came out of retirement to design Doha's Museum of Islamic Art.

49. "Increased Momentum," p. 229.

50. Ibid., p. 227.

51. Ibid.

52. Author interview, Doha, October 2011.

53. Gina Coleman, "Qatar Survey," *The Middle East,* August 1998, p. 30.

54. "Qatar Targets Tourism," *Middle East Economic Digest,* December 1, 2000.

55. Gina Coleman, "Qatar: The Fastest Growing Economy in the World," *The Middle East,* April 2011, p. 26.

56. Ibid.

57. Pamela Ann Smith, "Qatar Pledges $20 Billion for Tourism and Culture," *The Middle East,* July 2010, p. 36.

58. Ibid.

59. "New Frontiers," in Oxford Business Group, *The Report: Qatar 2011*, p. 231.

60. Ibid.

7

Qatar in the International Arena

The small states of the Gulf all face opportunities and challenges by virtue of their political geography: from regional strategic rivalry among major states; from the US role in the region, for both better and worse; and from the inherent linkages between domestic imperatives and foreign policies in the small Gulf shaikhdoms. Christopher Davidson has noted in the case of Dubai and by implication the United Arab Emirates (UAE) more widely, but with equal validity to Qatar: "[Dubai has] a somewhat unfortunate location—although widely marketed as being an ideal 'bridge between east and west,' Dubai is between a rock and a hard place, surrounded by extremely unstable neighbours and the elements within them."[1] Like Dubai, Qatar has an ambitious economic development and diversification strategy that relies on business and investor confidence and stable state-society relations, which in turn rely on at least a basic level of regional stability and predictability. This strategy is global in nature, given that in the past Qatar has had problems asserting its own foreign policy separately from that of Saudi Arabia in particular. However, Qatar retains a strong interest in engaging with other Arab Gulf states, and in engaging with security or economic architecture such as the Gulf Cooperation Council (GCC), to the extent that it promotes the stability and cooperation demanded by Doha's development strategy. Unsurprisingly, there is little interest among policymakers in Doha in making concessions to or allowing constraints from the Gulf to impact a strategy that they see as being far broader and ambitious than Qatar's subregional role.

As a result, Qatar has pursued a balanced foreign policy—one that at times has meant displeasing its friends and neighbors—because this best serves the state's economic and security strategies. As a late rentier state with a rather responsive and benevolent but essentially undemocratic new state capitalist dynamic, Qatar needs to ensure that foreign relations are stable and that they contribute to economic performance and opportunity and reinforce diversification and globalization on Qatar's terms. Qatar's microstatism connects its foreign policy to its economic strategy in two ways. The first is as a small state or microstate in a tough neighborhood, where it faces genuine direct security challenges. Yet second, as a microstate with a relatively small and tight political elite sharing a stake in the state capitalist structure of the political economy, it is able and motivated to build and expand commercial links, with the state taking a leading role in so doing. As explored in the previous chapter, this accounts in part for why and how Qatar brands itself as it does. Moreover, it is an *activist* microstate—that is, it brands itself, pursues strong foreign policy goals, and seeks to punch above its weight—because of the security dynamics and complex international relations of its neighborhood: to be reactive or isolationist in such a setting would be counterproductive both to the physical security of the state and to the state's security against domestic opposition.

At the more predictable level, the state seeks security from the United States as a major power, in effect gaining security for the Al Thani elite and their commercial as well as political interests. It also, not surprisingly, uses foreign policy tools and processes to pursue commercial interests; arguably, in fact, it does this more actively than do many other states. However, it also seeks to build regional ties with the GCC, where these deliver commercial and other benefits, and seeks, seemingly somewhat contradictorily, to build sound links with larger regional actors such as Iran and Iraq. Yet as mentioned, since its economic and nationalist goals are global in nature, Qatar looks far beyond its own subregion. It seeks to gain attention and send a (branding) message of uniqueness and importance so that its economic position is enhanced and developed, and it builds wide links with other states such that there is a breadth of international actors with strong interest in the stability and durability of Qatar itself and specifically in the core ruling and business elements and the family branches of the Al Thani family at its helm. Beyond a basic, unwritten survival contract with the United States, Qatar relies on few states for survival, yet needs strong links with a great many states in order to optimize and sustain the economic bases of the regime and underwrite its long-term robustness.

Cooperation and Competition with the GCC

Three dynamics are especially important in informing Qatar's approach to and relations with the Arab states of the Gulf. One is the desire to link with the region, but only to the extent that this contributes to a basic level of security and offers trade, investment, and other economic opportunities that otherwise would not be available. Qatar's relations with its neighbors have varied in recent decades and contributed to a somewhat aloof tendency toward them, in particular the border dispute with Bahrain over the Hawar Islands, which was not resolved until 2001. Second, Qatar has long sought to shift away from Saudi Arabia's influence and instead assert its own foreign policy and avoid what it sees as a propensity by the Saudis to seek a central, even domineering, role among the Gulf monarchies. Emir Khalifa is seen as having yielded to Saudi dominance during his time in power, for example. Finally, Qatar has sought to balance its relations with other regional states and with the Middle East more widely because Qatar has important trade and investment relationships beyond the GCC. The most obvious dynamic here is Qatar's commercial relationship with Iran and its desire to see some inclusion of Iran in the region and stability in Iran-GCC relations. This marks Qatar as distinct from major states such as Iraq and Saudi Arabia, which fear Iran and strategically compete with it, and some of the smaller Gulf states that have territorial disputes with the Islamic republic or see it as a destabilizing force. As a result of these factors, Qatar has sought to develop a solid level of engagement with the GCC and the states that comprise it, but has also kept its distance on some subregional initiatives and is not as active in the GCC or as close to it as some might expect or as its public rhetoric often claims it is seeking to be.

If this sounds as though Qatar has little interest in constructing ties with the GCC, it is worth recalling that relations between Qatar and the other GCC states have improved markedly under Hamad. Historically, Qatar had quite poor relations with the other Arab shaikhdoms of the Gulf,[2] especially with Bahrain but earlier with the UAE over border disputes and with Saudi Arabia over unclear borders and the sense in Doha that the Saudis were seeking to dominate Qatar. Rather strangely, Qatar's relations with Iran were as strong as those with many Arab Gulf states, perhaps because the trade relationship between the two states was solid, perhaps because Iran did not intervene in Qatar nor was seen as being interventionist toward Qatar, or perhaps because the Iranian population in Qatar itself usually behaved in a politically and socially innocuous way.[3] This view generally persisted until after the 1978–1979 Iranian revolution. In contrast, Qatar's relations with its other Arab neighbors varied but were not always so strong. In the 1950s and especially the 1960s and 1970s, Qatar had a dispute with Bahrain over the Hawar Islands as well as over Bahrain's lingering claim of sovereignty over the town and surrounding area near al-Zubara in Qatar. At the same time, Qatar's border with Saudi Arabia was undemarcated, and there was a Saudi claim over part of southern Qatar, until the early 1970s.

Finally, Qatar had a dispute with Abu Dhabi over royalties from some oil fields along their shared maritime border, which lasted until the early 1970s as well.[4] These issues were managed so that even where they created hurdles in some of Doha's bilateral relations, they did not completely pollute them. Yet they were important determinants nonetheless in the somewhat stale and tepid relationships that Qatar had with some neighbors in the lead-up to independence and the decade or more after it.

The formation of the GCC in 1981 only partly improved intra-Gulf security among the member states. It was initially a response to the power of Iran and Iraq and the instability and perception of threat created by the 1980–1988 Iran-Iraq War, and the Saudi desire to offset this power and the smaller states' need for security guarantees. The GCC allowed for the formation of a very basic security architecture and, subsequently, for some steps to be taken toward closer economic relations; however, problems continued to plague Qatar's relations with some GCC states. In the case of Saudi Arabia, these have been mostly minor issues, but their number and commonness has meant that the relationship between Qatar and Saudi Arabia was rocky for much of the period beginning in the 1980s and continuing until a deliberate attempt to improve the relationship was made by Qatar after 2007.[5] These problems dated back to the era of Emir Khalifa, who, although he was on generally good terms with the Saudis, faced a particular strain in relations in 1992 when a clash along the eastern end of the Saudi-Qatari border at Al-Khufus occurred, in which two Qatari border guards were killed. Qatar accused the Saudis of undertaking the attack deliberately—that they had captured a third Qatari border guard in the incident lent credibility to the claim, even though the Saudis claimed that the incident was the result of tribal clashes in the area—and ceased its security cooperation with the kingdom, including temporarily withdrawing its small contribution to the GCC's Peninsula Shield joint rapid-deployment force, based in Kuwait. While this particular incident was mediated and resolved, border problems persisted, including two clashes in 1994 that led to renewed tensions. Around the same time, hints that Qatar would build economic ties with Israel, including selling it gas, added to the tensions between Doha and some of the other GCC states.

Relations were often tense or hobbled by specific issues after Hamad took power as well. There was suspicion in Qatar that the attempted countercoup by Khalifa against Hamad in early 1996 had Saudi backing or support. As mentioned previously, Al-Jazeera managed to offend the Saudis multiple times in its early years of operation.[6] This reached the point in 2002 where the Saudis withdrew their ambassador from Doha because of anger over an Al-Jazeera report. Conversely, a couple of times in the 2000s the Qataris were offended by claims made by the Saudi-owned London-based newspaper *Asharq al-Awsat.* Even into the middle of that decade, there were issues over the Saudi objection to the Dolphin Project[7] and the fact that for some years the Saudis blocked a major contract for the Qatari sale of gas to Kuwait.[8] Saudi Arabia's dominant role in the Gulf had always been a worry for Qatar, but increasingly so under Hamad as Qatar has sought to develop a more independent and global foreign policy and an economic profile beyond the Gulf. This is why Qatar has been quite close to Iran, at least commercially, and has often sought to exploit the rivalry between Iran and Saudi Arabia for its own advantages.[9]

However, Qatar was not successful in ignoring or trying to outmaneuver this Saudi influence and, realizing that it could not act without some reference to the GCC's main actor, sought to improve relations with Riyadh, starting with a visit by the Qatari emir and the prime minister together to Saudi Arabia in September 2007.[10] This served Qatar's economic strategy in particular, given that this visit paved the way for closer economic ties, including a joint commission covering economic and trade cooperation and led by the states' crown princes. By 2010, air transport connections between the two states had expanded markedly, commercial links were improving because of greater contacts between the two business communities, and Qatar's successful bid to host the 2022 World Cup held out the possibility of Saudi firms, both state-owned and private, winning major infrastructure and other contracts.[11]

Relations with Bahrain have followed a similar trajectory, first dominated by problems stemming from the dispute over the Hawar Islands chain and al-Zubara, but then improving after 2001. The disputes did not dominate the relationship but were a serious thorn in its side. However, both matters were resolved by the International Court of Justice's decision on March 16, 2001—after deliberation on the dispute for some seven years—to confirm Qatari sovereignty over al-Zubara and Bahraini sovereignty over the Hawar Islands. With the matters concluded, relations between the two states subsequently improved. This is another example of a deliberate attempt by the Qatari emir, and especially the prime minister and minister of foreign affairs (a double portfolio), who is widely seen as the central architect of Qatar's foreign policy, to renew and expand ties with Bahrain. The commercial relationship between the two has improved, although whether as a result of diplomatic efforts is uncertain, and major projects such as a bridge and rail line spanning the two states have been proposed for construction in the 2010s and after.[12] It is notable that Qatar still has its suspicions toward Bahrain, perhaps because of the latter's closeness to Saudi Arabia, and because Doha still occasionally resurrects the supposedly resolved Hawar Islands issue for tactical diplomatic advantage.[13]

Qatar's relations with the lower Gulf states under Hamad's rule have been somewhat stronger.[14] At the popular level in Qatar, there is a positive view toward the lower Gulf states, perhaps because these states are, like Qatar, closer to Iran and less dominated by Saudi Arabia than are states such as Bahrain. Although historically there was some tension between Qatar and Abu Dhabi over the maritime boundary, and a sense perhaps that Abu Dhabi was seeking to be the dominant political force in the lower Gulf region after Saudi Arabia, Qatar has typically had friendly ties with Dubai and Oman, and its relations with Abu Dhabi, as the central government of the UAE, began improving as of the late 1990s. Prominent is the Dolphin Project, which both supports and reinforces the Qatari-UAE relationship, and with Oman included in the Dolphin Project[15] and investment among southern and central Gulf states having increased during the oil booms of 2003–2008, there is the potential for a tightly knit southern Gulf economy to develop. As examples of this trend, beginning around 2007, Qatar expanded its investment links with the UAE and Oman, with new initiatives specifically seeking to collaborate in areas of strength such as energy and to diversify the various economies.[16] At the same time, the UAE and Qatar were lukewarm on plans for a GCC common currency,[17] something that is now in hiatus and unlikely to reemerge and cover all GCC states for some considerable time.[18] This arguably was at least partly due to the economic and investment competition between Qatar and the UAE.

Given these dynamics, Qatar's links to the GCC are not especially ambitious, particularly when compared to its much greater aspirations regionally and globally. To the extent that it improved ties with the GCC under Hamad, it did so predominantly in the interests of its wider economic interests and strategy and because a Qatari occupied the secretary-generalship of the GCC from 2002 to 2010. During this time the GCC had some economic successes in moving toward closer economic integration and improving trade and labor mobility across the member states, but made few true strides toward political integration and only modestly improved the GCC's security role.[19] Arguably there was more to be lost than gained by Doha from being too aloof from the GCC and its initiatives, given this closer integration within the GCC. Its rationale therefore was to consolidate its image for stability, locate and exploit new intra-GCC investments and policy reform initiatives, and use the union as a further mechanism for closer relations with states such as the UAE and Oman, with which Qatar already had good relations. Yet at the same time, Doha appears to have been cognizant of the competition that underlies some of the economic development strategies of the Gulf states, and this, along with the limited complementarity of the energy-based Gulf economies, explains why true, deep economic integration still has not occurred within the GCC. Security is, of course, a consideration for Doha in engaging as it does with its Arab neighbors, but the GCC is, to Qatar, much more about underwriting economic security and locating new economic opportunities. Issues of physical national security and defense are more complex and mostly drawn from other relationships.

Qatar and Regional Security and Military Issues

Accounting in large part for the nature of Qatar's foreign relations within the Gulf and with some external actors such as the United States, and complicating these relationships at times, too, is the geostrategic vulnerability of the state: its microstatism in terms of geographic size and small population, in other words, coupled with the nature of the Gulf's geopolitics too, especially the combination of rivalry between major regional actors (Saudi Arabia, Iran, and in the past Iraq), external intervention and links in the region, and the perception of vulnerability among the smaller states seemingly reinforced by the experiences of Iraq's 1990 invasion of Kuwait and Qatar's sense in the past of an underlying threat from Saudi Arabia. However, as mentioned, Qatar also engages with the Gulf subregion in pursuit of commercial goals, reinforcing that foreign policy and political economy are deeply interrelated in the case of Qatar.

Qatar is unable to defend itself from any significant regional military threat. Despite some qualitative advantages in its weapons platforms and military technology, which it has been able to develop largely because of oil and gas rents, it has the second smallest military in the region in terms of personnel and the smallest number of key weapons systems and platforms of any Gulf state, as shown in Table 7.1. Notable are two features of the Qatari armed forces. First is the small size of the forces at its disposal: the total number of personnel amount to only 11,800 or so, of whom a large majority belong to the army (some 8,500); the air force and navy are very small in size by any measure.[20] This is partly due to a deliberate policy of having only a modestly sized military, and is also a reflection of a recruitment problem. The military has difficulty attracting Qataris to join, despite some 6,400 or more Qatari nationals reaching military age each year.[21] Such is the recruitment problem that about 75 percent of military personnel are foreign nationals.[22] A second feature of the Qatari military—linked to its small size—is its emphasis on qualitative capability, and especially its procurement of high-quality platforms; as a result, its nominal defense expenditure, for such a small state, has been quite high over the past two decades and has risen sharply, from around US$1 billion per annum in the second half of the 1990s to over US$2.4 billion in 2005.[23] Despite a small decline in the years after that, due to annual fluctuations in major defense purchases, Qatar's defense spending is large for its size: for most of the period from 1997 to 2009, it was the third-largest Gulf state, after Saudi Arabia and Oman, in defense spending measured as a percentage of gross domestic product.[24] Notable in qualitative terms are the Emiri Air Force's twelve Dassault Mirage 2000-5DAs, a multirole fourth-generation aircraft; the Emiri Army's main battle tanks, self-propelled artillery, and various MANPAD ground-to-air missiles; and the Emiri Navy's patrol vessels and fast-attack craft.[25] This emphasis on quality is to offset the small numbers involved. It may also reflect a caution by the emir or elite about the risk of a coup d'état by senior figures were the military to be much larger.

The military thus cannot guarantee the physical protection of the state from external existential or major threats, although the likelihood of Qatar facing a traditional external invasion is exceptionally thin. Thus the military exists with that type of goal prominent in its remit, but in reality this is a minor focus of its strategy. It is important in a limited respect because there is still an underlying if modest level of mistrust toward Saudi Arabia, in particular, among the Qatari elite. While Saudi Arabia is unlikely to pose a direct military threat to Qatar, there remains a fear of this remote possibility among some foreign policy elites, not to mention a wider view that a basic, high-quality level of military capability acts to reduce the risk of the state being threatened or coerced by an external actor.[26] Furthermore, important if to a lesser extent is the concern in Doha toward Iran in recent (namely, post-2004) years as its strategic position in the Gulf has expanded as a result of events in Iraq and the perception of a more influential Iran in parts of Iraq and, through proxies such as Hezbollah and others, elsewhere in the Middle East. Unlike in, say, Bahrain, in Qatar there is no realistic fear of a threat of invasion from Iran, but its military nonetheless provides a sense of security because of its potential to contribute to security in a worst-case scenario of military conflict within the Gulf region, or if the security environment were markedly damaged by events such as military conflict between Iran and the United States or Israel. In other words, the existence of the Qatari military represents the fact that the Gulf is contested political and strategic terrain, with a lack of security architecture, and characterized by large states engaged in strategic rivalry and smaller ones that feel either threatened by, or at least unable to ensure their full

Table 7.1 GCC Military Capabilities Compared, 2010

	Bahrain	Kuwait	Qatar	Oman	Saudi Arabia	United Arab Emirates
Total armed forces (number of personnel)	8,200	15,500	11,800	42,600	233,500	51,000
Army	6,000	11,000	8,500	25,000	75,000	44,000
Navy	700	2,000	1,800	4,200	13,500	2,500
Air force	1,500	2,500	1,500	5,000	36,000	4,500
National guard, royal guards, and other	0	7,100	0	8,400	109,000	0
Main battle tanks	180	293	30	117	565	471
Armored personnel carriers	375	260	226	206	1,800	892
Artillery pieces	151	218	89	233	855	561+
Naval surface vessels	1	0	0	1	7	0
Submarines	0	0	0	2[a]	0	10[a]
Patrol and coastal vessels	12	11	7	13	30	17
Fighter and attack aircraft	39	66	12	54	296	178
Helicopters	55	42	42	46	91[b]	66

Source: Derived from statistics in International Institute for Strategic Studies, *The Military Balance 2012*.
Notes: a. Swimmer delivery vehicles, not combat submarines.
b. Includes both air force and navy helicopters.

security and independence in the face of, the competition between these larger neighbors as well as some external actors.

Of far more importance than existential protection of the state in explaining the Qatari military's role, and its likely increase in size and capability in the coming decades, are two factors, one rather common to the region, the other more unusual. The first, more traditional role of the Qatari military is in providing a level of domestic protection for the regime against societal elements. This is a feature of much of the Gulf: it is a largely unspoken goal of most Arab Gulf, and indeed most Arab, militaries. There is a very low threat of revolutionary upheaval against the Al Thani family—arguably, Qatar is one of the most stable states in the region in this regard—but there remains a need for the emir and elite to have a military capable of addressing more specific threats such as from extremist and transnational terrorist elements, small armed opposition groups that could emerge in the absence of a military capability, and the albeit very unlikely risk of a sizable insurrection against the political order. This accounts in some part for the existence of the military but, in the absence of plausible external existential threats to Qatar, for its relatively modest size and its emphasis on qualitative rather than quantitative capability.

The more unusual justification for Qatar's military capability is its role in promoting Qatar's profile internationally and in its role in branding the emirate as discussed previously. Again, while the small geographic and demographic size of the country makes a large expeditionary or peacekeeping force impossible, the state promotes its image and reputation internationally, in both diplomatic and military settings, through its military. This explains the expanding international relations activities of the military, and its very high-profile role in actions such as the North Atlantic Treaty Organization (NATO)–led campaign of support for the Libyan opposition in the uprisings against the Muammar Qaddafi regime from March to October 2011. Its involvement in such activities is meant to signal an engagement with the international community, including with Western powers. It may seem strange that during the Arab Spring the Qatari elite supported oppositional forces in countries such as Libya and Syria, given that it is a soft authoritarian state itself with few democratic institutions or processes; however, it arguably did so for exactly this reason—specifically to build an image of Qatar as being committed to reform and populist change, whatever the reality in the case of political change in Qatar itself.

Such actions are useful in raising the profile of the regime in diplomatic circles, which encourages external actors to think of the emir and the Qatari regime more favorably than otherwise, and even to consider the international community as having a stake in Qatar's stability and in its ongoing engagement internationally. More broadly it helps in winning wider (that is, nonelite) support elsewhere, earning international media attention that it otherwise would not have gained. Note the near-mythological status that Emir Hamad gained at the popular level in post-Qaddafi Libya itself in late 2011.[27] In these respects, and in the purchases of military hardware and in goodwill and other such activities, Qatar's military activities also contribute to and reinforce its broadly Western-aligned but fairly independently inclined foreign policy, which has the protection and expansion of economic interests as one of several core goals.

Qatar's Relationship with the United States

Despite Doha occasionally frustrating the United States or there being some differences of perspective between the two, Washington arguably is Qatar's most important ally. This is the result of the two core strategic dynamics faced by Qatar as previously discussed: it derives a basic security guarantee from its relationship with the United States, which helps to address the defense limitations it possesses from its small size; and ties with a major power are important to securing it greater independence within the Gulf, especially given its fears of Saudi domination over its diplomatic orientation otherwise. This does not mean that Doha blindly follows or agrees with US policy. The relationship has had its share of strains, and Qatar maintains a fairly independent foreign policy, including in its dealings with Washington, even if it is ultimately reliant on its ally for protection in a worst-case security threat scenario.

Recall that Emir Hamad was minister of defense and commander-in-chief prior to seizing power, roles that gave him a sense of the strategic vulnerabilities and opportunities faced by Qatar, and that certainly were useful in helping him build links with external actors in the military context. Hamad was integral in Qatar's diplomatic role in condemning the August 2, 1990, Iraqi invasion of Kuwait and supporting its repulsion through military action in January–February 1991. Qatar provided a small military force to the anti-Iraq coalition, an act that won (for both itself and Hamad) wide popular support in Qatar after its success at the battle for Khafji in late January 1991, where Qatari forces helped defeat the Iraqis and took a number of them prisoner.[28] During the conflict, Qatar hosted US (and Canadian and French) forces on its soil as well. In June 1992, Hamad concluded a long-term bilateral defense agreement that allowed the United States access to Qatari bases, gave the United States the right to preposition equipment in Qatar (which it subsequently did), and set out agreement on joint military exercises. It is a document that proved central in Qatar's aim of ensuring that its security would be underwritten by a major power. Hamad was key in the development of the defense relationship with the United States prior to 1995, and since assuming power has supported the relationship at a strategic level but also in other political and economic spheres as well.

In fact, Hamad has presided over a strengthening of the bilateral relationship with Washington. Qatar stood to gain from the September 11, 2011, attacks in the United States and the subsequent war on terrorism, and apart from some criticism by US officials of Al-Jazeera's reporting on the war on terrorism and especially the 2003 Iraq War, Qatar has managed the relationship well and it has been strengthened by the greater US engagement with and involvement in the Middle East in the period since 2001. Hamad visited the United States not long after the terrorist attacks, in early October 2001, where he reiterated Qatari support for the United States in the war on terrorism. This was followed by a mutual defense pact with the United States signed on December 11, 2002, which went further than the 1992 agreement. It in effect made Qatar, and specifically Al-Udaid air base and Camp Saliyah to the west of the capital, the centers of operations in the Gulf for US Central Command (CENTCOM) and dramatically diminished the importance of Prince Sultan air base in Saudi Arabia to CENTCOM. Al-Udaid and Qatar would be integral to the US role in the Gulf after that time, and to how the US military fought the 2003 Iraq War.

Taking a central role in the 2003 Iraq War was important to Doha for several reasons, including setting Qatar apart from its larger neighbor Saudi Arabia in Washington's eyes—since Riyadh had not allowed any sizable numbers of US forces to fight the 2003 war from Saudi territory—and it also cemented the US-Qatari defense relationship in a way that helped ensure Qatari security would be underwritten by a long-term US military presence in the country. It is notable that the June 4, 2003, visit to Qatar by then–US president George W. Bush was the first-ever presidential visit to Qatar and the only stop that Bush made in the Gulf on that trip, and was a direct result of Qatar's support for the Iraq War.[29] It also sent a message of a closer bilateral relationship between the two states more broadly, and was a chance for the United States to characterize Qatar as the type of reformist state that Bush's policies were seeking to encourage in the Middle East:[30] Qatar was rapidly becoming an economic success story in 2003, and at that stage its profile as a democratizing state was higher than it would become subsequently. The visit symbolized, in other words, the growing mutual benefit that Qatar and the United States were obtaining from their closer bilateral relationship.

The US relationship has been pursued since then, despite some controversy about policies such as the support provided to the United States in the 2003 Iraq War. The oil boom of the 2004–2008 period saw Qatar develop and quickly expand its sovereign wealth investments abroad, and Qatari investment in the United States has begun to form an underlying feature of the relationship. The diplomatic and military relationship continued essentially unchanged after the transition to the Barack Obama administration in the United States in January 2009. Nonetheless, Qatar has still sought to maintain an independence from the United States. Hamad is not by any means seeking simply to become a US puppet, nor even to place Qatar so firmly within the US alliance that it overshadows other relationships. As previously mentioned, despite US talk of the importance of free speech and free media, senior US officials have at times been frustrated or angered by reporting by Al-Jazeera. Moreover, some other foreign policy initiatives or actions by Qatar have angered Washington. Qatar has, for example, been supportive of some Islamist groups that the US opposes, including Palestinian Hamas and other Palestinian groups[31] (despite Qatar seeking to establish a functional relationship with Israel, more on which shortly). It has also hosted the exiled Egyptian cleric Yusuf al-Qaradawi, who is closely connected to the Egyptian Muslim Brotherhood and has been a strong critic of Israel,[32] and has hosted visits to Qatar by figures such as the Iraqi Shiite leader Muqtada al-Sadr in May 2010.[33] In January 2012, it was announced that the Afghan Taliban would open an office in Qatar, something painted at times as contentious by the media but that the United States seemed to welcome if it would lead to more formal peace talks.[34] It was also a sign of the extent to which Qatar by the early 2010s had become an important international actor and mediator.

Perhaps in light of these sorts of characteristics in Qatari politics and diplomacy, it has been suggested that the expansion of the relationship with Washington is less about Qatar truly shifting toward the United States and is more a ploy by the emir to keep the US administrations thinking positively about Qatar and associating it with a reformist agenda. This, the argument goes, reduces the risk of US criticism of Qatar's record in areas such as human rights, foreign workers' conditions, and suchlike. An alternative view is simply that Qatar possesses a very personalized style of political rule and thus a sclerotic foreign policy susceptible to abrupt change and the specific whims of the emir. In fact, neither of these arguments is very convincing. In terms of the US relationship, the emir is truly promoting liberalism and cosmopolitanism, as various examples throughout this book have illustrated. The modernization of education, the expansion of the base of the economy, and the active response to globalization all suggest that a genuine reformism, at least in socioeconomic areas, is central to Hamad's strategy for Qatar. The idea that this and the closer US relationship are all a mirage is not plausible. Closer ties with Washington are consistent with a reformist emir who is seeking to protect his economic interests, send a message of political reformism too (if less actually implement such change), and engage with the world's largest major power—but on his own terms. Arguably Hamad wants to avoid being under the US thumb just as much as he detests the idea of being under the Saudi thumb. In a similar way, what appears as a confused or sclerotic foreign policy to a Western audience accustomed to states fitting neatly into a particular camp instead looks to many Qataris like a state and leader who are trying to undertake a balanced portfolio of foreign relations and not be overly tagged or burdened by a particular relationship or policy.[35] Perhaps it is just that such independence in small state diplomacy that Qatar demonstrates is very rare.

Qatar's Relationship with Iran

Hamad has deliberately sought to maintain a solid relationship with Iran at the same time as he has moved Qatar closer to the United States. In fact, the historical links between Qatar and Iran, dating back into the middle and even early twentieth century, and the lack of sectarian troubles that Qatar has faced, have meant that the two states enjoyed a cordial set of ties both before and after the 1978–1979 Iranian revolution, despite the tensions created by Qatar leaning toward Iraq in the 1980–1988 Iran-Iraq War. The bilateral commercial relationship has always been strong, founded on a complementarity in the trading relationship and strengthened by the Iranian community in Qatar and by direct sea links and, more recently, good air transport links. That both states were members of the Organization of Petroleum Exporting Countries (OPEC)—Iran a founding member in 1960, but Qatar joining quickly, in 1961—probably also reflected and reiterated an alignment of their interests in the energy sector. They have also both been members of the Non-Aligned Movement (NAM) and the Organization of the Islamic Conference (OIC). Iran recognized the sovereignty of Qatar quickly after its independence, which helped the diplomatic relationship and reinforced ties at the top political level.

However, and perhaps most important, in both symbolizing and reinforcing the functionality and cordiality of the Qatari-Iranian relationship, was the fairly painless way in which the exploitation of the North Dome/South Pars gas field was agreed by the two sides, and the fact that exploitation of the gas has occurred with very little disagreement emerging between the two states. Both Doha and Tehran have abided by the 1969 maritime boundary agreement, which has informed the border between the North Dome and South Pars and the exploitation by the two sides of the field, although on a couple of occasions Qatar became tense after Iran claimed that Qatar was overexploiting the field, for example in 2004.[36] Moreover, underlying the issue also has been the potential for greater competition to emerge between the two gas powers,[37] although Iran's slower development of its side of the field has so far constrained this risk from emerging. In general, however, the two states have developed their respective gas sectors with different links into the global gas sector (particularly, targeting different partners and buyers), and thus with little dispute between them on energy matters.

The Qatari and Iranian leaders maintain quite cordial ties, even if some tension exists between them. Iranian president Mahmoud Ahmadinejad visited Qatar twice during his presidency, and Hamad visited Iran at least four times up to 2011.[38] Statements by senior figures have been important too, including Qatar's public encouragement for the United States and Iran to resolve their disagreements, including on Iran's nuclear program, peacefully and directly.[39] To call on them to do so "directly," given the sanctions that the United States has in place against Iran and the lack of formal diplomatic engagement, in effect makes statements such as this lean in favor of Iran. Even more crucial than such visits in aiding in the relationship with Iran has been the fact that during the Hamad period, Qatar has refrained from foreign policy actions that Tehran might find objectionable or abrasive. The closer ties that Qatar has pursued with the United States have not come at the expense of other relations, nor been seen to have done so. The development by Doha of other ties, including with other states in the Arab world and with emerging powers such as China, has not had any negative impact on relations with Tehran either. And in marked contrast to Qatar's active support for opposition groups during the 2011 Arab Spring, Qatar deliberately avoided any involvement or even substantial comment on the 2009 protests in Iran.[40] If anything, initiatives such as Qatar's more ambitious diplomacy in the Levant and its much more aggressive attempts to influence politics in the Arab world, including during the 2011 Arab Spring, have annoyed Saudi Arabia rather than Iran and been seen by Riyadh rather than Tehran as upsetting the natural power dynamics in the region.[41]

In fact, as it developed its ties with Iran, Qatar distinguished itself by formalizing its strategic links with Tehran through a defense cooperation agreement signed in February 2010. This is much simpler than the defense pact with the United States—it must be stressed that Qatar remains under the US security umbrella—and the agreement with Iran covered antiterrorism and rudimentary-level training, exchanges, and other such cooperation, rather than more substantial matters such as joint defense or exercises.[42] Yet this pact is important. The deal meant that in effect Qatar then had one of the closest defense relationships with Iran of any Arab state, probably second only to Syria after that time and until mid-2011. It also was important in demonstrating that even while possessing security guarantees from the United States, Qatar is willing to go to great lengths to pursue, and formalize, a diplomatic and security agenda that is separate from its US relationship and in many ways very independent. Doing so assists it because it enhances economic opportunities, but also, as with its strategic development of broad investment linkages, it expands the number of states that have a stake in Qatar's security and stability and therefore helps underwrite both the economic and the physical security of the regime. Potentially, this gives Doha the advantage of being a bridge or link between the Arab world and Iran, and even between the United States and Iran, although the latter in particular is a high-risk strategy, too, given the risk of military conflict between those two.[43] It also serves as a means for offsetting some of Saudi Arabia's influence in the Gulf and over Qatar, which has both strategic and economic advantages for Qatar as it seeks to expand its economic role and ensure its economic and trade security.

Qatar's Relationship with Israel

It is for similar reasons that Qatar has sought to have a functioning, if by no means complete, relationship with Israel. This is one of the more contentious aspects of Qatari foreign policy with other Arab states in particular, and more than once has caused open tension with the other GCC states and others. However, the relationship is significant and essentially spans Hamad's time in power, having commenced with the creation of trade links between the two states in 1996, when then–Israeli prime minister Shimon Peres visited Qatar in April that year to open the trade office in Doha.

In the period after Qatar and Israel first established trade ties, the links between the two evolved into meetings on noncommercial matters and other broader links, while still remaining very modest in scope compared to what would occur in a full, normal diplomatic relationship.[44] The optimism that attended the Oslo peace process in the 1990s, at least until late in that decade, meant that Qatar initially pursued enhanced ties with Israel. It invited Israel to attend the Middle East and North Africa (MENA) Economic Conference that Doha hosted in 1997, for example, which caused overt tension with Saudi Arabia and displeasure with other Arab states. As the Oslo process became increasingly stalled, however, Qatar began to distance itself further from Israel; while Qatar left the trade office in place in Doha, its leaders' criticism of Israel increased, a request by Ehud Barak to visit Qatar in 1999 was declined, and Qatar was especially direct in its criticisms of Israel after the Al-Aqsa intifada broke out in September 2000. The Israeli trade office in Doha was eventually closed in November 2000 after Qatar came under increasing pressure to cut its ties with the Jewish state—Saudi Arabia and Iran threatened to boycott the OIC meeting that Doha was hosting that month if the office remained open—although several meetings between the two sides occurred in the years following.[45] Israel supported Qatar's nonpermanent membership in the United Nations Security Council in 2006–2007, although arguably it was not rewarded for this support; Qatar's criticism of the 2006 Israeli war in Lebanon is an example from the period, and Qatar's abstention from the vote on Security Council Resolution 1757 of 2007, which called for the creation of an international tribunal to investigate the 2005 assassination of former Lebanese prime minister Rafiq Hariri, is another. Qatar and Israel had occasional meetings around the time that kept the relationship going, such as the April 2008 visit to Qatar by Israel's then–foreign minister, Tzipi Livni, during which she met the Qatari emir and several of his ministers. Yet Qatar began to further distance itself from Israel not long after this. The turning point was Israel's Operation Cast Lead attacks on Gaza in December 2008 and January 2009, which prompted Qatar to sever its links with Israel. In the couple of years following that, the two states remained estranged; Qatar wanted Israeli agreement for it to ship supplies to Gaza if relations were to resume and the Israeli presence in Doha to be reestablished, something to which the Israelis would not agree.[46] Presumably Qatar's relationship with Hamas and other groups was a consideration too, being something that had long annoyed key Israeli figures.

Fully and satisfactorily explaining the exact strategy behind Qatar's engagement with Israel has eluded scholars, and there is fierce debate as to why Qatar chose to engage with the Jewish state as and how it did so over the period from 1996 onward. To some, Qatar hoped to make a long-term gas supply agreement with Israel.[47] While plausible, it is unlikely that commercial energy considerations would be so dominant as to push Qatar to defy regional diplomatic and popular opinion to such an extent. Besides, much of its gas is exported under long-term contract, often through the firms that have entered joint venture arrangements in particular gas investment projects. To others, it was an attempt by Qatar to impress itself on the United States and expand its ties with Washington. If so, this is a failed policy, not because there are any real problems in the Qatari-US relationship, but simply because the Qatari-Israeli relationship has had so little impact, for better or worse, on Qatar's relationship with the United States. The latter relationship has developed because of the imperatives and interests of Doha and Washington, not because the United States has wanted to support an Arab Gulf state to work with Israel, even if initially the new ties between Israel and Qatar would have been viewed positively by US policymakers.

The most likely explanation for Qatar developing the links it did with Israel is, yet again, that this allowed Doha to assert the independence of its foreign policy and mark itself out from other Arab states[48]—that is, to assert and brand itself in a unique way—while at the same time position itself as an intermediary between Israel and the bulk of Arab states, something with potential benefits to its diplomatic situation. In involving itself in negotiations with Israel over supplies to Gaza after Cast Lead, for instance, Doha was in effect operating as a regional diplomatic actor alongside much more powerful states such as Egypt. It is notable, for example, that Qatar not only was active diplomatically during the 2006 Israeli war in Lebanon but also contributed some 300 peacekeepers to southern Lebanon after the conflict,[49] while this was also the time around which Doha started to more openly liaise with Hezbollah. These all add weight to the likelihood that its diplomatic engagement was about raising its international profile and being seen in a positive light by a range of states and actors.

Ultimately such a role may offer potential flow-on benefits to Qatar's economy, if the investment relationship with Israel or its allies is boosted by it or if new trade opportunities emerge, but it is much harder to make the case for an economic strategy underlying the Qatari-Israeli link. Moreover, as with its engagement with Iran, Qatar's engagement with Israel has been a high-risk strategy: it backfired a couple of times, in late 2000 in particular but also following Cast Lead and the anger in the region toward Israel because of it, and to date there are virtually no economic dividends evident for Qatar, and few political ones apart from its regional profile, which arguably would have developed similarly anyway in the absence of Doha's engagement with Israel. Yet if a small-scale engagement with Israel provides even a remote possibility of political or economic advantage, it may simply be that the emir has judged a basic engagement to be worthwhile, especially since Qatar does not shy away from controversy with other Arab states and as a microstate would gain nothing—not even much attention, presumably—from isolating itself from Israel and simply screaming at or about it. And as *The Economist* put it in 2006: "One reason Qatar can challenge Israel is that it, unlike most Arab countries, maintains discreet, low-level relations with [Israel]."[50]

An interesting event in October 2012 was the visit by Emir Hamad to the Gaza Strip, the first such visit by a head of state since Hamas took control of the strip in 2007. During the visit, Hamad met with key political figures, made a public call for Palestinian unity, and pledged US$400 million in assistance for construction projects.[51] Not surprisingly, Israel condemned the visit, and Palestinian Authority president Mahmoud Abbas expressed concerns about it as well, given his claim to represent all Palestinians as president. What is interesting, however, is that the visit signified how quickly Qatar seized the opportunity to step in and mark a role for itself in Israeli-Palestinian dynamics. With an end to Syrian support for Hamas, given the civil war that the Damascus regime was fighting by mid-2012, and with Iran having sidelined itself by ceasing support for Hamas after the group failed to openly support Syrian president Bashar al-Assad in the face of the Syrian uprising, the visit suggests that Qatar is pursuing a more mature but riskier regional foreign policy, willing as it is to irritate Israel and Iran if the benefit instead is greater leverage in Arab politics. While Qatar is not usually Machiavellian in its foreign relations, it is often very aggressive and candid, and this visit probably symbolizes an increased tolerance for risk in the pursuit of a regional role far beyond that normally afforded to such a small state.

Qatar's Relationship with China and Emerging Asian States

If Qatar's ties with Israel are confusing and presumably driven by image and branding considerations rather than direct economic strategy, then its rapidly expanding links with emerging powers, especially China, are the opposite. The relationships with China in particular, but also India and some Southeast Asian states, are overwhelmingly driven by commercial considerations, albeit also possessing some diplomatic and other advantages for Doha if global power dynamics ultimately shift markedly from the Western Hemisphere to the Eastern.

China and India have both grown sharply in economic importance to Qatar since around 2002 or 2003. This is commensurate with the growth in Qatar's international trade. Qatar's total exports jumped from QR68 billion (US$18.7 billion) in 2004 to almost QR206 billion (US$56.6 billion) in 2008 and its imports climbed from slightly under QR20 billion (US$5.5 billion) to over QR91 billion (US$25 billion) in the same period.[52] Of course energy exports dominated this impressive trade growth, especially as the major gas projects began coming on-stream at the time. Gas exports feature prominently in Qatari exports to India; by volume, Qatari gas exports to India rose from 2 million tons in 2004 to 7.5 million tons in 2008.[53] These sales were the result of the sales and purchase agreement with Petronet in India as part of the RasGas 2 project. As Qatar expanded its gas production, it also actively sought to develop gas exports to China.[54]

Yet Qatar also imports significant volumes of goods from both, but especially by the late 2000s from China, reflecting the growth of wealth in Qatar, mostly because of the development of the gas sector, and the greater purchasing power of both individuals and the state. There is also a good complementarity in the trade relationship: Qatar's imports from China and India include goods such as mechanical and electrical products, new technologies, and some consumer goods and simple manufactures—that is, goods that it does not yet produce very efficiently itself, but that as an energy exporter it has a high demand for. This meant, in a foreign relations context, that commercial ties between Qatar and both China and India gained greater depth and diversity over the first decade of the 2000s, especially given the enormous demand for energy by both states at the same time, reflecting the rise of both China and India, and including a more deliberate and strategic attempt by China in particular to build and diversify its trade and investment ties with the Gulf starting around the middle of the decade.[55] Table 7.2 shows the growth in Qatar's trade with both China and India in that key period.

Table 7.2 Qatar's Trade with China and India, 2001–2010 (QR millions)

	Qatar-China Trade		Qatar-India Trade	
	Qatar's Exports to China	Qatar's Imports from China	Qatar's Exports to India	Qatar's Imports from India
2001	1,190	396	560	323
2002	421	467	365	440
2003	938	605	536	561
2004	751	668	3,655	514
2005	1,369	1,892	3,203	1,412
2006	1,444	3,483	5,995	1,642
2007	1,213	4,975	9,697	2,419
2008	2,064	7,327	10,379	3,282
2009	2,260	7,159	13,449	3,314
2010	8,044	7,658	23,096	2,553

Source: Derived from statistics provided by the Qatar Information Exchange, http://www.qix.gov.qa/portal/page/portal/QIXPOC/Documents/QIX%20Knowledge%20Base/Publication.

The issue of diversification is also of interest to China, in particular its desire to ensure diversity in where it sources its energy and in the types of energy upon which its economy relies. As one Chinese official noted in 2006: "We have made it clear we are pursuing the diversification of our supply sources. . . . If we just source crude from one region, this will lead to even higher oil prices, and no-one really benefits. For the purposes of long-term stability, we are looking at Australia, the Caspian and elsewhere, and not just at oil and gas."[56]

There is also consistency between, on the one hand, the globalization of Qatar and its attempts at liberalizing and expanding its international economic and diplomatic role, and on the other, the rise of China and India as economic powers, especially as exporters of manufactures, and simple technology and services, respectively. From Qatar's side, this rise in trade with China and India occurred at the same time as its role as a hub began expanding; note that air transport by passengers and freight began increasing sharply as of about 2004,[57] which was soon followed by Qatar developing its maritime and ports capacity and further developing its already sound logistics and shipping industries.[58] As previously discussed, this was also the time when the Asian Games helped boost Doha's international profile and its desire to play a more activist international role.

The investment relationship too is becoming increasingly important for Qatar, especially with China. This has moved in both directions; both Qatar and China have overall trade surpluses and active sovereign wealth funds looking for new investments beyond the Atlantic states or domestic sources. Both also take a strategic view of such investment. For Qatar it is a way to invest downstream in the energy sector and thus gain greater value and diversification from its energy production. For China, investment provides a useful means by which to expand its foreign economic links, especially to underwrite its energy security through more diverse links with energy supplier states, and at the same time offset a balance of payments surplus that at times has been very high. As examples of the investment relationship, Qatar's sovereign wealth fund, for example, is the largest nonstate investor in the Agricultural Bank of China, having invested in 2010[59] and apparently keen to remain engaged with an investment strategy that covers both the financial sector and indirectly the agricultural sector as well.

As China and India become wealthier, it is likely that Qatar, given its interests in both more diverse investment and in ensuring its own food security, will be increasingly keen on investments in new sectors in China and India. In fact, when the Qatar Investment Authority (QIA) was the subject of a cable published by WikiLeaks in mid-2011, the cable showed that this was exactly the QIA's 2010 strategy. A QIA official told the US ambassador to Qatar, according to the cable, that "the first area of the QIA's investment efforts will be the commodities sector. . . . [The QIA official] shared [the US ambassador's] view that a structural change is underway in the commodities sector, strongly suggesting long-term price increases. The growth in the middle class of emerging countries such as China and India, for example, suggests higher food prices over the long term."[60] It is also notable that the same cable confirmed a commonly held view[61] about "China's ability to quickly make major spending decisions, particularly related to large scale infrastructure."[62] This could also be said of Qatar and other emerging, new state capitalist political economies, and partly as a result of this the Qatari-Chinese investment relationship is likely to grow in the future as Qatar places more funds in China and as China becomes more actively invested in Qatar. In the case of India, there is less investment and arguably less capacity for inward investment to Qatar from India, but the prospects of Qatar investing in India are high.[63] Already the QIA has entered or looked at energy, infrastructure, and agribusiness projects there,[64] and has an office in Mumbai, as it does in Shanghai.

Qatar's relationships with China and India demonstrate further and reiterate how political economy dynamics and foreign relations are interrelated. In the case of both China and India, and growing from the basic commercial relationships that had long existed between Qatar and these two countries, Qatar's rise as an energy exporter and its openness to inward investment and desire for economic diversification have given it a strong complementarity with the commercial goals of China and India. At the same time, however, there is scope for both trade and investment, but especially the latter and in both directions, to increase, given that all three states have developed balance of payments surpluses as their economies have boomed and given that, on their current trajectory, these states are likely to maintain such surpluses overall in the 2010s. The global financial crisis and associated weakness in the economies in the United States and Europe into the 2010s have further prompted these states to look at new sectors and new states for their investment.

For the time being, Qatar does not have a military or strategic relationship of any note with either China or India, nor is any significant one foreseeable. The expansion of China did not mean a greater military involvement in the Indian Ocean or further afield in the first decade of the 2000s, even if China has a small presence in Burma and despite its strategic reach being likely to grow in the 2010s. Traditionally, India and China have had a lukewarm relationship at best: the two fought a border war in 1962 and had a frosty relationship for many years after that, but after the turn of the century, they began to develop the relationship. For a long time they have maintained sufficiently cordial ties by avoiding strategic competition, and especially by retaining their strategic and naval forces close to home, usually on their respective sides of the Straits of Malacca. In the longer term, however, there is always a risk of strategic rivalry between them, or involving the United States as well as it develops links with India to offset China's rising power in greater Asia, but this is not likely to impact Qatar's political economy any more than it would the political economy of any other Gulf state. It is likely that Qatar would remain as aloof as possible from any such rivalry anyway, given its strong economic interests in China and India but its minimal security interests in them.

Qatar and the Arab Spring

One of the most interesting elements of Qatari foreign policy was its policy toward the 2011 Arab Spring. While its military forces had previously been used to engage with the Arab world, as during the 1990–1991 Gulf War or later during the peacekeeping contingent sent to southern Lebanon, the very small size of Qatar and its armed forces makes a highly activist role internationally, and not least of all a military role abroad, seem very peculiar when it happens. Yet Qatar took a direct military role in Libya in 2011 and was a crucial state in verbally backing the opposition in Syria. Not surprisingly, Doha was much quieter in the case of the uprising in Bahrain, which included Saudi and UAE military intervention in March 2011 in support of the minority-Sunni ruling Al Khalifa dynasty there, but even so its involvement in Libya in particular looks disproportionately activist and strong.

The Western- and then NATO-led Libyan intervention ran from March 19 to October 31, 2011, and was a somewhat controversial military intervention in support of UN Security Council Resolution 1973, which was passed after the Libyan uprising and then civil war became increasingly bloody and the fate of civilians in Libya of increasing international concern. The military involvement was mostly by naval and air forces from the United Kingdom, United States, and France, including a naval blockade and air strikes against Libyan military assets that were being used against the rebels. Despite the dominance of Western militaries in the media reporting about the conflict, and the sheer size of air forces in particular that they were able to deploy in the operation, Qatar nonetheless played a crucial role in the intervention. For its small size, the Qatari contribution was large: the Emiri Air Force provided six of its Mirage 2000 fighter aircraft and two C-17 large transport aircraft, stationed in Crete, Greece, to efforts to enforce the no-fly zone over Libya authorized by Security Council Resolution 1973. This commitment amounted to around half of its operational air capability and thus was a major contribution even if modest in overall size.[65] Importantly, as the conflict progressed, Qatari special forces reportedly assisted in training the Tripoli Brigade, a well-equipped core force within the Libyan National Liberation Army, which was probably important in the growing ability of opposition forces to win ground battles against the Libyan army in the latter stages of the conflict. Other assistance included some US$400 million in financial help to the opposition and assistance with the export of oil from Benghazi. Doha's involvement continued after the end of hostilities, with aid and other support agreed upon, including a memorandum of understanding between the Qatari government and the National Transitional Council, Libya's post-Qaddafi transitional government, for Qatar to assist in developing the institutions, laws, regulations, and skills of staff involved in public administration and justice. Other aid and support is likely in the future.[66]

Qatar also was vocal in supporting opposition forces or in criticizing governments engaged in conflict elsewhere during the Arab Spring. It is interesting, for example, that this included Doha distancing itself markedly from the Syrian regime through 2011 as the protests there continued, to the point that Doha reportedly started arming Syrian opposition forces in 2012,[67] possibly with clandestine US involvement as well.[68] Qatar had built quite solid ties with Damascus under Hamad, partly through diplomatic contact—as much in the service of Qatar's relationship with Iran, some would argue—but ties were especially strong in the realm of trade and investment links.[69] Qatar became a key Arab investor in Syria, and at times was vocal in its support for the Syrian regime in political and other noncommercial matters too. Although the Qatari government was initially quiet after protests began in Syria in early 2011, it quickly and sharply reversed its previous policy of building ties with the al-Assad regime; by mid-2011 Doha had recalled its ambassador in Damascus, was making public comments critical of the Syrian regime, and was allowing Al-Jazeera to do the same in its broadcasts. A few months later, the Qatari-Syrian diplomatic relationship had virtually collapsed,[70] followed in 2012 by a report that Doha had offered military support to Syrian rebels. By late 2012, Doha was openly backing the Syrian rebels against the al-Assad regime, calling on the United Nations in October to support the rebels more aggressively, and holding a conference of opposition groups in November.

Why Qatar took the positions that it did during the Arab Spring remains contested. To some there is a natural financial advantage, consistent with political economy arguments as a central source of Doha's foreign policy. Such views tend to argue, in the case of Libya, either that Doha ultimately wanted to shore up its power as a gas producer by winning post-Qaddafi gas contracts from a new Libyan government, or that Doha instead was seeking to advantage its diversification policy by winning future nongas contracts (especially in infrastructure and reconstruction) in Libya instead. This could have been a consideration but is unlikely to have been the only driver, especially given the size of the aid and the military contribution that Qatar provided the rebels.

As with some other foreign policy positions and actions, Doha probably had three other outcomes in mind in its policies toward Libya, Syria, and other states at the center of the Arab Spring, all of which are economically beneficial or related but none of which are centrally matters of trade or economics. First, it was a chance for Doha, and the emir, to reiterate to both an Arab and a Western audience Qatar's willingness to contribute to regional initiatives. Its involvement in Libya strengthened its ties with NATO and other states' militaries, and raised its public profile too, while also reinforcing its role as an *Arab* contributor to enforcing the no-fly zone and protecting civilians in Libya. Second, Doha may well take a preemptory view of such commitments, in particular that they allay the risk of Qatar being criticized for its very limited political liberalization, despite the promises of such that have been made by the emir since he seized power, or even criticism of Qatar as behaving globally in a trade and investment context but not being willing to engage diplomatically, militarily, or in other such ways. Such arguments have been raised to explain Qatar's policy toward both Libya and Syria. Finally, Doha was probably motivated, again, by the issue of branding. This was an opportunity not just to brand the country in general, but particularly to reinforce a couple of specific messages. One is its model of blending soft authoritarianism with an openness to globalization and (some) economic sectors and reforms, and in this sense is not markedly different from the idea of its response to the Arab Spring being a preemptory act by the regime. Another element, however, is Doha's common support for Islamism. Not only has it hosted meetings and figures from Hamas, Hezbollah, and other such groups, but also, as some argue, its support for Islamic groups in Libya during and after the civil conflict and external intervention there may be a sign of its support for Islamism, specifically of an attempt to create a balanced, fairly strict, but not radical Islamist model for the region. Proponents of this argument sometimes point to the Wahhabi tradition in Qatar as justification for this. Again, while this may be part of the explanation for Qatari policy toward Libya, Syria, and others during the Arab Spring, it is only one of several factors: in and of itself there is insufficient evidence to support this as a foreign policy driver, and no sign that the regime is seeking to mark Qatar out in a religious sense except as a conservatively oriented but appropriately open Sunni society.

Influence, Protection, Microstatism, and Qatar's Balancing Act

Foreign policy and foreign relations need to be incorporated into a study of Qatar's political economy for several reasons. Most obvious is the fact that several aspects of its foreign policy are driven by economic considerations, including many of its ties with the GCC, its relationship with Iran, and its growing links with China and India. Important, however, is the wider dynamic of its broad, at times seemingly almost contradictory, foreign relations and alliances backing the regime and the system over which it rules. Its foreign policy thus acts as a tool to protect Qatar's interests, and to ensure maintenance of the status quo. It is for this reason that it engages with the outside world, that it brands the country clearly and appropriately, and that it builds a core set of both major and regional actors that have both economic and other stakes in Qatar and its political and economic status quo.

In a statement to the Oxford Business Group elicited for its 2011 report on Qatar, Emir Hamad noted: "In terms of our work abroad, Qatar's foreign policy has always been based on strengthening our bonds and cooperation with all countries and peoples in a way that promotes mutual interests. . . . Our top priority is to build up the pillars of security and stability in the Gulf region, as well as the wider Middle East."[71] However, he made these remarks in regard to a report that focused on implementing the *Qatar National Vision 2030* and the emir's goals for the economy and for social development, almost as if foreign relations were simply a reinforcing tool for socioeconomic development and regime maintenance. Diplomacy is, of course, much more than that, but in Qatar's case there is an especially strong economic motivation behind its foreign policy, driven as with the wider political economy by the nature of the late rentier regime; the dynamics of Qatar's new state capitalism, especially the central role of the state and a small group of individuals at its summit; and of course the fact that Qatar is a microstate, situated in a tough neighborhood and wanting to be close—but never too close—to the major powers that provide both insurance against security threats and the economic opportunities that help sustain the regime.

Notes

1. Davidson, *Dubai,* p. 7.

2. This observation and what follows are noted in several sources, including, for example, Anthony, *Arab States of the Lower Gulf,* pp. 88–93.

3. Anthony, *Arab States of the Lower Gulf,* pp. 89–90, suggests a combination of these factors, and the links created by the Qatari elite visiting Iran for educational, social, or other reasons in the decades up to the mid-1970s. Multiple other sources focus on the lack of Iranian interventionism and lack of territorial conflict between the two states; unlike the elites in other Gulf states, most Qatari elites do not view Iran as expansionist in its goals; see the sources discussed in Lawson, "From Here We Begin," pp. 340–342.

4. Anthony, *Arab States of the Lower Gulf,* p. 91.

5. What follows on problems and tensions in the Saudi-Qatari relationship is from Dargin, "The Dolphin Project," pp. 19–24; Jeremy M. Sharp, "Qatar: Background and U.S. Relations," Congressional Research Service, US Library of Congress, RL31718, updated March 17, 2004, available online at http://fpc.state.gov/documents/organization/33741.pdf; and Sultan Sooud al-Qassemi, "How Saudi Arabia and Qatar Became Friends Again," *Foreign Policy,* July 21, 2011, http://www.foreignpolicy.com/articles/2011/07/21/how_saudi_arabia_and_qatar_became_friends_again.

6. Sharp, "Qatar," p. 6.

7. On the Saudi opposition to and disengagement from the Dolphin Project specifically, but also on wider issues in the Saudi-Qatari bilateral relationship, see Dargin, "The Dolphin Project," pp. 19–24.

8. al-Qassemi, "How Saudi Arabia and Qatar Became Friends Again."

9. More on this follows, plus see Wehrey et al., *Saudi-Iranian Relations Since the Fall of Saddam,* pp. 48–51.

10. "Reconciliation Benefits All," *Middle East Economic Digest,* October 5, 2007; al-Qassemi, "How Saudi Arabia and Qatar Became Friends Again."

11. al-Qassemi, "How Saudi Arabia and Qatar Became Friends Again."

12. The Gulf-wide GCC rail network was long planned but often delayed. See Ed Blanche, "Gulf Rail Network: The Dream Becomes Reality," *The Middle East,* February 2011, pp. 12–16.

13. "United Front Still Falters," *Middle East Economic Digest,* July 9, 2010.

14. Tom Owen, "Qatar Leads the Way," *The Middle East,* September 2000, pp. 4–7.

15. As discussed earlier, Oman is attached to the project, but technically receives gas from the United Arab Emirates via a separate asset, the 128-kilometer pipeline between Al-Ain and Fujairah.

16. See, for example, "Qatar and Oman Establish Joint Venture Investment Company," *Middle East Economic Digest,* May 18, 2007; "UAE and Qatar Co-Invest," *Middle East Economic Digest,* June 15, 2007; and some of the discussion in "Independent State," *Middle East Economic Digest,* August 14, 2007.

17. On the common currency idea and some of the issues of economic incompatibility that undermined its prospects, see al-Jasser and al-Hamidy, "A Common

Currency Area for the Gulf Region"; and Hanna, "A New Fiscal Framework for GCC Countries Ahead of Monetary Union."

18. "IIF: Gulf Currency Union Faces Delay," *Khaleej Times,* May 19, 2010; and author interviews, Doha, October 2011. Two interviewees mentioned that key Qatari elites had, as of 2011, distanced themselves from the single currency publicly, claiming that for reasons of saving face, a reversal back to supporting its implementation was unlikely for many years.

19. "United Front Still Falters," *Middle East Economic Digest,* July 9, 2010.

20. International Institute for Strategic Studies (IISS), *The Military Balance 2012,* pp. 344–345.

21. This figure is an estimate from Central Intelligence Agency, *The World Factbook 2011,* available online at https://www.cia.gov/library/publications/the-world-factbook/geos/qa.html.

22. IISS, *The Military Balance 2012,* p. 344.

23. Cordesman and al-Rodhan, "The Gulf Military Forces in an Era of Asymmetric War: Qatar," p. 3.

24. Cordesman and Nerguizian, "The Gulf Military Balance in 2010," pp. 36–37. Yemen spends a higher percentage of GDP on defense than Qatar too, if it is counted as a Gulf state.

25. See various tables in Cordesman and Nerguizian, "The Gulf Military Balance in 2010," pp. 17–35.

26. Author interview, Doha, October 2011.

27. "All Too Friendly," *The Economist,* November 12, 2011.

28. "Qatar: Profile—Shaikh Hamad bin Khalfa Al Thani: Key Regional Role," *Middle East Economic Digest,* August 28, 1995.

29. "Special Report: Qatar—A Special Relationship," *Middle East Economic Digest,* October 17, 2003.

30. Ibid.

31. Hugh Eakin, "The Strange Power of Qatar," *New York Review of Books,* October 5, 2011, http://www.nybooks.com/articles/archives/2011/oct/27/strange-power-qatar/?page=1.

32. Ibid.

33. Ibid.

34. Matthew Rosenberg, "Taliban Opening Qatar Office, and Maybe Door to Talks," *New York Times,* January 3, 2012.

35. Author interviews, Doha, October 2011.

36. el-Gamal and Jaffe, *Oil, Dollars, Debt, and Crises,* p. 64.

37. Ibid.

38. "Improving Regional Diplomacy," *Middle East Economic Digest,* June 4, 2010.

39. See, for example, Blanchard, "Qatar: Background and U.S. Relations," p. 5.

40. Ibid.

41. Ibid.; "Independent State."

42. "Improving Regional Diplomacy."

43. "Doha Offers Iran a Bridge to the West," *Middle East Economic Digest,* February 5, 2010; "Doha's Delicate Balancing Act," *Middle East Economic Digest,* February 5, 2010.

44. Most of the details that follow, on the history of Qatari-Israeli relations since 1996, unless indicated otherwise come from Rabi, "Qatar's Relations with Israel."

45. Rabi, "Qatar's Relations with Israel," p. 452.

46. "A Shameful Rejection," *Haaretz,* May 10, 2010.

47. This point and the others in this paragraph are also to be found in Rabi, "Qatar's Relations with Israel," p. 443.

48. "Independent State."

49. Rabi, "Qatar's Relations with Israel," p. 454.

50. "A Bouncy Bantam," *The Economist,* September 7, 2006.

51. "Qatar Emir Calls for Palestinian Unity on Visit to Gaza," *BBC News,* October 23, 2012, http://www.bbc.co.uk/news/world-middle-east-20037203.

52. QNB Capital, *Qatar Economic Review 2010,* p. 33.

53. Ibid., p. 34 (tab. 5.3).

54. Simeon Kerr, "Qatar Targets Increased Gas Exports to China," October 27, 2009, http://www.ft.com/intl/cms/s/0/4644013a-c350-11de-8eca-00144feab49a.html#axzz1ebwQqMKl.

55. "Trade Routes," *Middle East Economic Digest,* July 7, 2006.

56. Quoted in ibid.

57. World Bank, *Strengthening China's and India's Trade and Investment Ties to the Middle East and North Africa,* pp. 64–65 (especially figs. 3.7, 3.8).

58. "The Birth of a Gas Shipping Giant," *Middle East Economic Digest,* March 4, 2005.

59. "Qatar Said to Invest $2.8 Billion in AgriBank IPO to Tap Growth—Sources," *Reuters,* June 21, 2010, http://www.swfinstitute.org/swf-news/qatar-said-to-invest-2-8-billion-in-agribank-ipo-to-tap-growth.

60. "Qatar Investment Authority's 2010 Investment Strategy Outlined," November 25, 2009, released by WikiLeaks on August 20, 2011, http://wikileaks.org/cable/2009/11/09DOHA691.html.

61. Author interviews, Doha, January 2011 and October 2011.

62. "Qatar Investment Authority's 2010 Investment Strategy Outlined."

63. Author interviews, Doha, April 2012.

64. See the examples provided through the articles and links on the Sovereign Wealth Fund Institute website, at http://www.swfinstitute.org/fund/qatar.php.

65. "Qatar Deepens Support of Post-Qadhafi Libya," Economist Intelligence Unit, November 1, 2011, http://country.eiu.com/Qatar.

66. Ibid.

67. Karen DeYoung, "Saudi, Qatari Plans to Arm Syrian Rebels Risk Overtaking Cautious Approach Favored by U.S.," *Washington Post,* March 2, 2012.

68. Eric Schmitt, "C.I.A. Said to Aid in Steering Arms to Syrian Opposition," *New York Times,* June 21, 2012.

69. Anthony Shadid, "Qatar Wields an Outsize Influence in Arab Politics," *New York Times,* November 14, 2011.

70. Ibid.

71. Sheikh Hamad bin Khalifa Al Thani, "A Solid Core," in Oxford Business Group, *The Report: Qatar 2011,* p. 25.

8

Challenges for the Future

Having outlined some of the trends in and explanations for Qatar's political economy since the 1990s, attention now shifts in this final chapter to an outline and assessment of the future for Qatar. The main issues to be covered are those that the state and society are likely to confront in pursuing social, economic, and political development in the coming couple of decades. In the process, some comment on current thinking about these issues is offered, especially as some are fiercely contested. In undertaking such a challenge as this, it is easy to fall into the trap of either being too optimistic or too pessimistic in the analysis: too often, too many scholars are keen to play Cassandra and be the first or most assertive to have predicted a problem, failing, or even a political or economic collapse, while many policymakers and businesspeople, both external observers and many Qatari officials, are too keen to brush aside potential problems and talk only of the country's successes. To be sure, there are a great many successes in Qatar's story, but at the same time, no transition as profound and rapid as Qatar's comes without problems, and Qatar has a great many that will dominate its politics and development in the future.

Those problems and challenges that will be explored here include the management of the economy during and after the global financial crisis and whether there are any macroeconomic vulnerabilities still faced by the government, as well as the problems stemming from both high domestic population growth and a large expatriate work force. These include labor market issues, the question of how to preserve Qatari identity as the indigenous become a smaller percentage of the population, and how to meet the expectations of youth and women about the future. Perhaps most important is democratization: Is Qatar transitioning toward greater democracy? Or closer to the "pluralized autocracy" that Daniel Brumberg identified,[1] wherein promises of reform are routine but true reform of the system is deliberately immobilized by the state? Will the social change that necessarily follows such dramatic economic change as experienced by Qatar mean that some sort of political change is certain too? All of these questions are explored in the context of an academic debate that after more than two decades still rages.

The final part of the chapter is concerned with the question of whether there is a "Qatar model" of development. Specifically, does the collection of policies and strategies adopted by Qatar after 1996 constitute a specific program of economic development, and, perhaps equally important to those concerned with the challenges of Arab development, does this set of strategies and policies constitute a model or package that can be transferred to other states? Much has been made of a "Dubai model,"[2] for example—and the question of whether this is in part derived from a "Singapore model," and in turn is broadly a model that has informed post-1996 Qatar—and so the wider question of development models is also explored in the process of assessing Qatar's experience. The ultimate argument is that Qatar has copied or adapted *some* of Dubai's policies, but has also sought to develop on its own terms and distinctly from Dubai, and moreover, that there is limited transmissibility of Qatar's "model"—if it can even be called that—because there are too many unique or specific features to Qatar's experience, from its oil and gas wealth, to its specific political structure, to its historical experiences with social and political change and with development. While Qatar affords some lessons in development for other states, it has not found any magical policy wand that any state can wave and enchantingly have development unfold neatly before it. Qatar is a success story on the whole, but a distinctive one, and still one that is not without its problems.

Qatar, the Global Financial Crisis, and the Economy

The first and perhaps most obvious question about Qatar's economic transition has to do with its macroeconomy: Is its economy as healthy and dynamic as the high, sometimes double-digit, growth figures from 2000 to 2011 might suggest? Further, are there underlying problems either caused by or separate from this growth? In fact, as a general observation, the Qatari economy *is* in fairly good condition. Its nominal rate of gross domestic product (GDP) growth in the period from 2004 to 2008 averaged

37 percent.[3] Its real growth rate—that is, growth after inflation—was over 7 percent from 2003 onward, including double-digit levels in 2008 and 2010. That said, this was mostly the result of new gas projects coming online, and therefore it was a feature of the specific period. This high growth, with it being the product of energy exports moreover, meant that it also contributed to high inflation in that same period, especially in 2007 and 2008. Table 8.1 shows GDP (at purchasing power parity), real growth rates, and inflation rates for the period 1999–2011. Growth in the 2010s, until new gas projects possibly come online late in the decade, probably will be far more modest, perhaps only 1–2 percent per annum in real terms.

To the extent that there are macroeconomic problems or risks facing Qatar, only two stand out as warranting note. One is the risk of inflation—a common problem with energy exporters and, along with the "Dutch disease" (a high exchange rate pushed up by higher demand than for currency to pay for energy exports from the energy-exporting state), considered a

Table 8.1 Qatar's GDP, Real GDP Growth Rate, and Inflation Rate, 1999–2011

	GDP (PPP) (US$ billions)[a]	Real GDP Growth Rate (%)[b]	Inflation Rate (%)[c]
1999	12.3	1.5	2.0
2000	15.1	4.0	2.5
2001	16.3	5.6	2.0
2002	17.2	3.4	1.9
2003	14.5	8.5	2.3
2004	19.5	8.7	3.0
2005	24.5	8.8	8.8
2006	26.4	7.1	7.2
2007	71.4	8.4	13.7
2008	91.3	13.4	15.1
2009	100.8	9.5	–4.9
2010	150.6	16.3	1.1
2011 est.	184.3	18.8	1.9

Source: Derived from statistics in Central Intelligence Agency, *The World Factbook,* various editions, https://www.cia.gov/library/publications/the-world-factbook.

Notes: For more detail on GDP and inflation at current prices, see the figures in International Monetary Fund, "Qatar: 2010 Article IV Consultation," Country Report no. 11/64; and International Monetary Fund, "Qatar: Statistical Appendix," Country Report no. 10/62.

a. Gross domestic product at purchasing power parity (PPP) measures the value of goods and services produced within a country over a particular year, taking into account variations in both incomes and expenditures and (roughly) equating them across different economies.

b. This is the annual rate of change in gross domestic product, adjusted for inflation.

c. This is the annual rate of inflation for consumer goods.

typical feature of the "oil curse." Qatar has avoided currency problems by tying the rial to the US dollar—it remained at 3.64 to the US dollar for over a decade after 2001—which, along with the stimulus provided by a dramatic rise in rent income, meant a high inflation rate; as Table 8.1 shows, inflation from 2005 to 2008 was especially high, worrisome above all at the height of the boom period in 2007 and 2008 when major new gas projects were coming online and rents flowed into prices in the property/housing sector and food especially.[4] Inflation hit 13.7 percent in 2007 and over 15 percent in 2008. The pressure from this was significant, adding around 52 percent to average consumer costs in the four years covering 2005 to 2008, and it was only the slowdown in new gas rent sources and the global financial crisis that reduced this rate to a more manageable level in the years after that. Had the inflation rates of 2007 and 2008 continued, it almost certainly would have had a serious negative impact on non-energy areas of the economy and especially on private sector export competitiveness.[5] For the next period of energy production expansion, which may come in 2015 to 2020 if the North Dome is opened to new projects after 2014 or may simply result from a sharp jump in demand and a price boom as was seen with oil from 2003 to 2008, Qatar will need a more coherent and considered plan to handle inflation.

A second question about Qatar's economy in recent years has been the rise in public debt and, by the late 2000s, the high levels of private debt too. Certainly, when the basic figures are considered, as laid out in Table 8.2, they superficially show a dramatic increase in public debt starting in 2009. However, it is important to consider the debt figures also as a percentage of GDP, in which case they are far more manageable than the sheer numbers alone might suggest. Government debt as a sheer number increased some three-and-a-half-fold over 2005 to 2009, but, at 16.8 percent of GDP in 2009, remained at a very manageable level given the virtually guaranteed income that the state has from energy rents.

Private debt, at some 38 percent of GDP in 2011, is more of a worry, but even so, it is not at the level seen in many Western economies. It is also important to note that a significant amount of nongovernment debt is held by firms that are partially state-owned. Moreover, this debt is often productive debt—that is, debt accrued toward income-earning projects, or for major capital works that will repay a socioeconomic benefit over the very long term and probably beyond the life of the specific loan.[6] Such lending is far less of a concern than private borrowing for consumption or even for property or portfolio investment, and certainly Qatar has seen nothing like the growth in debt that characterized Dubai's economy in the years leading up to the global financial crisis that began in 2008.[7] Nonetheless, the

Table 8.2 Qatar's External Debt: Composition and Value, 2005–2012 (US$ millions)

	2005	2006	2007	2008	2009	2010	2011 est.	2012 est.
Total external debt excluding banks	14,989	19,486	24,762	33,452	50,259	70,757	87,409	89,535
As percentage of GDP	38.4	32.2	31.1	29.1	51.5	55.6	50.5	49.8
Government external debt	3,743	3,333	2,871	3,868	12,760	16,995	21,397	22,710
As percentage of GDP	8.7	5.5	3.6	3.4	13.1	13.3	12.4	12.6
Debt service, as percentage of GDP	4.8	4.4	4.2	2.8	3.3	4.9	3.1	2.7

Sources: International Monetary Fund, "Qatar: 2010 Article IV Consultation," Country Report no. 11/64, p. 25 (tab. 1); International Monetary Fund, "Qatar: 2012 Article IV Consultation," Country Report no. 12/18, p. 27 (tab. 1).

levels of private debt became more concerning in the late 2000s, and in February 2010 the government placed strict lending limits on unsecured private borrowing by individuals in an effort to address it. Done at the same time as reforms to sharia-compliant banking, it was seen as an attempt to tighten up personal borrowing and to ensure that individuals did not develop unserviceable levels of debt, nor institutions develop large amounts of unsecured loans on their books.

In September 2011 the state announced an immediate pay increase of 60 percent for most public sector employees, and 120 percent for those in senior military and security positions and 50 percent for other military and security personnel.[8] Many state-owned firms and some private ones felt compelled to offer a similar pay increase as well, to remain competitive as employers with the state.[9] Although this was probably motivated in part by the 2011 Arab Spring, and in effect therefore was classic rentier co-optive behavior toward society, it also suited the government's concerns about debt, since the constraints on unsecured borrowing, which had been linked to multiples of an individual's salary, were not immediately eased, suggesting a government hope that some of the pay increase would go toward retiring private debt. Certainly this was how the pay increase was in part justified at the time and commonly painted by officials afterward.[10]

In other respects, Qatar survived the global financial crisis rather well, for a number of reasons. One is that with the large budget and current account surpluses—the "twin surpluses"[11]—that it had enjoyed through the 2003–2008 oil boom and even throughout the 2008–2009 global financial crisis, the economy was able to absorb some shocks and the state was able to step in and reinforce some key areas such as the finance and property sectors. Second, the state had built up enormous investments through the sovereign wealth fund, meaning that while there was a sizable amount of public and private foreign debt on Qatar's books as the global financial crisis began in 2008, the net position of the state was positive. If anything, the Qatar Investment Authority used the global financial crisis as an opportunity to invest in some new assets and countries, even after the costs of investing into the domestic banking sector and shoring up some other sectors. Third, Qatar had a specific advantage as a gas producer, given that the long-term and costly nature of large gas projects meant that they could not easily be cut back or canceled when the global financial crisis began, and given the fact that gas contracts were, anyway, mostly long-term ones that may be affected but are not normally wrecked by immediate economic fluctuations.[12] It probably helped also that investors view gas as an emerging and growing energy source and Qatar as an emerging giant in gas. Qatar was also, by 2008, gaining an international reputation as a hub in the

Gulf, and its diversification strategy was starting to give it a new commercial reputation in sectors such as transport, finance, leisure, and tourism, which some commentators have suggested may have assisted it during the global financial crisis.[13]

Moreover, the current profile of the economy looks promising for Qatar, especially the ongoing likelihood of gas dominating it and of gas being in high demand as developed economies increasingly try to shift away from coal and oil. It suggests that even with the environmental and energy security pressures that are likely to impact hydrocarbon-producing states in the 2010s and 2020s, Qatar will have a large rentier income guaranteed for a long time into the future. In fact, it is the dynamics of this that ought to be of much greater concern to the Qatari regime and society than macroeconomic conditions. While minor macroeconomic problems are likely to crop up occasionally, such as periods of problematically high inflation, it is the socioeconomic impact of Qatar's rentier structure and the dynamics that the rentier pathology creates that are far more important problems. Ensuring social stability, socioeconomic development, and cultural harmony is a challenge, not *despite* rents and the political order and state capitalism they have fostered, but *because* of them.

Many of Qatar's challenges in the coming decades will stem from demography, including the small population of the country overall, the small number of Qatari nationals in comparison to the large number of expatriate workers, and the expected rise in absolute numbers of both but especially—in political terms, of most concern to the state—of Qatari nationals. These population changes will bring new pressures for socioeconomic infrastructure, while the growth in the indigenous, or national, population will lead to pressures to make economic diversification and Qatarization succeed, where until now they for the most part have not. When demographic change is linked with globalization, and with the changing global environment into which young Qataris especially are increasingly connected, then there is a likelihood that the state will face increasing pressure for reform not only from society in general, but also from specific groups of citizens such as youth and women. The chapter now turns to these issues and what they might mean and entail.

Problems of the Labor Market and Qatarization

Intimately linked to both economic development and sociopolitical harmony are the dynamics of the Qatari labor market and the efficacy of the state's labor market policies. Two main dynamics here are likely to be important in the coming generation: the reliance on expatriate workers, especially with major events such as the 2022 World Cup dictating further massive infrastructure projects over the 2010s and into the 2020s; and the problems of Qatarization, including the weakness of it in policy terms and its failure to work effectively in light of problems of business culture, education and training, and other impacting factors.

The Qatari government does not publish exact or reliable figures on the number of Qatari nationals. The population of Qatar in 2010 was 1,696,563 according to the census that year.[14] Of these, around 280,000–300,000 were Qatari citizens,[15] a figure consistent with what the majority of estimates suggest and given the labor market dynamics, gender balance, and other indicators of Qatari versus expatriate population sizes. If true, then about 1.4 million residents of Qatar are foreigners, perhaps half from South Asia, and the majority of them single males. The total economically active population in 2010 was about 1,262,000, and of these perhaps only 100,000 were Qataris[16]—less than one in a dozen people in the work force—given the rapid population growth and large numbers of housewives and full-time students among the Qatari population. Thus the dynamics of the workplace, and business culture, are already impacted by this large majority of non-Qataris dominating the labor force, although Qatari dominance at the highest ranks gives them an influence disproportionate to their small numbers overall. However, it is a problem that "Qataris and non-Qataris essentially work in separate labor markets."[17] This is a hobbling factor for economic development and specifically for labor market development and skills transfer, and it is a social problem as well because it limits communication and potentially social harmony across the Qatari/non-Qatari line.

What is even more profound is that estimates of future population magnify this dynamic even more markedly. According to most estimates, the total Qatari population when the World Cup occurs in 2022 will be around 3 million, though some estimates place the population as high as 5 million. Assuming that the Qatari population grows at the current rate, and even with increasing numbers of young Qataris entering the work force in the coming two decades, perhaps between 150,000 and 200,000 Qataris will be working around 2030, out of a total work force of as many as 4 million if the population of 5 million is reached. Such a case, where Qataris would constitute only 3–5 percent of the work force, presents something of a paradox. At one level, it suggests that good jobs will be found for any Qataris who want them, simply because there will be so few Qataris as a share of the work force. Yet in fact, such population growth is likely to place even greater pressures on Qataris. Both economic diversification and

Qatarization remain crucial to the absorption of these Qataris. First, those Qataris who work will be greater, in sheer number, than at present and so they will need to be appropriately qualified and skilled if they are to obtain the positions that they expect. The education system will have to produce world-class graduates, otherwise Qataris will not gain the positions they aspire to. Educational reforms under Hamad are headed in this direction, but the perception remains that secondary education, especially, is not up to international par,[18] and that higher education, while more globally competitive, is expensive and its benefits are limited to a relatively small number of people. Qatarization can never be a substitute for this. If a simple quota system continues to be the effect of the Qatarization policy, then Qataris will not find themselves in positions that give them truly meaningful work. Finally, since so much of GDP comes from the energy sector, which is not a large employer, and since much of the population growth over the 2010s will involve importing labor for the construction sector, which does not employ a large number of Qataris either, diversification will still be absolutely essential. In fact, diversification will need to be achieved to a much greater extent than at present to ensure sufficient numbers of skilled, prestigious positions for Qataris.

This all touches on the fact that both the laws covering foreign laborers, and the Qatarization policy, have not been very successful by most measures. In terms of expatriate workers, the current rigidity of the sponsorship system, together with the power that this gives employers, is a problem, because it stops the best-qualified people from moving into employment easily and even allows some to be excluded from the economy for two years by their employers if they depart those employers on poor terms, or simply because the employers fear that the expatriates will be employed by competitors. It makes economic sense to liberalize the laws on expatriate workers, but to do so except in a few minor ways would be unpopular among Qataris, especially the most influential of them, and thus remains unlikely.[19]

Other laws, especially given the power that Qatari sponsors and business owners possess under both labor law and contract law, are also a problem where disputes or behaviors damage Qatar's reputation. The control that Qataris have over expatriates in both labor and contract disputes is an example, above all the common requirement for expatriates to obtain exit permits to be able to travel abroad. Most Western expatriates in Doha are aware of the various cases of Western executive expatriates being held in Qatar and not being permitted to leave, often for months or even a year or more, because of a dispute with a former employer or other person with whom the expatriate has entered into a contract.[20] Perhaps the most famous case was that of the Belgian Philippe Bogaert, who was imprisoned for almost a year before escaping Qatar by sailboat in September 2009 after a court in June of that year had found him guilty of deliberately bouncing checks and sentenced him to three years in prison.[21] His sponsor had been able to stop him from leaving the country lawfully because of the dispute between the two.

Of course, for poorer, unskilled expatriates the experience can be worse, as they are often housed and fed by their employers at remote locations near a worksite, or bused to and from work, and so have very little chance to gain information about how their conditions compare to those of others or what their rights are. Again, however, there is little desire on the part of employers to give workers any new or additional powers and no wish by the state to create conditions in which there might be labor unrest or under which unrest might more easily occur. In an environment where there are enormous disparities in incomes, and where the citizenry is the state's only real political concern, stability is the first goal of labor law. Thus, as much as some Qataris are very good employers, there is little prospect of formal reform to the laws governing expatriates, and least of all the laws governing the poorest of workers, apart from perhaps some very superficial reforms if negative media reporting about the issue reaches a strong enough tempo.

The second issue, Qatarization, is also a case where reform is needed but is unlikely to happen until real economic pressures make resistance to reform unjustifiable. If the goal was simply to find positions for Qataris and to keep them busy and politically content, then perhaps Qatarization has been a marginal success. By any other (read, developmental) measure, Qatarization has failed. Qatarization commenced on June 1, 2000, as a rolling five-year policy and plan.[22] Under the policy, state-owned firms and larger foreign firms engaged in joint ventures with the state have quotas, depending on the sector, for the number of Qataris they must employ; the long-term aim of the policy is to increase the opportunities for Qataris and reduce the reliance on expatriates, and especially to reach at least a 50 percent level for Qatari nationals in the key sectors of energy and various industrial sectors. Often in these sectors employers will fulfill the legal requirement placed on them by the policy, but are not truly engaged with such staff or willing to fully develop them as employees. Western businesspeople affected by Qatarization routinely say that they treat the policy as a form of taxation or as a cost of doing business, and that they recruit Qataris to meet the required quota but do not give them the same responsibilities or opportunities that they would an expatriate in the same role.[23] Some claim that they have to recruit an expatriate anyway to "shadow" the Qatari and perform or supplement some of his or her work.[24] Businesspeople running smaller firms where there is no Qatarization requirement typically do not recruit Qataris at all; this is the case not just with Western businesspeople but with many Qatari employers and managers as well.

The problems of Qatarization are partly the result of the "manager (*mudir*) syndrome," although this is often overstated, and partly due to weaknesses and failings in the policy itself. This syndrome, named by Daryl Champion,[25] and described by other authors,[26] is the characteristic that some claim exists in the Gulf in which nationals feel that their country is wealthy enough that it ought to give them an easier life—specifically, more generous working conditions and a more prestigious position than otherwise. It is often equated with rentierism,[27] even if the two do not have to be linked. However, the *mudir* syndrome is contentious, partly because it is very difficult to measure, and partly because it occurs to some extent in many societies. It is certainly a feature of business culture and a dynamic of the workplace that Qataris prefer not to work in manual labor roles or in positions that lack social status,[28] but that arguably is the case in most developed economies, not just in rentier ones. The *mudir* syndrome is perhaps most important because of its influence. Regardless of its precise characteristics, if employers feel that it exists and is important as an indicator of the likely performance of a potential employee, and if this in turn affects hiring or training decisions, then it has an impact by virtue of its image if nothing else. Employers certainly take this view of it as a problem.[29]

The more important consideration with Qatarization is whether it is a flawed policy doomed to failure, at least in its current guise. There are several reasons to take this view. Perhaps the most important weakness of it is that, in the absence of true economic diversification and an expansion of the private sector as an employer, Qatarization is simply a policy that requires some wealthy but non-labor-intensive sectors, dominated by state-owned firms, to have more Qataris on their books. The policy in this sense does little to reduce the role of the state as an employer, nor does it decrease the attraction of working for the state (arguably the opposite, if getting a prestigious position is easier with a state-owned firm than a private one). Thus to implement Qatarization requirements without providing genuine incentives for private sector development, and without making private sector employment more attractive or the public sector less so to the bulk of Qataris, is to set the policy up to ultimately fail. The pay increases of between 60 and 120 percent in September 2011 were almost certainly counterproductive to Qatarization in this regard, too, sending a message as they did that the state is a better and more generous employer than the private sector.

Likewise, education policy is linked to Qatarization outcomes. At present, a very small number of Qataris are given a world-class higher education at Education City or increasingly through Qatar University. However, Qataris are not being graduated at the rate necessary to help Qatarization, and especially, Qataris often lack the skills and quality of experience to work in the private sector in more technical roles.[30] Just as important is the fact that some two-thirds of graduates are women, who often leave the work force earlier than men, whether by choice or social pressure, and even when they stay in employment they are usually underutilized by employers. If more men are not able to complete the requirements for a world-class degree, then for Qatarization to succeed, alternatives have to be found where appropriate work is available for these men, in roles that they are willing to work hard in and will find meaning in doing. None of this seems to have been given appropriate consideration in the implementation of Qatarization.

Resolving these issues is crucial because they will impact the long-term future of Qatar. Even if the rents accruing to the state continue or expand further in per capita terms, there is little point in creating meaningless or unnecessary employment positions for Qataris just so that they have a job on paper. This would mean creating a nation of well-educated, wealthy, but in effect idle people, which would be counterproductive for the economy and potentially politically destabilizing as well if rents remained varied or if Qataris began to demand more meaning in their work. Likewise, subsidizing jobs in new areas of the economy using rents is economically undesirable, and is not sustainable in the long term anyway. Of the current debates in Qatar, those of economic diversification and Qatarization are perhaps the most crucial and contested. Some argue that they are flawed policies that need to be scrapped and redesigned from scratch. Others see this as too harsh a criticism of policies that are inherently very long term: both policies, they argue, require intergenerational change so that attitudes toward education, workplace dynamics, and what positions and sectors are prestigious all have time to shift. A Qatari noted that it is not the policies that need changing, but the political and business cultures that currently form the environment in which the policies are implemented: "Changing these cultures," he noted, "is a proposition not for the next two or three years, or even two or three decades, but rather for the next two or three generations."[31]

Questions of Qatari Culture and Identity

Just as important to a political economy as economic performance and dynamics is the question of political culture, which in turn stems at least in part from cultural identity. In much of the Gulf, identity is complicated by the minority status of nationals, and this is the case in Qatar as it is in most Arab Gulf states. Tellingly, it is also something to which the state has paid great attention over the past two decades or so, in part out of a desire to avoid the same social and cultural outcomes that Dubai has experienced, and in part because a strong national identity is central to political stability in a society that is changing rapidly and given a political elite that has historically been fractured. When demographic change is mixed with globalization and the social change that has occurred in the past couple of decades, including some changes such as a rise of consumerism and a sense of greater "Westernization" of public space among some Qataris, it is little wonder that the state has become concerned with matters of cultural identity.

This is why the *Qatar National Vision 2030* makes such a strong statement about culture within its second pillar, social development: this includes a commitment to "preserve Qatar's national heritage and enhance Arab and Islamic values and identity" and a goal to engage internationally—to brand the country, that is, but also to enhance its self-image and the domestic sense of Qatari-ness—including the aim of "intensification of cultural exchange with the Arab peoples in particular and with other nations in general."[32] It is also why the state has put so much effort into the symbols of national identity and into reinforcing a sense of nationalism among the citizens. The development of grand national facilities and sites has been integral to this too, whether the redevelopment of Souq Waqif or construction of the new Qatar National Museum in the case of Qatari national identity, or the Museum of Islamic Art as an Arab and Islamic symbol of identity. While these are part of the effort at international branding by the state, they are also an attempt at reinforcing Qatari identity and nationalism, something equally important to long-term stability as branding.

However, the nature of political power and the political economy dictate that culture and identity be constructed in a particular fashion. It would be a double-edged sword, after all, for the emir or the Al Thani elite to promote a Qatari identity that recalled the dominance of the Al Thani, or the fragmentations within the extended family, or the disputes that have sometimes characterized Al Thani relations with some of the other large families and tribes. Thus the type of identity that is promoted is centered on a globalized, open, tolerant image of the country, and as a country with a specific national identity but that nonetheless forms part of a wider Arab and Muslim identity. Historical settings or claims may be drawn upon to build this image, but as with all such historical narratives, they are interpretations that are weaved and presented according to current needs.

Culture and identity stem, like labor market challenges do, from the twin issues of demographic change and population growth. Qataris are already a minority in the country, constituting barely one-sixth of the overall population and, given the high number of expatriates and the rapid population growth rate, well less than one-sixth of adults. There is a fear that Qatari identity, or Qataris' agreed and shared values, may be threatened by their minority status in the country, all the more so as the population grows further in the coming decades. Many Qataris view Dubai as an example of the risks of unbridled expansion and openness: while the economic performance of Dubai, until the 2008–2009 global financial crisis at least, was something that appealed to Qataris, the sense that Dubai had become too socially liberal, perhaps because of the dominance of foreigners, and Emiratis too small and obscure a minority in their own land—some 4 percent by one estimate around 2007 or 2008[33]—was not something that Qatar wanted to emulate. Some Qataris feel that trends such as the relaxation of rules on the serving of alcohol and the growing dominance of English in public space are signs that a traditional culture is being eroded and replaced by a more globalized, Westernized one.[34] That said, this trend has not been an uninterrupted one: the decision by Qatar University in early 2012 to switch from English to Arabic as its primary language of instruction, for example, was probably motivated in part by a concern that places such as the university campus were too cosmopolitan and not reflective enough of local perceptions of Qatari identity.

Some of the issues that are emerging in Qatar are similar to those in other Gulf states where the indigenous population is a minority, but the debate and the sense of cultural penetration are not as stark as Christopher Davidson notes in the case of Dubai.[35] Instead, the state's policies for promotion of a national identity, albeit a reconfigured one that only partly matches most Qataris' self-identity and understanding of their shared history, have been closer to the deliberate anchoring of the country in an historical narrative and the promotion of an identity that suits the political status quo that Marc Valeri describes in Oman under Sultan Qaboos bin Said.[36] Whether this reassertion of traditionalism and of constructed identity will succeed remains unclear, however: certainly in terms of identity and nationalism there is a sense of "Qatari-ness" and a sense that Qatar is different from other Gulf states, not to mention Arab states. How much of this is the result of the state and the Al Thani imposing itself as an allocative force over society, however, and how much is a genuine sense of shared cultural identity as members of a set of tribes who have lived for some time on the small finger that is the Qatar peninsula, is impossible to tell. As with elsewhere in the Arab world, loyalty often is ultimately much more local than national; it is to family, tribe, and the like, before it is to the state. In contrast with many other Arab states, however, Qatar has had to work especially hard to construct a historical narrative and to guide society's view of its own culture.

Social Change: Future Roles for Women and Youth

Among Qatari nationals, the two important groups for future development—and arguably the two who feel most aggrieved about some aspects of the political economy and social structure—are women and young people. In both cases, as a generalization, dynamics are complicated by the expectations on the one hand that the state will continue in its rentier role as a provider of social benefits, employment opportunities, and other advantages, while other expectations are expanding, with young people and women expecting greater opportunity and equality at work and in some cases a greater voice with the state as well.

The position of women in Qatar is complicated by the clash between traditional roles and expectations on the one hand, and the requirements of the economy and the growing level and quality of female education on the other. In the past, women mostly played traditional family roles in Qatar, and to a large extent this continues to the present time, even though the growing wealth of most Qataris arguably allows women the time and opportunity to pursue a career if they wish. Still, Qatari women, especially those of childrearing age, are very likely to withdraw from the labor market and focus on domestic duties, whether due to their own choice or to pressure from family. This is inconsistent, however, with the growth of educational accomplishment by women, although this varies greatly across generations; while on average women are better educated than men,[37] this is accentuated by age group. Currently, older Qatari women are actually less educated than men of the same age, while for those currently in middle age the figures are about equal, and among younger Qataris a far greater number of women than men are tertiary-educated: those aged twenty-five to twenty-nine who held a postsecondary qualification in 2004 outnumbered men by a ratio of roughly 1.8 to 1.[38] As discussed in Chapter 5, by 2009 women comprised over three-quarters of students at Qatari higher education campuses, now a long-term trend given that even in the mid-1990s there were around twice as many women compared to men at Qatari universities.[39] At the secondary level, since about 2000 both men and women have completed high school studies at roughly the same rate, since most Qataris complete their secondary schooling, but again and as with many other countries, women outperform men in their secondary school results[40] and have a reputation for being more diligent.

The issue with gender is predominantly one of social expectations. Under Qatari law, for example, women have had the right to access government jobs on the same basis as men and with the same employment conditions since Law no. 9 of 1976.[41] However, at that time, and extending to the present, there was societal opposition to the idea of women taking on the same public roles as men, especially if they had families, even though women are becoming increasingly essential if economic diversification and Qatarization are to succeed, given the shortages of appropriately skilled Qataris in the labor market.[42] Societal opposition to women in the work force probably comes not from economic concerns, therefore, but from social ones: a worry by some about women working with men, perhaps, or about the consequences for men of the upper echelons of the labor market becoming more feminized.

Thus there are several issues involved in encouraging women into a larger number of roles in the work force. One is that well-educated women are clustered into specific sectors of the work force, especially education, social work, administrative office roles, and government positions, even if increasingly they appear in professional roles as well.[43] Second is the challenge of getting women into the private sector: this is an issue with Qataris generally, but it is especially challenging to get women into private sector roles because often there is less predictability in tenure and working hours. Conversely, however, when faced with discrimination or limited opportunities in formal employment, increasing numbers of women (albeit a small number overall at present) are engaging in self-employed work.

Finally, and perhaps more important in encouraging more Qatari women into the work force, is the need to combine economic imperatives with social expectations. This is gradually changing as increasing numbers of expatriate women take up roles in Qatar—often senior roles—and as local women see more potential from their rising educational achievements and though the Internet and other communications tools. There are also now some high-profile female figures in public life, including Hamad's wife, Shaikha Muza, of course, as well as women such as Shaikha bint Abdallah al-Missnad, the president of Qatar University; Shaikha Mayassa bint Hamad bin Khalifa Al Thani, chair of the Qatar Museum Authority; and a large number of women in top positions in nongovernmental organizations.[44] Despite some expansion of the public role of women in the past decade or so, they remain hobbled by their dominance in only particular sectors.[45] When they do obtain public sector positions in particular, they are often underutilized in those roles and not given the same experience, training opportunities, or access to promotion as are men.[46] As a Qatari government agency survey noted more generally, this clash between economic needs and social values and behavioral norms in the workplace is acute and is something that disadvantages women and places in a difficult position those who would like the situation to change:

> Despite the openness of Qatari society; and women occupying some leadership positions including a minister post; and woman-to-woman support and encouragement, women are still confused and live [in] hesitation [over] whether to accept such situation [of social pressures as to their roles]; to relinquish their cultural heritage, and to act freely and openly in the society, or otherwise to decline and accept cultural [norms], which cannot be easily abandoned.[47]

However, it is very likely that this will change, if gradually, over time. Women now so outperform men in higher education, and are so central to the long-term prospects for economic diversification, that the economic imperatives for them to take a greater role in the work force are becoming inexorable. Moreover, as families become wealthier and yet have fewer children, which is the trend now, there will be less of a case to be made that women need to play traditional roles at home. Besides, women playing more active economic roles might seem to be a diversion from their recent home-centered roles, but in fact would be a reversion to the pre-oil past, when women routinely played economic roles outside the home, especially during the often-lengthy periods of male absences during the pearling season. If this happens, it will not be something foreign to the culture, but rather a reversion to the greater commercial and civic roles that women played as recently as a couple generations ago. It will not happen quickly, however, and it is likely to take several decades for women's roles in the work force to shift profoundly.

In some ways, young males carry many of the same grievances as young women who currently would like to play a greater professional role or have the same opportunities as older male counterparts at work. Just as women are economically underutilized, the same could be said of young males. Many young professionals feel as though they are not treated seriously in the workplace, or that they are expected to yield to less educated (or less skilled) senior managers rather than express their own views and contribute to the organization.[48] One Qatari, aged around thirty and possessing two international degrees, expressed it as an ongoing frustration: "What was the point of sending me to study management and business overseas for six years, if I am going to then be put into a role back here [in Qatar] and told to keep my mouth shut and do what I'm told?"[49] The same interviewee made the point that it is extremely rare to have a human resources department in most Qatari firms, and even in the large state-owned firms where such a department does exist, human resources is not taken seriously and the departments are not of the standard normally found in large US or European firms, and they are functional units rather than providing much if any strategic contribution.[50]

Such a problem exists for a couple of reasons. One is the high power distance within Qatari firms, a feature of most Arab organizations, but especially of bureaucracies and state-owned firms that have well-defined structures and hierarchies.[51] Power distance is a measure of the degree to which people accept that inequalities in power exist within a society, and in general the Arab world rates quite highly on such measures—that is, there is a strong acceptance of a distance between the more and the less powerful in society and in organizations, and thus there is more likely to be a very tiered or hierarchical structure to larger organizations in particular. This is the case in most large firms in Qatar, regardless of ownership and with few having an organizational culture that is flat or democratic. However, there is another intergenerational dynamic at work in Qatar, that of education. In the 2004 census, around 9 percent of men and 2 percent of women aged sixty to sixty-four reported having higher degrees, compared with 26 percent of men and 46 percent of women aged twenty-five to twenty-nine.[52] It is quite common for a young Qatari to enter employment, especially in a major firm in the public sector, with a top degree from a Western university or from Qatar University that has included study of the latest ideas in a particular field, but to report to more senior managers who are unaware of such thinking or who may even lack the educational qualifications or intellectual skill of the subordinate. Many managers assume that new, young staff want an easy workload and time for the family, and are surprised and resistant when these staff expect a more inclusive or democratic workplace where they can express their views and be taken seriously. Thus there is often a difference both in educational perspective and sometimes also in work-life perspective or views on corporate culture, as well, between younger and older employees in many firms.

The question here is whether change is occurring at such a speed that older workers cannot keep pace with it, or whether younger workers are developing unreasonable expectations because of their educational opportunities and the more globalized environment in which they live and work in the twenty-first century. Perhaps it is both. A similar difference in workplace culture and values arguably exists in some US and European organizations between Baby Boomers and Generation Y employees due to both varying perspectives on work and changes in education over the past four decades. This could be the case in Qatar, too, especially given the educational variations across generations and the expectations that this creates, not to mention of course the variations in how different generations have viewed and responded to globalization and the social and technological changes it has brought. This is a potential problem because of the negative political repercussions inherent in raising societal expectations, or the expectations of some members of society, but then dashing those expectations because of cultural norms, workplace dynamics, or simply the self-interest of entrenched elites.

The Challenge of Political Change After the Arab Spring: Is Democratization Inevitable?

The other important area in which expectations have been created by Emir Hamad and some key reforms since 1996, but where actual change has been far slower, is in political reform and democratization. The question of political liberalization and democratization has been a central one in scholarship on the Middle East since 1991 or so, and has largely been concomitant with a greater rhetorical emphasis given to political liberalization by Arab leaders and the political elite. Thus the debate has shifted from a question of what kinds of democracy might work best in the region and from where true democratic reform might come to the question of transition, specifically to whether democracy is an endpoint or a process, and whether democratic transition can be a permanent or very long-term process used by leaders as a distraction rather than a true basis of reform and accountability.

What has been a common feature of the wealthier, rentier states is reform that is constructed not as a mechanism for political liberalization or more democratic policymaking but as what Daniel Brumberg has called "pluralized autocracy."[53] By this he means a situation in which the state settles into a permanent mode of pluralized but not democratic or transitional rule: "The trademark mixture of guided pluralism, controlled elections, and selective repression" that "is not just a 'survival strategy' adopted by authoritarian regimes, but rather a type of political system whose institutions, rules, and logic defy any linear model of democratization."[54] Such a description fits Qatar well, where the regime is an authoritarian, but *soft* authoritarian, one, genuinely interested for both self-preservation and out of benevolence in listening to society and incorporating what societal wishes it can into policy, but at the same time, not surrendering any genuine political power to society. Certainly, there is no likelihood of the Al Thani or Hamad's line within it voluntarily withdrawing from the central position they occupy in the political order.

This is not to say that there has not been any political reform in Qatar or that no more will emerge in the future. As already discussed, Hamad's early years in power were characterized by some significant political reforms, and an optimism that genuine political liberalization would occur under his leadership.[55] Examples of his reforms included polls for elected municipal officers for the twenty-nine-seat Central Municipal Council,[56] and Chamber of Commerce members being allowed to elect their own board as of 1996.[57] Important too of course was the referendum vote in April 2003 to approve the new constitution.

In theory the new constitution allowed for significant further reform, including the separation of executive, legislative, and judicial power and the popular election of thirty of the forty-five members of the legislature.[58] However, an expected wider political liberalization has not emerged. The elections for the thirty legislative members did not follow the passage and implementation of the new constitution, and despite regular assurances that the polls would take place, they still had not occurred by the start of 2013 but were being promised for later that year.[59] The term of the existing appointed Consultative Assembly was extended in June 2010 for a further three years. This, and the enduring centrality of the emir and the royal family in the political order, strongly support Brumberg's idea of a pluralized autocracy in the case of Qatar. Even when legislative polls do take place, they are likely to provide just enough of an outlet for popular frustration and just enough room for consultation and co-optation that they are seen as a positive sign of democratization and of greater state accountability to society. However, they will not develop into a process by which elements of society can construct a genuine power base within state institutions, or above all through which societal forces would have any reasonable chance of seizing power from the Al Thani dynasty.

There is little political imperative for a genuine democratic transition in Qatar. The emir is by no means unpopular, and few Qataris seem interested in challenging him or the Al Thani dynasty. The co-optive means available to the state and the royal elite through the development of gas in particular is so great, and likely to endure for so long, that there seems little prospect of rent fluctuations placing real and long-term strain on state-society relations, in contrast with some other rentier states such as Saudi Arabia. The reforms during Hamad's first decade in power were probably driven by several factors: by a genuine desire on the part of the emir for *some* reforms, by the emir's need to build and reinforce his own legitimacy after seizing power, by the economic strains caused by low oil prices in the late 1990s, by the emir's attempts at branding and his desire to appear a magnanimous and reformist leader both to his own people and regionally, the growing political language of reform both in the state and by societal and civil society actors and forces, and perhaps by Qatar's support for the United States in the lead-up to and during the 2003 Iraq War.[60] The pace of reform then slowed because these imperatives were either removed or much reduced.

The question is whether democratic pressures are arising anew as a result of the 2011 Arab Spring, and specifically whether this accounts for the renewed focus on parliamentary elections and the promise as of late 2012 of a legislative poll in 2013. Certainly the Qatari elite reacted in fairly expected rentier fashion after the uprisings in the Arab world began in late 2010. The September 2011 pay increase for public sector workers—in effect for all Qataris, given the flow-on of these pay increases to the private and nonprofit sectors—looked like very typical rentier co-optation, even if other arguments such as high personal debt could be made to justify the pay increases too. Given that the impacts of the global financial crisis on Qatar have so far been minimal, and that rents remained high through much of the same period, including throughout the Arab Spring, this suggests a co-optive motivation behind these renewed promises of political reform and democratization.

That noted, one of the features of Qatar has been the relative lack of popular propensity to joint the Arab Spring uprisings. Arguably the capacity existed for Qataris to do so, at least in a limited way, given the regime's relative openness to political debate. There was one case of a local poet, Mohammed ibn al-Dheeb al-Ajami, who was arrested in November 2011 and, after a long time incommunicado, reportedly brought to secret trial in late 2012 for his criticism of Arab regimes, including by implication the Qatari one. However, he was one of a rare number of such cases, and more broadly, the almost complete absence of oppositional activity marked out Qatar as quite unique, even in the Gulf. The lack of opposition does speak to an emir who is genuinely popular among the majority of Qataris, and also to the co-optive capacity of the state, both of which perhaps allowed the regime to be more sanguine and unperturbed about the risks of the Arab Spring. Neighboring states such as Bahrain, Kuwait, and Saudi Arabia were more nervous because, although they also possess co-optive means, they have different political dynamics from Qatar: Saudi Arabia and Kuwait have sizable sectarian minorities, in contrast with Qatar, and the Saudi regime is far less popular than the Qatari one. The Bahraini regime, meanwhile, faces a Shiite majority who are politically and economically marginalized, and a Sunni population who are disillusioned with the king for political reforms that were promised but that never materialized. In Qatar, the co-optive bargain has been better for society but, just as crucially, has been clearly articulated and generously sustained by the regime.

Still, the Arab Spring and the regime's response to it support the late rentierism argument about Qatar: the state is not autonomous from society, and the Arab uprisings demonstrated a need to continue to listen to and respond to society. While in effect buying off society is relatively easy and common in Qatar as in all such rentier states, Qatar still needs to avoid revolutionary pressures and cannot completely ignore regional change or domestic social and political pressures. Thus there is a genuine political reform of sorts under way in Qatar because of the imperative to be responsive to society, if not democratic. There is a genuine increase in the number of institutions that include voting in their selection of members. There is the likelihood of a more influential legislature emerging if it is partially freely elected. Corruption, although it exists in Qatar, by any common measure is less when compared to most other Gulf states. There is certainly much greater freedom of political expression permitted in Qatar compared with other Gulf states; while the emir and some dynamics of politics are essentially off-limits to criticism, people are otherwise relatively free to speak critically in public about politics, policy issues, and matters of social or economic change and reform. This will continue for as long as the need for the state to listen and react to societal pressure exists.

Is There a "Qatar Model" of Development?

While Qatar broadly shares its late rentier, new state capitalist, and microstate features with other small Gulf states, there is much about it that is unique or at variance with these other states. In that light, should Qatar's development strategy and policies since 1996 be considered to constitute a specific "Qatar model" of development? Some have suggested that this is indeed the case,[61] and certainly a comparison with the more studied and arguably more accepted "Dubai model"[62] is likely in the future as Qatar becomes increasingly well known and debated in popular, media, and scholarly circles. Is the idea of a "Qatar model" convincing, however? At one level there is a collection of policies and a strategic approach that, all combined, is unique and original enough to qualify as a model for the purposes of description. Qatar's experience, however, cannot simply be transplanted to other states, and in this sense it is not a development model in the sense formally meant by the term *model*.

The uniqueness of the Qatar model stems from several of the characteristics that have been explored here. Perhaps most obvious, while Qatar is a rentier state and is heavily state capitalist, it has a uniquely ambitious and activist approach to globalization, to international trade and investment ties, and to playing a disproportionately large role in international affairs and in major events. Other states either have taken a different approach to positioning themselves—think of Dubai positioning itself as a regional business center and tourist destination, which has been very different to what Qatar has done even if for similar ultimate political ends—or in the cases of states such as Kuwait and Oman, have simply not been as successful as Qatar in engaging with the global economy and in the international realm.

Second, the sectoral focus in Qatar and the way in which it has pursued economic development are different from the path pursued in other Gulf states. While some features such as a desire to expand downstream oil and gas, higher education, and transport are common to several Gulf states, Qatar has pursued these things astutely, and moreover has sponsored other, more novel sectors too. It has adroitly developed its capability in emerging energy technologies—its gas trains are world class, it is a world leader in gas-to-liquids, and it is rapidly developing capacity in renewable energy—while also effectively developing other sectors such as banking, sports, leisure, (niche) tourism, and the like. It has also developed its higher education sector carefully and strategically, avoiding either a free-for-all higher education market where standards might decline or be variable, as arguably has been the case in Dubai, or an overly rigid structure that lacks responsiveness to global and social change, as arguably remains the case in Saudi Arabia. Qatar University is now among the best higher education institutions in the Gulf, and there is nothing like Education City in the other Gulf states.

Third, Qatar has managed to implement a set of development policies and reforms that draw on the examples and lessons of Dubai and other states, but without simply copying them. The Qatari leadership has been quite successful in marking Qatar as distinct from other Gulf states and city-states. It has also avoided outright competition with states such as Dubai, Abu Dhabi, and Bahrain. While some competition exists in some economic sectors, these states, broadly speaking, collaborate more than they compete, and areas of seeming competition such as in the development of their global airlines have in fact not led to a great deal of direct competition; instead, these airlines are more of a threat to those based in hubs elsewhere in the world. In key economic sectors, likewise, Qatar has taken elements of policy from elsewhere, but has not simply copied another state's model and then sought to outperform it in open competition. Qatar has learned from the mistakes of Dubai's development, especially in ensuring that new sectors are chosen for development on the basis of comparative advantage; that its debt is more productively incurred; and that globalization and cosmopolitanism occur at a more comfortable pace than has been the case in places like Dubai.

Finally, the political openness in Qatar does mark it out from other Gulf states. While not a political model in any sense, its openness, when combined with economic, diplomatic, and other dynamics, does help form part of the Qatar model, because this is a way in which the state marks out the country against other Gulf states. Qatar is famous for Al-Jazeera, of course, and there are political as well as economic goals behind this trend-setting broadcaster that are unique to Qatar or that have been uniquely pursued through it.

Seemingly Qatar has handled both its energy wealth and its economic transition deftly. It has done what many scholars recommend of energy exporters looking to transition to a post-energy economy: it has adopted strategies to plan for a decline in energy income in the future, to diversify the economy, and to prepare the citizenry for a longer-term post-energy transition, all the while maximizing the wealth it does obtain from its energy exports.[63] What is far more problematic is making an argument that this "model" somehow is a wider development model that other states might copy or use as a template or guide in their own economic development. Scholars often seem obsessed with finding a model of development, perhaps out of habit in looking for patterns in the study of politics, or perhaps simply out of a desire to see the Middle East, as a region that has struggled with economic development challenges in the twentieth century, find a feasible, indigenous path to development. Previous attempts at economic development were initially state-led ones, as characterized the Middle East from the post–World War II period up to the 1970s and into the 1980s, only to be replaced by market-oriented ones beginning with Tunisian reforms in the late 1960s and especially the Egyptian *al-infitah* (economic opening) from 1974 onward, which by the 1990s were a feature of most Arab political economies.

The attempts at finding alternative, and especially indigenous, models of development have been largely unsuccessful. A broad concept of "good governance" might be applicable to all of the Middle East (and elsewhere) as something to aspire to, but even in strictly configured settings that replicate the structure of a model, it is not a model per se.[64] Islamic models of economics are problematic because they need to be isolated from other economic systems, especially where *riba* ("usury," but in effect, interest) is involved. The idea that China might provide a "Beijing model" of development is equally problematic: the Chinese themselves do not talk about or claim to have invented such a model, making the idea of one strange if not fallacious.[65] The idea of a Dubai model is actually problematic in a similar way, since much of what it says is generic: the late-late development of Dubai is a feature common to much of the Gulf, where energy rents allowed the economy to bypass industrialization, and common to much of the smaller Gulf states are ideas such as government-led development, rapid decisionmaking by senior figures, labor market flexibility (among expatriates at least), and a focus on investment relations.[66] Even the branding of the state that many associate almost exclusively with Dubai has been a feature of Qatar for almost as long, as outlined here. The idea, therefore, that Qatar has adopted a Dubai model—if one even exists—is thus erroneous, since some of the Dubai model consists of generic or widely adopted policies shared by several Gulf states; these began in Bahrain in the 1970s rather than in Dubai a decade or more later. Bahrain tried to configure itself as a commercial, financial, transportation, and communications hub in the Gulf as early as 1975.[67] Furthermore, some other elements of what Dubai has done, especially allowing a debt bubble to expand with so little economically productive activity behind it and permitting the degree of social liberalism that it has, have not been adopted by Qatar and in fact have been deliberately eschewed.

Both proponents and opponents of marketization let the debate about economic liberalization dominate discourse on development over the generation from the 1980s to the global financial crisis, neglecting the transformation in many Gulf states, including Qatar, toward a more hybrid approach. Qatar and its small neighbors have not undertaken full economic neoliberal reform, nor have they shunned any such restructuring. Rather, they have embarked on selective reforms, including marketization reforms, that make parts of the economy more competitive and that especially make prices much more likely to be set by supply-and-demand dynamics. They are also much more business-friendly, efficient, and open to investment than they were a generation ago. However, the centrality of the state as an owner in the economy has remained, as has a prominent regulatory role for it. Such new state capitalism is not unique to Qatar, even if some of the elements of it may be.

Given all of this, Qatar possesses many unique characteristics, but is not unique enough that there is a "Qatar model" that can simply and neatly be adopted by other states as a transposable, generic hybrid prototype or exemplar of development. The centrality of gas rents and the power that this gives the state are enormous, but high rents and rentierism are hardly unique in energy states. Yet the exact nature of Qatari late rentierism varies from that of other Arab Gulf states, with a Qatari state that, facing little challenge from merchants or clerics but with historical threats to the ruler from within the extended royal family, is comparatively liberal and benevolent toward society. Qatar has the advantage of having moved early and effectively in some of the ways in which it has branded itself; it is unlikely that other states could, or would choose to, compete directly with Qatar in the realms of international media or major sports events. Among countries of similar size and economic power, Qatar has many emulators but little real competition in key sectors and initiatives. Qatar has, to a large extent, charted its own development course, paying attention to the experience of other states and being informed by those experiences, but copying them only to a limited extent and not, certainly, in terms of an overall model. It chose a development path from its own point of departure, as other states will invariably have to do.

Conclusion: Past, Present, and Future

Qatar is not a simple country or polity, yet much of the attention that it has received, especially popular media attention, is relatively unsophisticated or one-dimensional. Some of it is a straightforward rendition of the economic success story, pointing out the rapid rise in GDP after the year 2000, mostly because of gas rents coming online, and presenting this as a rags-to-riches story, sometimes reinforcing the stereotype of a cashed-up oil shaikhdom suddenly swimming in opulence and ambitiously, even overeagerly, chasing new infrastructural and social works programs funded by this new wealth. Other reports, especially with a focus on the political system, add a further layer to the economic success story by contrasting it with an endurance of social conservatism or linking it to a strengthening of the authoritarian capacity of the state, in effect positing a simple rentier-state argument, but typically with little or no acknowledgment of or detail on the social and other changes that have taken place in Qatar under Hamad. There is a growing amount of this type of reporting, as Qatar's image has developed since it gained the 2022 World Cup, as it has sought to host the Olympics, and in 2011 when it became an increasingly active regional diplomatic actor during the Arab Spring. Yet as noted at the outset of this book, Qatar has received little other attention, above all scholarly attention, of late, despite the changes in its economic position, social dynamics, diplomatic posture, and regional socioeconomic role since the mid-1990s.

In fact, Qatar has an interesting story to tell. Indeed it is an economic success story of sorts, but the dynamics behind that success and the caveats that remain attached to it are equally important and thought-provoking. It provides an example (as do some other small Arab Gulf states) of the challenges of energy-fueled development, especially the enduring pathologies of rentierism and of social problems stemming from the capital-intensive nature of the energy sector and the need for genuine—as opposed to energy-subsidized—economic diversification. Qatar has learned a lesson similar to that learned by Saudi Arabia in the 1980s, that economic diversification is easy enough to subsidize but very difficult to achieve and sustain by itself and on its own terms. Qatar still faces problems, along the lines of those encountered in other small energy-exporting states, notably youth dissatisfaction and underemployment, macroeconomic susceptibility to energy shocks and a reliance on energy to set the economic tone, and a largely unsuccessful attempt at replacing expatriate workers with locals through a national employment program. Yet Qatar is not the same as the other Arab Gulf states; indeed, there are limits to the degree to which it can be compared to them in a political economy framework. For all the challenges of energy-centrism in the economy, for example, Qatar nonetheless is constructing a reputation in a select set of other sectors such as sports, transport, and media, and arguably, at a modest level, in some other sectors such as healthcare and renewable energies. Rather than surrender to its energy reliance, or pointlessly fight it, Qatar seems instead to have made a peace of sorts with it. Qatar has encouraged and grown its gas sector in particular, while also thinking beyond the present era of high rents to a post-hydrocarbon economy. If it has been slow in diversifying the economy and has suffered from problems in trying to do so, this has not been unexpected given the challenges of developing an energy-driven economy. Such is the hydrocarbon wealth of Qatar, especially the gas reserves of the North Dome field, that it is tempting to argue that even if economic diversification and Qatarization take two or three more generations to achieve, which would certainly not be the ideal, Qatar probably nonetheless can afford to proceed at such a slow pace.

Just as interesting are the paradoxes that abound in Qatar's political economy, and the insights that stem from these. Perhaps the most important here—which confounds the political science literature in many ways—is the fact that the political economy has had such a narrow elite structure in the past and yet such a reformist emir and elite since the mid-1990s. As discussed, a merchant class never emerged in Qatar—at least not a group of businesspeople with the political coordination and clout of a class—nor did an indigenous religious elite develop. The centrality and size of the Al Thani meant, furthermore, that other tribes were never especially strong, and the key shaikhly figures and other notables who did arise did so with the blessing, if not the outright support, of the emir. In the Qatar of the 2010s, Emir Hamad, his wife Muza, Prime Minister Hamad bin Jassim, and maybe post-2003 Crown Prince Tamim had become the main figures in the political economy and arguably the only figures of any profound importance in the strategic direction of the country.

What is curious is why the emir in particular, but backed by key elements of his family, has so actively sought to expand and diversify the economy, and especially to globalize it, often in the face of both family and popular opposition to some aspects of this globalization. The conventional argument of the literature, especially rentier-state theory, has typically been that in the presence of large rents and the absence of domestic reform pressures on the elite, or absence of an impending end to rents, leaders have very little motivation to reform the political economy. Such reform, the argument goes, would needlessly introduce and empower new bases of political power, strengthen existing sources of opposition or alternative power holders, and as a result potentially create new challenges to the regime.

Likewise, the emir's active foreign policy, especially his involvement in regional peace initiatives and in supporting opposition forces in the 2011 Arab Spring, above all the military and financial support to the Libyan opposition to the Qaddafi regime, is according to conventional theoretical explanations unnecessarily activist and interventionist for a small state with strategic vulnerabilities of its own. In fact, such dynamics reinforce the uniqueness of Qatar and the need to analyze it on its own terms. In part this has been the aim here in expanding the discussion beyond the narrower, stricter definitional confines of political economy to focus as well on issues such as branding as a strategy and international relations and diplomacy as policies driven by political economy interests and imperatives. In such ways, along with the specifics of how energy and its rents have been handled by the state, and other sectors of the economy managed, Qatar is a unique development model within the Gulf and internationally. It is not simply a close copy of the Dubai model of development, as argued in the previous chapter, even if Qatar has adopted some of Dubai's policies and strategies or developed very similar ones itself. Qatar's political economy since 1995, and the development strategies that have underlain it, are not all unique, but as a conglomeration they need to be assessed on their own terms and from their own points of departure.

The theoretical approach proposed here is based on this uniqueness and on the broad applicability to Qatar of some extant explanations, especially elements of rentier-state theory and the emerging debate about a new state capitalism, and yet the need for these approaches to be refined, given their inadequacy in fully explaining post-1995 Qatar, and further developed, given their potential to inform other studies of the contemporary Arab Gulf states. In the case of rentier theory, Qatar needs to be seen as a "late rentier" state; indeed, it is probably the consummate example of a late rentier state. As demonstrated, the basic systemic characteristics of the rentier state are present in Qatar, including a centralization of rents and tight control of their dispersal; an absence of democratic institutions, strong civil society organizations, or other such alternative power bases to the regime; and a set of relatively weak state institutions co-opted by rents and by strong patron-client bureaucratic networks. Yet the "late" aspect of Qatar's rentierism is that its politics are more complex than traditional rentier arguments would assert or allow. The emir and his inner circle—the regime—clearly worry about the wider political and social threats from rentierism and from a dissatisfied youth population in particular. They also clearly want to build a polity and a legacy that go beyond simple regime maintenance and that are seen as having contributed to a stable, wealthy, and developing Qatar and a profound and expanded role for it regionally and globally. Given this, traditional rentier-state theory is inadequate in explaining Qatar since the 1990s, because its experience has demonstrated that the state is not autonomous from society, nor does it lack an economic or development plan for the country, nor does it operate aloof from societal input. Rents have allowed the state to purchase more autonomy and concede less political power to institutions than it might otherwise have had to do, but Qatar's desire for development and willingness to risk political change in supporting and encouraging it is a sign of a much more sophisticated state-society relationship than simpler models of rentierism previously accommodated.

The Qatari state is also at variance with some other Arab Gulf states, and different to what it was in the pre-Hamad era, because of the salience of the new state capitalism in its political economy. However this is viewed—as patrimonial capitalism, *asabiyya* (kinship) capitalism, or just a new, financially efficient form of family-centered state enterprise—it is a break from the traditional understanding of "state capitalism," which assumed strong central planning, bureaucratization, and a *dirigiste* role for the state. It is also a break from the past in the Gulf, when institutional development and nationbuilding were often considered more important goals than economic efficiency and profitability in state-owned firms, and when a state's protectionist bargains with merchants were stronger and more crucial to regime survival than was a desire to globalize and diversify the economy. Thus, while the state and the ruling royal families have always been key owners of a large proportion of the means of production in the economies of the Gulf, the "new" state capitalism—which is new in that it is a feature almost exclusively of the 1990s and afterward—has allowed for, even dictated, a (selected) opening and reform of economies, greater efficiency in state-owned firms and even increasingly in public sector departments, and new initiatives to develop education, public services, infrastructure, and other capital that will enhance economic performance and development. This also defies traditional rentier arguments that the state will not bother with such reform so long as it possesses sufficient rental income. It is curious that such significant change has occurred in Qatar when there is seemingly so little pressure for reform on the emir. In a rentier sense, Hamad's reforms have been driven by the desire to manage rentier dynamics and ultimately move beyond them, and in this way the need for a late rentier approach and an understanding of the new state capitalism and its links to rentierism are both crucial.

Finally, viewing Qatar through the microstate lens, specifically as an activist microstate, is important too. It is a state that despite—in fact, because of—its small size, seeks constantly to punch above its weight and to have stable and positive relations with all the key regional and major power states that can most impact its security and stability. But equally crucial, given the late rentier and new state capitalist characteristics of Qatar's political economy, its activism on the world stage, whether in diplomacy, sovereign wealth fund investment, or culture, media, and major events, is also informed by commercial interests. Security and stability are obviously the first order of preserving the regime and the commercial benefits accruing to the elite. Beyond this, both Doha's international branding efforts and foreign policy have links to its economic strategy and its attempts to tie the political economy into the global economy, to diversify beyond oil, gas, and petrochemicals, and to promote and broaden the opportunities for the citizens on whom the emir and his Al Thani dynasty's legitimacy and durability—despite the capacity for co-optation and repression brought about by rentierism—rest. There ought to be little surprise, then, that such a small state is so active internationally, even in parts of the world or on issues where it would seem to have little direct interest. Its interests, arguably, are as broad as its elite's ambitions and imagination will allow.

There is little point, given all of this, in seeking to overstate or understate Qatar's prospects or to dwell on its strengths or weaknesses at the expense of assessing the other. Too many works—especially popular or media pieces—that do so end up being either unjustifiably hagiographic about or overly critical toward the emir and his family. Too many scholars, arguably, are too keen to play Cassandra, or occasionally Pollyanna. When soberly assessed, Qatar's political economy is important for several reasons: for the characteristics that it shares with the Gulf and yet the uniqueness that characterizes many of its political and economic dynamics; for the enormous wealth that it possesses and is likely to enjoy for several generations into the future, which will invariably provide it with greater international influence as well; and yet the underlying risks to its stability that remain—despite its rising wealth and prominence—from both energy, as the very source of that wealth, and enduring and emerging political and social challenges to the political order, to social dynamics, and to national identity and culture. Steering Qatar through these trials will be a far more multifaceted and compounded endeavor than most observers of Qatar assume, and far more complex than simply deciding how to spend an energy windfall, and will remain a challenge—and in some facets a contested one—long after Hamad's rule as emir has passed.

Notes

1. Brumberg has written extensively on this and similar ideas; see, for example, Brumberg, "The Trap of Liberalized Autocracy."
2. Perhaps the most important piece on the Dubai model, and written by arguably its greatest proponent, is Hvidt, "The Dubai Model."
3. Moin Siddiqi, "Qatar Stands Firm in the Face of Global Financial Storm," *The Middle East,* July 2009, p. 47.
4. Ibid.
5. Ahmed Gad, "Is Qatar's Economy Recession-Proof?" *The Middle East,* April 2009, p. 47.
6. This point was made to me in interviews in Doha, January 2011 and October 2011.
7. This point about Dubai has been widely made, but see, for example, Ellaboudy, "The Global Financial Crisis," pp. 182–183.
8. See, for example, Habib Toumi, "Public Sector in Qatar to Get 60 Per Cent Pay Rise," *Gulf News,* September 7, 2011.
9. Major firms such as Qatargas, Nakilat (Qatar Gas Transportation Company), Qatar Navigation, Qatar National Hotels, and others followed suit quickly.
10. Toumi, "Public Sector in Qatar to Get 60 Per Cent Pay Rise"; and author interviews, Doha, October 2011.
11. Term cited in Moin Siddiqi, "Qatar: A Beacon of Stability in Troubled Times," *The Middle East,* June 2010, p. 36.
12. This point is made in Gad, "Is Qatar's Economy Recession-Proof?" pp. 47–48.
13. Gad, "Is Qatar's Economy Recession-Proof?" p. 48, makes this point, although it is not a very convincing one given that debt levels and banking exposure were of far greater importance than economic diversification in how most states fared during the initial few years of the global financial crisis.

14. See the figures published in Qatar Statistics Authority, *Annual Statistical Abstract,* available online at http://www.qix.gov.qa/portal/page/portal/QIXPOC/Documents/QIX%20Knowledge%20Base/Publication/General%20Statistics/Annual%20Abstract. The most recent is the 2009 abstract, available online at http://www.qix.gov.qa/portal/page/portal/QIXPOC/Documents/QIX%20Knowledge%20Base/Publication/General%20Statistics/Annual%20Abstract/Source_QSA/Annual_Abstract_QSA_AnBu_AE_2009.pdf.

15. This is my own estimate, but this figure is consistent with most estimates made in the media and by scholars and observers of Qatar, who around 2010 were typically estimating the citizen population to be roughly or "approaching" 300,000.

16. QNB Capital, *Qatar Economic Review 2010,* p. 8.

17. Berrebi, Martorell, and Tanner, "Qatar's Labor Markets at a Crucial Crossroad," p. 432.

18. Author interviews, Doha, October 2011.

19. Ibid.

20. Ibid. There are a range of websites and the occasional media article on the topic; see, for example, articles such as "Held Hostage in Qatar," *International Schools Review,* April 4, 2011, http://internationalschoolsreviewdiscuss.wordpress.com/2011/04/21/held-hostage-in-qatar; and various websites, Facebook posts, and Twitter feeds related to "economic hostages" (the website Friends to Free Nasser, https://sites.google.com/site/qatarhostages, was particularly high profile in late 2011).

21. Bogaert subsequently wrote a book on the experience, titled *Exit Permit.* See also Loveday Morris and David George-Cosh, "Belgian Jailed for Three Years After Company Fails," *The National* (Abu Dhabi), June 25, 2009, http://www.thenational.ae/news/worldwide/middle-east/belgian-jailed-for-three-years-after-company-fails; and Bogaert's Twitter site, http://twitter.com/#!/hostageinqatar.

22. On the policy, see the official Qatarization website, at http://www.qatarization.com.qa/Qatarization/Qatarization.nsf/en_Index?ReadForm.

23. Author interviews, Doha, October 2011.

24. Ibid.

25. See Champion, *The Paradoxical Kingdom,* pp. 200–202. Champion was writing on the case of Saudi Arabia, although other writers, both scholars and journalists, have argued along the same lines but without using the term "*mudir* syndrome" itself.

26. Such as Nora Bensahel and Daniel Byman in *The Future Security Environment in the Middle East,* pp. 113–114, who cite Champion.

27. An argument along the same lines as that of the *mudir* syndrome is made in Beblawi, "Gulf Industrialization in Perspective," p. 188: "[rentierism] embodies a disconnect in the work-reward relationship."

28. Berrebi, Martorell, and Tanner, "Qatar's Labor Markets at a Crucial Crossroad," p. 436.

29. Ibid.; and author interviews, Doha, October 2011.

30. Berrebi, Martorell, and Tanner, "Qatar's Labor Markets at a Crucial Crossroad," p. 436.

31. Author interview, Doha, October 2011.

32. Qatar General Secretariat for Development Planning, *Qatar National Vision 2030,* p. 23.

33. Davidson, *Dubai,* p. 190.

34. Author interviews, Doha, October 2011. It is interesting that both Western and Qatari interviewees often asserted this issue of cultural change as being a matter of contention in society, but often claimed that they personally did not object to it.

35. Davidson, *Dubai,* pp. 193–206.

36. See Valeri, *Oman,* especially pp. 120–147. There are very important distinctions, of course, between the two states in how history and tradition are manufactured by incumbent regimes, at least in part for the purposes of nationbuilding in the interests of regime maintenance. However, both Oman and Qatar share a broadly similar style and aim in situating and justifying their relatively new status as nation-states as part of their very long historical narratives. As well, their promotion of a shared Arab and Muslim identity is very similar to such identity promotion elsewhere in the region, but both Oman and Qatar mark out their societies as possessing unique traits and customs.

37. Berrebi, Martorell, and Tanner, "Qatar's Labor Markets at a Crucial Crossroad," p. 425 (tab. 2).

38. Ibid., p. 426 (tab. 3).

39. See Tables 5.2 and 5.3. This issue is also discussed in Qatar Planning Council, *Labor Market Strategy for the State of Qatar;* and Stasz et al., *Post-Secondary Education for Qatar.*

40. Wendy Wallace, "Qatar Invests in a Vision," *The Middle East,* July 2005, p. 58.

41. Saud, *Qatari Women,* pp. 182–183.

42. Berrebi, Martorell, and Tanner, "Qatar's Labor Markets at a Crucial Crossroad," pp. 428–429.

43. As an indication, see Qatar Statistics Authority, *Labor Force Sample Survey 2008,* p. 40 (graph 11), p. 44 (graph 13), and p. 50 (graph 16), available online at http://www.qix.gov.qa/portal/page/portal/QIXPOC/Documents/QIX%20Knowledge%20Base/Publication/Labor%20Force%20Researches/labor%20force%20sample%20survey/Source_QSA/Report%20Labor%20Force%20Sample%20Survey_AE_QSA_2008.pdf.

44. Author interviews, Doha, October 2011.

45. See the survey results in al-Ghanem, *Qatari Women and Leadership Challenges,* available online at http://www.scfa.gov.qa/studies.

46. Author interviews, Doha, October 2011.

47. al-Ghanem, *Qatari Women and Leadership Challenges,* pp. 5–6.

48. Author interviews, Doha, October 2011.

49. Ibid.

50. Ibid.

51. Much has been written on power distance in works on organizational psychology and organizational culture. See, for example, Carl, Gupta, and Javidan, "Power Distance."

52. Berrebi, Martorell, and Tanner, "Qatar's Labor Markets at a Crucial Crossroad," p. 426 (tab. 3).

53. See Brumberg, "The Trap of Liberalized Autocracy," pp. 56–68.

54. Ibid., p. 56.

55. Neil Ford, "Qatar: A Trailblazer for Democracy?" *The Middle East,* January 2004, pp. 20–22.

56. See Lambert, "Political Reform in Qatar," especially pp. 90–94.

57. Crystal, "Political Reform in Qatar," p. 120.

58. Ford, "Qatar: A Trailblazer for Democracy?" p. 21.

59. Ian Black, "Qatar to Hold First National Election," *The Guardian,* November 2, 2011, p. 19.

60. These arguments are drawn from several sources: Crystal, "Political Reform in Qatar," especially pp. 123–130; Lambert, "Political Reform in Qatar," pp. 95–99; some of the ideas in Mitchell, "Political and Socioeconomic Transformation in the GCC"; and author interviews, Doha, January 2011 and October 2011.

61. Shadi Hamid, "The Qatar Model: A New Way Forward in the Middle East?" *The Atlantic,* December 13, 2010, http://www.theatlantic.com/international/archive/2010/12/the-qatar-model-a-new-way-forward-for-the-middle-east/67908.

62. See Hvidt, "The Dubai Model."

63. This in effect is the argument that J. E. Peterson makes about what the Gulf oil and gas exporters need to do in the transition away from oil reliance. See Peterson, "Life After Oil."

64. Khan, "Is 'Good Governance' an Appropriate Model for Governance Reforms?"

65. William Hurst, "A China Model or Just a Broken Mould?"

66. Hvidt, "The Dubai Model," pp. 401–408.

67. Looney, "The Omani and Bahraini Paths to Development," p. 12.

Bibliography

Aarts, Paul, and Gerd Nonneman (eds.). *Saudi Arabia in the Balance: Political Economy, Society, Foreign Affairs*. London: Hurst, 2005.

al-Ghanem, Kaltham Ali. *Qatari Women and Leadership Challenges*. Doha: Supreme Council for Family Affairs, 2008.

al-Jasser, Muhammad, and Abdulrahman al-Hamidy. "A Common Currency Area for the Gulf Region." In Bank for International Settlements, Monetary and Economic Department, *Regional Currency Areas and the Use of Foreign Currencies*. Basel, May 2003, pp. 116–120.

al-Nawawy, Mohammed, and Adel Iskandar. *Al-Jazeera: The Story of the Network That Is Rattling Governments and Redefining Modern Journalism*. Boulder: Westview, 2003.

Ali, Syed. *Dubai: Gilded Cage*. New Haven: Yale University Press, 2010.

Amara, Mahfoud. "2006 Qatar Asian Games: A 'Modernization' Project from Above?" *Sport in Society* 8(3), 2005, pp. 493–514.

Anscombe, Frederick. "The Ottoman Role in the Gulf." In Lawrence G. Potter (ed.), *The Persian Gulf in History*. Basingstoke: Palgrave Macmillan, 2009, pp. 261–276.

Anthony, John Duke. *Arab States of the Lower Gulf: People, Politics, Petroleum*. Washington, DC: Middle East Institute, 1975.

Askari, Hossein, Faranghees Abbas, George Jabbour, and Dohee Kwon. "An Economic Manifesto for the Oil Exporting Countries of the Persian Gulf." *Banca Nazionale del Lavoro Quarterly Review* 59(239), December 2006, pp. 363–388.

Bahry, Louay Y. "Elections in Qatar: A Window of Democracy Opens in the Gulf." *Middle East Policy* 6(4), June 1999, pp. 118–127.

———. "The New Arab Media Phenomenon: Qatar's Al-Jazeera." *Middle East Policy* 8(2), June 2001, pp. 88–99.

Barrett, Raymond. *Dubai Dreams: Inside the Kingdom of Bling*. Boston: Nicholas Brealey, 2010.

Beblawi, Hazem. *The Arab Gulf Economy in a Turbulent Age*. London: Croom Helm, 1984.

———. "Gulf Industrialization in Perspective." In Jean-François Seznec and Mimi Kirk (eds.), *Industrialization in the Gulf: A Socioeconomic Revolution*. London: Routledge, 2011, pp. 185–197.

———. "The Rentier State in the Arab World." In Hazem Beblawi and Giacomo Luciani (eds.), *The Rentier State: Nation, State, and the Integration of the Arab World*. London: Croom Helm, 1987, pp. 63–82.

Beblawi, Hazem, and Giacomo Luciani (eds.). *The Rentier State: Nation, State, and the Integration of the Arab World*. London: Croom Helm, 1987.

Behrendt, Sven. "Sovereign Wealth Funds: The Governance Challenge." Washington, DC: Carnegie Endowment for International Peace, January 21, 2010.

Bensahel, Nora, and Daniel L. Byman. *The Future Security Environment in the Middle East: Conflict, Stability, and Political Change*. Santa Monica: RAND, 2004.

Berrebi, Claude, Francisco Martorell, and Jeffrey C. Tanner. "Qatar's Labor Markets at a Crucial Crossroad." *Middle East Journal* 63(3), Summer 2009, pp. 421–442.

Blanchard, Christopher M. "Qatar: Background and U.S. Relations." Washington, DC: Congressional Research Service, May 16, 2011.

Bogaert, Philippe. *Exit Permit*. Brussels: Le Cri, 2011.

Bremmer, Ian. *The End of the Free Market: Who Wins the War Between States and Corporations?* New York: Portfolio, 2010.

Brewer, Dominic J., Catherine H. Augustine, Gail L. Zellman, Gery Ryan, Charles A. Goldman, Cathleen Stasz, and Louay Constant. *Education for a New Era: Design and Implementation of K–12 Education Reform in Qatar*. Santa Monica: RAND–Qatar Policy Institute, 2007.

Brumberg, Daniel. "The Trap of Liberalized Autocracy." *Journal of Democracy* 13(4), 2002, pp. 56–68.

Carl, Dale, Vipin Gupta, and Mansour Javidan. "Power Distance." In Robert J. House, Paul J. Hanges, Mansour Javidan, Peter W. Dorfman, and Vipin Gupta (eds.), *Culture, Leadership, and Organizations: The GLOBE Study of 62 Societies*. Thousand Oaks, CA: Sage, 2004, pp. 513–563.

Champion, Daryl. *The Paradoxical Kingdom: Saudi Arabia and the Momentum of Reform*. London: Hurst, 2003.

Chatham House. *The Gulf as a Global Financial Centre: Growing Opportunities and International Influence*. London: Royal Institute for International Affairs, 2008.

Chaudhry, Kiren Aziz. *The Price of Wealth: Economics and Institutions in the Middle East*. Ithaca: Cornell University Press, 1997.

Cook, M. A. (ed.). *Studies in Economic History of the Middle East*. London: Oxford University Press, 1970.

Cordesman, Anthony H., and Khalid R. al-Rodhan. "The Gulf Military Forces in an Era of Asymmetric War: Qatar." Washington, DC: Center for Strategic and International Studies, June 28, 2006.

Cordesman, Anthony H., and Aram Nerguizian. "The Gulf Military Balance in 2010: An Overview." Washington, DC: Center for Strategic and International Studies, April 22, 2010.

Crystal, Jill. *Oil and Politics in the Gulf: Rulers and Merchants in Kuwait and Qatar.* Cambridge: Cambridge University Press, 1990 (rev. ed., 1995).

———. "Political Reform in Qatar." In Mary Ann Tétreault, Gwenn Okruhlik, and Andrzej Kapiszewski (eds.), *Political Change in the Arab Gulf States: Stuck in Transition.* Boulder: Lynne Rienner, 2011, pp. 119–135.

Curtiss, Richard H. "The Arabian Gulf in 1997: With Ruling Family's Dispute Settled, Qatar's New Emir Charts Bold Course." *Washington Report on Middle East Affairs* 15(6), February 1997, p. 9.

———. "Qatar's New Ruler Breaks the GCC Policy Mold." *Washington Report on Middle East Affairs* 15(1), June 1996, p. 78.

Dargin, Justin. "The Dolphin Project: The Development of a Gulf Gas Initiative." Working Paper no. NG22. Oxford: Oxford Institute for Energy Studies, January 2008.

———. "Qatar's Natural Gas: The Foreign-Policy Driver." *Middle East Policy* 14(3), Fall 2007, pp. 136–142.

Davidson, Christopher M. *Abu Dhabi: Oil and Beyond.* London: Hurst, 2009.

———. *Dubai: The Vulnerability of Success.* London: Hurst, 2008.

Donn, Gari, and Yahya al-Manthri. *Globalisation and Higher Education in the Arab Gulf States.* Didcot: Symposium, 2010.

Drezner, Daniel W. "Sovereign Wealth Funds and the (In)Security of Global Finance." *Journal of International Affairs* 62(1), Fall 2008, pp. 115–130.

Economic and Social Infrastructures in the State of Qatar. Doha: Ali Bin Ali, 1984.

el-Gamal, Mahmoud A., and Amy Myers Jaffe. *Oil, Dollars, Debt, and Crises: The Global Curse of Black Gold.* Cambridge: Cambridge University Press, 2010.

el-Mallakh, Ragaei. *Qatar: Development of an Oil Economy.* London: Croom Helm, 1979 (reprinted as *Qatar: Energy and Development,* 1985).

el-Quqa, Omar M., Faisal Hasan, Chandresh Bhatt, and Bikash Rout. *Qatar Banking Sector.* Kuwait: Global Investment House KSCC, 2008.

Ellaboudy, Shereef. "The Global Financial Crisis: Economic Impact on GCC Countries and Policy Implications." *International Research Journal of Finance and Economics* 41, July 2010, pp. 177–190.

Energy Information Administration. "Country Analysis Brief: Qatar." Washington, DC: US Department of Energy, January 2011.

Foley, Sean. *The Arab Gulf States: Beyond Oil and Islam.* Boulder: Lynne Rienner, 2009.

Fromherz, Allen. *Qatar: A Modern History.* London: Tauris, 2012.

Gause, F. Gregory, III. *Oil Monarchies: Domestic and Security Challenges in the Arab Gulf States.* New York: Council on Foreign Relations, 1994.

Gray, Matthew. "The Politics of the 'New State Capitalism': The Origins and Aims of Gulf Sovereign Wealth Funds." Refereed paper for the 2009 Australian Political Studies Association annual conference, Macquarie University, Sydney. http://www.pol.mq.edu.au/apsa/papers/Refereed%20papers/Gray%20-%20Sovereign%20Wealth%20Funds%20etc.pdf.

———. "A Theory of 'Late Rentierism' in the Arab States of the Gulf." Center for International and Regional Studies, Occasional Paper no. 7. Doha: Georgetown University School of Foreign Service in Qatar, 2011.

Greenfield, Victoria A., et al. *Design of the Qatar National Research Fund: An Overview of the Study Approach and Key Recommendations.* Santa Monica: RAND–Qatar Policy Institute, 2008.

Gulbrandsen, Anders. "Bridging the Gulf: Qatari Business Diplomacy and Conflict Mediation." Master's subthesis. Georgetown University, Washington, DC, 2010.

Hanieh, Adam. *Capitalism and Class in the Gulf Arab States.* London: Palgrave Macmillan, 2011.

Hanna, Daniel. "A New Fiscal Framework for GCC Countries Ahead of Monetary Union." Briefing Paper no. IEP BP 06/02. London: Chatham House, May 2006.

Hanouz, Margareta Drzeniek, and Sofiane Khatib. *The Arab World Competitiveness Review, 2010.* Geneva: World Economic Forum, 2010.

Harik, Iliya, and Denis J. Sullivan (eds.). *Privatization and Liberalization in the Middle East.* Bloomington: Indiana University Press, 1992.

Held, David, and Kristian Ulrichsen (eds.). *The Transformation of the Gulf: Politics, Economics, and the Global Order.* Abingdon: Routledge, 2012.

Henry, Clement Moore, and Robert Springborg. *Globalization and the Politics of Development in the Middle East.* 2nd ed. Cambridge: Cambridge University Press, 2010.

Herb, Michael. *All in the Family: Absolutism, Revolution, and Democracy in the Middle Eastern Monarchies.* Albany: State University of New York Press, 1999.

Hertog, Steffen. "Defying the Resource Curse: Explaining Successful State-Owned Enterprises in Rentier States." *World Politics* 62(2), April 2010, pp. 261–301.

———. "The Evolution of Rent Recycling During Two Booms in the Gulf Arab States: Business Dynamism and Societal Stagnation." In Matteo Legrenzi and Bessma Momani (eds.), *Shifting Geo-Economic Power of the Gulf: Oil, Finance, and Institutions.* Farnham: Ashgate, 2011, pp. 55–74.

———. *Princes, Brokers, and Bureaucrats: Oil and the State in Saudi Arabia.* New York: Cornell University Press, 2010.

Heydemann, Steven (ed.). *Networks of Privilege in the Middle East: The Politics of Economic Reform Revisited.* New York: Palgrave Macmillan, 2004.

House, Robert J., Paul J. Hanges, Mansour Javidan, Peter W. Dorfman, and Vipin Gupta (eds.). *Culture, Leadership, and Organizations: The GLOBE Study of 62 Societies.* Thousand Oaks, CA: Sage, 2004.

Hurst, William. "A China Model or Just a Broken Mould?" In Robert Springborg (ed.), *Development Models in Muslim Contexts: Chinese, "Islamic," and Neo-Liberal Alternatives.* Edinburgh: Edinburgh University Press, 2010, pp. 13–25.

Hvidt, Martin. "The Dubai Model: An Outline of Key Development-Process Elements in Dubai." *International Journal of Middle East Studies* 41(3), 2009, pp. 397–418.

———. "Economic and Institutional Reforms in the Arab Gulf Countries." *Middle East Journal* 65(1), Winter 2011, pp. 85–102.

———. "Economic Diversification in the Gulf Arab States: Lip Service or Actual Implementation of a New Development Model?" In Matteo Legrenzi and Bessma Momani (eds.), *Shifting Geo-Economic Power of the Gulf: Oil, Finance, and Institutions*. Farnham: Ashgate, 2011, pp. 39–54.

International Crisis Group. "Popular Protests in North Africa and the Middle East (III): The Bahrain Revolt." MENA Report no. 105. Brussels, April 6, 2011.

International Institute for Strategic Studies. *The Military Balance 2012*. London, 2012.

International Monetary Fund. "Qatar: Statistical Appendix." Country Report no. 10/62. Washington, DC, March 2010.

———. "Qatar: 2010 Article IV Consultation—Staff Report; Staff Statement and Supplement; Public Information Notice on the Executive Board Discussion; and Statement by the Executive Director for Qatar." Country Report no. 11/64. Washington, DC, March 9, 2011.

———. "Qatar: 2012 Article IV Consultation—Staff Report; Information Annex; and Public Information Notice." Country Report no. 12/18. Washington, DC, January 2012.

Janardhan, N. "New Media: In Search of Equilibrium." In Mary Ann Tétreault, Gwenn Okruhlik, and Andrzej Kapiszewski (eds.), *Political Change in the Arab Gulf States: Stuck in Transition*. Boulder: Lynne Rienner, 2011, pp. 225–245.

Kahwaji, Riad. "Gulf Cooperation Council Threat Perceptions and Deterrence Objectives." *Comparative Strategy* 22(5), 2003, pp. 515–520.

Kamrava, Mehran (ed.). *International Politics of the Persian Gulf*. Syracuse: Syracuse University Press, 2011.

———. "Mediation and Qatari Foreign Policy." *Middle East Journal* 65(4), Autumn 2011, pp. 539–556.

———. "Royal Factionalism and Political Liberalization in Qatar." *Middle East Journal* 63(3), Summer 2009, pp. 401–420.

Kanna, Ahmed. *Dubai: The City as Corporation*. Minneapolis: University of Minnesota Press, 2011.

Kechichian, Joseph A. "The Gulf Cooperation Council: Search for Security." *Third World Quarterly* 7(4), October 1985, pp. 853–881.

———. *Power and Succession in Arab Monarchies: A Reference Guide*. Boulder: Lynne Rienner, 2008.

Kern, Nathaniel, Fareed Mohamedi, Lucian Pugliaresi, and Jean-François Seznec. "Symposium: Gulf Oil and Gas—What Are the Producers Thinking?" *Middle East Policy* 17(2), Summer 2010, pp. 1–23.

Khan, Muhstaq. "Is 'Good Governance' an Appropriate Model for Governance Reforms? The Relevance of East Asia for Developing Muslim Countries." In Robert Springborg (ed.), *Development Models in Muslim Contexts: Chinese,*

"Islamic," and Neo-Liberal Alternatives. Edinburgh: Edinburgh University Press, 2010, pp. 195–230.

Knowles, Warwick. *Jordan Since 1989: A Study in Political Economy*. London: Tauris, 2005.

Koren, Miklós, and Silvana Tenreyro. "Volatility, Diversification, and Development in the Gulf Cooperation Council Countries." In David Held and Kristian Ulrichsen (eds.), *The Transformation of the Gulf: Politics, Economics, and the Global Order*. Abingdon: Routledge, 2012, pp. 188–217.

Krane, Jim. *Dubai: The Story of the World's Fastest City*. London: Atlantic, 2009.

Lacey, Robert. *Inside the Kingdom: Kings, Clerics, Modernists, Terrorists, and the Struggle for Saudi Arabia*. London: Hutchinson, 2009.

Lambert, Jennifer. "Political Reform in Qatar: Participation, Legitimacy, and Security." *Middle East Policy* 18(1), Spring 2011, pp. 89–101.

Lawson, Fred H. "From Here We Begin: A Survey of Scholarship on the International Relations of the Gulf." *British Journal of Middle East Studies* 36(3), 2009, pp. 337–357.

Legrenzi, Matteo, and Bessma Momani (eds.). *Shifting Geo-Economic Power of the Gulf: Oil, Finance, and Institutions*. Farnham: Ashgate, 2011.

Looney, Robert. "The Omani and Bahraini Paths to Development: Rare and Contrasting Oil-Based Economic Success Stories." Research Paper no. 2009/38. Helsinki: United Nations University World Institute for Development Economics Research, June 2009.

Luciani, Giacomo. "Allocation vs. Production States: A Theoretical Framework." In Giacomo Luciani (ed.), *The Arab State*. London: Routledge, 1990, pp. 65–84.

Mahdavy, Hussein. "The Patterns and Problems of Economic Development in Rentier States: The Case of Iran." In M. A. Cook (ed.), *Studies in Economic History of the Middle East*. London: Oxford University Press, 1970, pp. 428–467.

Maloney, Suzanne. "The Gulf's Renewed Oil Wealth: Getting It Right This Time?" *Survival* 50(6), 2008, pp. 129–150.

Mansour, Ahmed Mustafa Elhussein. "Public Policy and Privatization: The Case of the Qatari Experience." *Public Administration and Development* 27(4), 2007, pp. 283–292.

Mehmet, Ozay, and M. Tahiroglu. "Growth and Equity in Microstates: Does Size Matter in Development?" *International Journal of Social Economics* 29(1–2), 2002, pp. 152–162.

Miles, Hugh. *Al-Jazeera: The Inside Story of the Arab News Channel That Is Challenging the West*. New York: Grove, 2005.

Mitchell, Jocelyn Sage. "Political and Socioeconomic Transformation in the GCC: Image and Reality." *History Compass* 8(3), 2010, pp. 275–302.

Moini, Joy S., et al. *The Reform of Qatar University*. Santa Monica: RAND–Qatar Policy Institute, 2009.

Moore, Pete W. *Doing Business in the Middle East: Politics and Economic Crisis in Jordan and Kuwait*. Cambridge: Cambridge University Press, 2004.

———. "Rents and Late Development in the Arab World." Paper prepared for the American Political Science Association annual meeting, September 2, 2004. http://www.allacademic.com/meta/p61099_index.html.

Nafi, Zuhair Ahmed. *Economic and Social Development in Qatar.* London: Frances Pinter, 1983.

Niblock, Tim, and Monica Malik. *The Political Economy of Saudi Arabia.* Abingdon: Routledge, 2007.

Niethammer, Katya. "Political Reform and Foreign Policy in Persian Gulf Monarchies." In Mehran Kamrava (ed.), *International Politics of the Persian Gulf.* Syracuse: Syracuse University Press, 2011, pp. 234–256.

Nugée, John, and Paola Subacchi (eds.). *The Gulf Region: A New Hub of Global Financial Power.* London: Royal Institute of International Affairs, 2008.

Okruhlik, Gwenn, and Mary Ann Tétreault. "Juxtapositions and Sticking Points." In Mary Ann Tétreault, Gwenn Okruhlik, and Andrzej Kapiszewski (eds.), *Political Change in the Arab Gulf States: Stuck in Transition.* Boulder: Lynne Rienner, 2011, pp. 291–307.

Onley, James. "Britain and the Gulf Shaikhdoms, 1820–1971: The Politics of Protection." CIRS Occasional Paper no. 4. Doha: Georgetown University School of Foreign Service, 2009.

———. "The Politics of Protection in the Gulf: The Arab Rulers and the British Resident in the Nineteenth Century." *New Arabian Studies* 6, 2004, pp. 30–92.

Oxford Business Group. *The Report: Qatar 2011.* London, 2011.

Peterson, J. E. *The Arab Gulf States: Steps Toward Political Participation.* New York: Praeger and Center for Strategic and International Studies, 1988.

———. "Life After Oil: Economic Alternatives for the Arab Gulf States." *Mediterranean Quarterly* 20(3), Summer 2009, pp. 1–18.

———. "Qatar and the World: Branding for a Micro-State." *Middle East Journal* 60(4), Autumn 2006, pp. 732–748.

Potter, Lawrence G. (ed.). *The Persian Gulf in History.* Basingstoke: Palgrave Macmillan, 2009.

Potter, Lawrence G., and Gary G. Sick (eds.). *Security in the Persian Gulf: Origins, Obstacles, and the Search for Consensus.* London: Palgrave Macmillan, 2002.

Qatar Central Bank. *Quarterly Statistical Bulletin.* Doha, various editions.

Qatar Financial Centre. *A Guide to the Qatar Financial Centre Authority.* Doha: Qatar Financial Centre Authority, 2011. http://www.qfc.com.qa/Files/Brochures%202011/Final%20General%20Brochure%20(low%20resolution).pdf.

Qatar General Secretariat for Development Planning. *Qatar National Vision 2030.* Doha, 2008.

———, Department of Social Affairs. "Social and Human Development Profile no. 2: Features of Education in Qatar—Trends and Patterns." Doha, March 2009.

Qatar Ministry of Foreign Affairs. *Qatar.* London: Stacey International, 2000.

Qatar National Bank. *Qatar Economic Insight 2012.* Doha, October 2012.

Qatar Petroleum. *Annual Report.* Doha, various years. http://www.qp.com.qa/en/homepage/mediacentre/publications/10-2015054360.aspx.

Qatar Statistics Authority. *Annual Statistical Abstract.* Doha, various years.

———. *Labor Force Sample Survey 2008.* Doha, December 2008.

———. *Labor Market Strategy for the State of Qatar: Main Report.* Vol. 1. Doha, 2005.

QNB Capital. *Banking Sector Review.* Doha, various years.
———. *Qatar Economic Review.* Doha, various years.
———. *The Qatari Banking Sector.* Doha, various years.
Rabi, Uzi. "Qatar's Relations with Israel: Challenging Arab and Gulf Norms." *Middle East Journal* 63(3), Summer 2009, pp. 443–459.
Rahman, Habibur. *The Emergence of Qatar: The Turbulent Years, 1627–1916*. London: Routledge, 2006.
Rathmell, Andrew, and Kirsten Schulze. "Political Reform in the Gulf: The Case of Qatar." *Middle Eastern Studies* 36(4), October 2000, pp. 47–62.
Richards, Alan, and John Waterbury. *A Political Economy of the Middle East*. 2nd ed. Boulder: Westview, 1996.
Saud, Abeer Abu. *Qatari Women: Past and Present*. Harlow: Longman, 1984.
Schwab, Klaus. *The Global Competitiveness Report, 2010–2011*. Geneva: World Economic Forum, 2010.
Schwarz, Rolf. *War and State Building in the Middle East*. Gainesville: University of Florida Press, 2012.
Seznec, Jean-François, and Mimi Kirk (eds.). *Industrialization in the Gulf: A Socioeconomic Revolution*. Abingdon: Routledge, 2011.
Shediac, Richard, and Hatem Sammam. *The Vital Role of Sovereign Wealth Funds in the GCC's Future*. Dubai: Booz, 2009.
Springborg, Robert (ed.). *Development Models in Muslim Contexts: Chinese, "Islamic," and Neo-Liberal Alternatives*. Edinburgh: Edinburgh University Press, 2010.
Stasz, Cathleen, et al. *Post-Secondary Education for Qatar: Employer Demand, Student Choice, and Options for Policy.* Santa Monica: RAND, 2007.
Tanaka, Yoshifumi. "Reflections on Maritime Delimitation in the Qatar/Bahrain Case." *International and Comparative Law Quarterly* 52(1), January 2003, pp. 53–80.
Tatchell, Jo. *A Diamond in the Desert: Behind the Scenes in Abu Dhabi, the World's Richest City.* London: Sceptre, 2009.
Tétreault, Mary Ann, Gwenn Okruhlik, and Andrzej Kapiszewski (eds.). *Political Change in the Gulf States: Stuck in Transition*. Boulder: Lynne Rienner, 2011.
Ulrichsen, Kristian Coates. *Insecure Gulf: The End of Certainty and the Transition to the Post-Oil Era*. London: Hurst, 2011.
Valeri, Marc. *Oman: Politics and Society in the Qaboos State*. New York: Columbia University Press, 2010.
Wehrey, Frederic, et al. *Saudi-Iranian Relations Since the Fall of Saddam: Rivalry, Cooperation, and Implications for U.S. Policy.* Santa Monica: RAND, 2009.
Wiegand, Krista E. "Bahrain, Qatar, and the Hawar Islands: Resolution of a Gulf Territorial Dispute." *Middle East Journal* 66(1), Winter 2012, pp. 79–96.
Wilkinson, Paul F. "Strategies for Tourism in Island Microstates." *Annals of Tourism Research* 16(2), 1989, pp. 153–177.
World Bank. *Doing Business in the Arab World, 2011*. Washington, DC, 2010.
———. *Strengthening China's and India's Trade and Investment Ties to the Middle East and North Africa*. Washington, DC, 2009.
Wright, Steven. "Foreign Policies with International Reach: The Case of Qatar." In David Held and Kristian Ulrichsen (eds.), *The Transformation of the Gulf:*

Politics, Economics, and the Global Order. Abingdon: Routledge, 2012, pp. 296–312.

———. "Foreign Policy in the GCC States." In Mehran Kamrava (ed.), *International Politics of the Persian Gulf.* Syracuse: Syracuse University Press, 2011, pp. 72–93.

Xu Yi-chong. "The Political Economy of Sovereign Wealth Funds." In Xu Yi-chong and Gawdat Bahgat (eds.), *The Political Economy of Sovereign Wealth Funds.* Basingstoke: Palgrave Macmillan, 2010, pp. 1–25.

Xu Yi-chong and Gawdat Bahgat (eds.). *The Political Economy of Sovereign Wealth Funds.* Basingstoke: Palgrave Macmillan, 2010.

Zahlan, Rosemarie Said. *The Creation of Qatar.* London: Croom Helm, 1979.

———. *The Making of the Modern Gulf States.* 2nd ed. Reading, Berkshire: Ithaca Press, 1998.

Zayani, Mohamed. *The Al Jazeera Phenomenon: Critical Perspectives on New Arab Media.* London: Pluto, 2005.

Index

About the Book

Located on a small isthmus in the central Arab Gulf, with barely 300,000 citizens and a total population of 1.7 million, Qatar has risen rapidly from obscurity to become the world's wealthiest country per capita. Matthew Gray traces this spectacular rise, exploring the development of Qatar's economy, the patterns of its politics, its role on the world stage, and its prospects for the future.

Matthew Gray is associate professor at the Centre for Arab and Islamic Studies at the Australian National University. He is author of *Conspiracy Theories in the Arab World: Sources and Politics*.